RHETORIC: READINGS IN FRENCH

RHETORIC: READINGS IN FRENCH LITERATURE

MICHAEL HAWCROFT

OXFORD
UNIVERSITY PRESS

OXFORD
UNIVERSITY PRESS
Great Clarendon Street, Oxford OX2 6DP

Oxford University Press is a department of the University of Oxford.
It furthers the University's objective of excellence in research, scholarship,
and education by publishing worldwide in

Oxford New York

Athens Auckland Bangkok Bogotá Buenos Aires Calcutta
Cape Town Chennai Dar es Salaam Delhi Florence Hong Kong Istanbul
Karachi Kuala Lumpur Madrid Melbourne Mexico City Mumbai
Nairobi Paris São Paulo Singapore Taipei Tokyo Toronto Warsaw

and associated companies in Berlin Ibadan

Oxford is a registered trade mark of Oxford University Press
in the UK and in certain other countries

Published in the United States
by Oxford University Press Inc., New York

British Library Cataloguing in Publication Data

Data available

Library of Congress Cataloging in Publication Data

Data available

ISBN 0–19–815984–6
ISBN 0–19–816007–0 (Pbk.)

1 3 5 7 9 10 8 6 4 2

Typeset by Hope Services (Abingdon) Ltd.
Printed in Great Britain
on acid-free paper by
Biddles Ltd,
Guildford and King's Lynn

100293957X

For
Olive Sayce

ACKNOWLEDGEMENTS

I am indebted to Adrianne Tooke, who commented on a draft of two chapters of this book, to David Maskell and Russell Goulbourne, who commented on drafts of the whole book, and to Olive Sayce, who read the proofs with a sharp eye. I am deeply grateful for the time they gave up and for the improvements they suggested.

I should like to thank the Librarian of the Taylor Institution, Oxford, for permission to reproduce on the jacket of the book the frontispiece of Boileau's *Traité du Longin* from a copy in the library's collection. I should also like to thank the Warden and Fellows of Keble College, Oxford, for granting me generous teaching relief in Michaelmas Term 1998 which enabled me to complete the writing of this book.

I dedicate the book to Olive Sayce as an expression of my gratitude for her friendship, her support, and her example.

MICHAEL HAWCROFT

Oxford, February 1999

CONTENTS

INTRODUCTION

Le monde est incroyablement plein d'ancienne rhétorique.

(Roland Barthes)

This book is about rhetoric as the art of persuasion, and aims to promote its use as a critical tool for the close reading of French literary texts. It is both a handbook and a demonstration of critical practice, and it is addressed to anyone with a serious interest in French literature.

The word 'rhetoric' has a variety of connotations in modern usage. Most commonly, it conjures up insincerity and verbal deceit, as in the injunction to drop the rhetoric and tell the truth. It sometimes refers to the expression of an ideology, as in the claim that the rhetoric of recent governments has constructed members of society as consumers. It has also been used by literary critics to evoke, usually with pejorative overtones, a kind of writing or speech that is highly wrought and pompous. None of these connotations applies to the use of the word 'rhetoric' in this book.

Ever since its beginnings in the ancient Greek world, rhetoric has been an academic discipline. It is the art of persuasion, as codified by ancient rhetoricians and synthesized, refined, and developed by their numerous successors in the Western world. This art, traditionally divided into five parts, teaches the techniques of finding appropriate material (*invention*), arranging it (*disposition*), expressing it in the most effective words (*elocution*), and, in the case of oral communication, memorizing it (*memory*) and delivering it (*action*). For hundreds of years, rhetoric was a core subject in the school curriculum. It shaped the writing and speech of all those who learnt it. Moreover, rhetoric not only taught the techniques of persuasive writing and speech; a useful and fundamental exercise was to use the framework of rhetoric to analyse the discourse of others (typically, famous writers of the past), and it is in this respect that rhetoric is of interest to the critic today.

Traditional rhetoric is the subject of this book. But the book aims to make no contribution to the history of rhetoric, which is now a vast field of scholarly endeavour in its own right.[1] Rhetoric is usually said to have been born in Sicily in the fifth century BC. After the expulsion of the tyrants, land had to be restored to those from whom it had been confiscated. The art of persuasion became a necessity for the Sicilians as they competed for land, and it was taught to them by Corax, and written down by his disciple Tisias. These early beginnings of rhetoric bear witness to one of the recurrent claims of its defenders: rhetoric is the mark of a civilized society; it is better to fight with words than with weapons.

Three names from the ancient world stand out for their contribution to rhetorical theory: Aristotle, Cicero, and Quintilian. Their works run in filigree through the hundreds of treatises that came after them. Principal among them are Aristotle's *Rhetoric*, various works by Cicero, most notably *De Oratore* and *Orator*, and Quintilian's substantial pedagogical treatise the *Institutio Oratoria*. To these canonical works should be added an anonymous treatise, long thought wrongly to be by Cicero, the *Rhetorica ad Herennium*.[2] Whilst remaining recognizably the same discipline, rhetoric adapted itself over the centuries to changing educational, political, and social circumstances.

Rhetoric's heyday in France was probably in the early modern period, when it was wielded as a powerful educational tool by the Jesuits and when, from the mid-seventeenth century onwards, it became available to all readers in a range of popularizing books about rhetoric written in French (as opposed to the Latin of the school textbooks). In the first half of the nineteenth century the Romantics, with their commitment to individual genius and imagination, were hostile to rhetoric. Yet, at least notionally, rhetoric remained on the school syllabus in France until 1902. For the first half of the twentieth century it was largely ignored, but interest has been revived in the second half of the century by literary critics keen to exploit its potential as a tool of critical analysis, and by educa-

---

[1] The works of G. A. Kennedy are indispensable, in particular: *The Art of Persuasion in Greece* (Princeton: Princeton University Press, 1963), *The Art of Rhetoric in the Roman World* (Princeton: Princeton University Press, 1972), *Greek Rhetoric under Christian Emperors* (Princeton: Princeton University Press, 1983). For the early modern period in France see M. Fumaroli, *L'Âge de l'éloquence: Rhétorique et 'res litteraria' de la Renaissance au seuil de l'époque classique* (Geneva: Droz, 1980). For an extremely useful and concise survey of rhetoric from classical to modern times (including synopses of many key treatises), see T. M. Conley, *Rhetoric in the European Tradition* (Chicago: University of Chicago Press, 1994).

[2] Editions of all these works (with translations) are listed in the Select Bibliography.

tionalists, who in 1995 restored rhetoric to the syllabus for the *baccalauréat* in the form of a test in argumentation.

The revival of interest has taken two forms. The first is an array of monographs exploring rhetoric in the work of individual writers, typically of the early modern period. There are important rhetorical studies of Ronsard, Montaigne, Corneille, Pascal, Racine, Diderot, and Rousseau, amongst others.[3] The second kind of interest in rhetoric is more theoretical. A number of writers, some associated with structuralism, saw rhetoric as a forerunner of a modern poetics, and have attempted sympathetically to understand and extend the writings of earlier theorists: witness Gérard Genette's editions of theoretical works by Dumarsais and Fontanier, and Roland Barthes's seminar and subsequent article on 'L'Ancienne Rhétorique';[4] witness, also, the interest of stylisticians in the third part of rhetoric, *elocution*.[5] Others, whose interests are more philosophical than literary, have proposed a new rhetoric of argumentation, going well beyond the theories of traditional rhetoric, and their work has been taken up most notably by Gilles Declercq, who has applied theories of argumentation to literary texts.[6]

---

[3] A. L. Gordon, *Ronsard et la rhétorique* (Geneva: Droz, 1970); M. M. McGowan, *Montaigne's Deceits: The Art of Persuasion in the 'Essais'* (University of London Press, 1974); S. Harwood, *Rhetoric in the Tragedies of Corneille* (New Orleans: Tulane University, 1977); M. Fumaroli, *Héros et orateurs: Rhétorique et dramaturgie cornéliennes* (Geneva: Droz, 1990); P. Topliss, *The Rhetoric of Pascal* (Leicester: Leicester University Press, 1966); P. France, *Racine's Rhetoric* (Oxford: Clarendon Press, 1965); M. Hawcroft, *Word as Action: Racine, Rhetoric, and Theatrical Language* (Oxford: Clarendon Press, 1992); P. France, *Rhetoric and Truth in France: Descartes to Diderot* (Oxford: Clarendon Press, 1972), which includes studies of Diderot and Rousseau.

[4] P. Fontanier, *Les Figures du discours*, ed. G. Genette (Flammarion, 1968); C. C. Dumarsais and P. Fontanier, *Des Tropes*, ed. G. Genette (Geneva: Slatkine Reprints, 1984); R. Barthes, 'L'Ancienne Rhétorique: Aide-mémoire', in *Recherches rhétoriques* (Seuil, 1970), 254‑333. The structuralist-inspired Groupe *mu* has published a *Rhétorique générale* (Larousse, 1970; Seuil, 1982).

[5] A number of recent introductions to stylistics published in France draw substantially on rhetorical terminology. See e.g. G. Molinié, *La Stylistique* (Presses Universitaires de France, 1993), and C. Fromilhague and A. Sancier-Chateau, *Introduction à l'analyse stylistique*, 2nd edn. (Dunod, 1996). For a useful handbook of stylistics, see K. Wales, *A Dictionary of Stylistics* (Longman, 1989).

[6] For the most significant attempt to produce a modern rhetoric of argumentation, see C. Perelman and L. Olbrechts-Tyteca, *Traité de l'argumentation: La Nouvelle Rhétorique*, 5th edn. (Brussels: University of Brussels, 1988), and C. Perelman, *L'Empire rhétorique: Rhétorique et argumentation* (Vrin, 1977). The work on argumentation by O. Ducrot (e.g. *Dire et ne pas dire: Principes de sémantique linguistique*, 2nd edn. (Hermann, 1980)) has directly influenced G. Declercq's approach to rhetorical argumentation in literary texts (see his *L'Art d'argumenter: Structures rhétoriques et littéraires* (Éditions Universitaires, 1992)). Declercq's work stresses argumentation at the expense of the other parts of traditional rhetoric.

This book does not follow in the footsteps of either the writers of monographs on rhetoric or the theorists working to produce a modern rhetoric. It is written in the belief that traditional rhetoric still offers a fruitful framework in which to approach any text that seeks to communicate with readers or audiences, regardless of the period in which that text was composed. Rhetoric does not cease to be useful just because a writer may not have had a rhetorical education. The book aims to explain traditional rhetoric and to illustrate its potential uses to the literary critic. It aims also to defend, promote, and stimulate rhetorical approaches to French literature. It is written for undergraduates and graduates studying French, but also for those professionally engaged in the study and teaching of French literature. Different categories of reader will need more or less of my illustrative analysis. But I hope that all readers will find it a useful guide to rhetoric and its applications to French texts. I shall be pleased if it sits on bookshelves as a work of reference: even readers not disposed to a rhetorical approach to texts will find in it a helpful store of rhetorical terminology. I shall be more pleased, however, if readers find its rhetorical analyses illuminating and are prompted to develop the insights provided by rhetoric in their own critical writing.

This book is not a *mise au point* of recent rhetorical criticism of French literature. It goes beyond the concentration on *elocution* which has characterized much rhetorical criticism. For historical reasons rhetorical study has focused primarily on this one part of rhetoric, to the detriment of the other parts and, indeed, of rhetoric as a whole.[7] *Elocution* is mainly about style. It is the part of rhetoric which, over the ages, has prompted theorists to be most inventive. But to look at *elocution* in isolation is to falsify the rhetorical enterprise. For the rhetorician, any discourse aims to make an impact, typically a persuasive impact, on a reader or an audience. Writers have to choose their material, its organization, and the words in order to make the most appropriate impact: it is with the same

[7] On the narrowing of rhetoric see G. Genette, 'La Rhétorique restreinte', in *Recherches rhétoriques* (Seuil, 1970), 233–53. See also the polemical defence of the scope of traditional rhetoric by B. Vickers in his excellent study *In Defence of Rhetoric* (Oxford: Clarendon Press, 1988), ch. 9, 'Epilogue: The Future of Rhetoric'. He is scathing about those modern critics who tamper with rhetoric and reduce it to a few tropes. The work of Paul de Man is particularly criticized. To counter the narrowing of rhetoric to *elocution* in modern studies, A. Kibédi Varga wrote in defence of *invention* and *disposition* in early modern French rhetorical theory (*Rhétorique et littérature: Études de structures classiques* (Didier, 1970)).

keen eye on an audience that the speaker must choose a mode of delivery.

This book presents rhetoric in its breadth as the art of persuasive communication. The notion of a communicative situation is central to the method adopted here.[8] If we consider the kind of discourse that the ancient orators had in mind when they composed their treatises, we can see clearly the importance of the communicative situation to anyone wanting to assess a writer's rhetoric. For instance, a barrister composes a speech to deliver to a jury to persuade them that his client is innocent. The communicative situation here is relatively straightforward. All the words are spoken by one voice, and are aimed at an identifiable audience. The reaction of that audience is likely to be in itself an adequate judgement of the speaker's rhetoric. Chapter 2 ('Oratory') takes examples of this kind of discourse: examining, for instance, the speeches of the prosecution and the defence in the trial of Flaubert, who was accused of offences against public morality in the publication of *Madame Bovary*.

This simple communicative model needs to be developed if it is to help critics in the rhetorical analysis of other kinds of texts. Most of what is called literature involves more than one speaker and more than one audience. The dramatist, for example, writes for a theatre audience; but a play typically shows several characters engaging in acts of communication with one another. It is usually vital for the theatre audience to think that the words of one character are addressed first and foremost to another character. In order to understand how the dramatist communicates with a theatre audience, the critic must first observe how the dramatist makes characters engage rhetorically with each other. Two axes of communication operate simultaneously: the writer-to-audience axis and the character-to-character axis. The critic must inevitably examine the character axis before being able to assess the writer–audience axis. Examples of rhetoric in drama are the subject of Chapter 3.

The communicative situation is even more complex for works of prose fiction. The writer often communicates to readers through the medium of a narrator; but the narrator often depicts other

---

[8] The most influential modern writer to outline the main constituents of communication is R. Jakobson in 'Closing Statement: Linguistics and Poetics', in T. A. Sebeok (ed.), *Style and Language* (Cambridge, Mass.: MIT Press, 1960), 350–77. An addresser sends an addressee a message in a given context, adopting a certain code. In the case of literary texts the model of communication can be much more complex.

characters engaging rhetorically with each other. Depending on the novel's narrative structure, the axes of communication in play can be more or less numerous, more or less complex.[9] The critic of rhetoric in the novel needs to attend to the various communicative structures which different examples of the genre adopt. Some examples are discussed in Chapter 4 ('Prose Fiction'). Similar communicative considerations apply to the kinds of writing examined in Chapters 5 ('Poetry') and 6 ('The Self'). Lyric poems often posit a speaking character addressing another character, whilst narrative poetry has the potential to develop all the communicative complexity of the novel. Those who write explicitly about themselves sometimes profess to do so without any particular eye to an effect on a readership; but examples of such writing, including autobiography and personal correspondence, suggest complex rhetorical patterns at work.

Establishing the communicative situations in the texts discussed is the preliminary step to examining the texts' rhetoric more closely. It can, of course, be difficult for the critic to pass any definitive judgements on the effect of a work's rhetoric on a reader or an audience. Yet, when rhetoric is represented within the fictional world of a play or a novel, the success of that rhetoric is usually made plain to the audience or the reader in the form of one character's reaction to another. Sometimes there is historical evidence about the success of a writer's rhetoric on his first or later audiences. We know, for instance, how the jury responded to lawyers speaking in the trial of Flaubert. We know how some of Madame de Sévigné's letters were received by her daughter, because she sometimes makes retrospective remarks on the subject. But how we, as modern readers and audiences, respond to the rhetoric of all the writers considered here will inevitably vary.

I hope, however, that readers will be persuaded of the interest of my rhetorical readings. Reading is not, of course, an innocent activity. In his most recent work on French verse, Clive Scott surveys the many modern attempts to produce a theory of reading.[10] What

---

[9] This is the domain of narratology. See esp. G. Genette, *Figures*, vol. 3 (Seuil, 1972), and S. Rimmon-Kenan, *Narrative Fiction: Contemporary Poetics* (Routledge, 1983).

[10] C. Scott, *The Poetics of French Verse: Studies in Reading* (Oxford: Clarendon Press, 1998), 1–9. Some key texts in the theory of reading are W. Iser, *The Implied Reader: Patterns of Communication in Prose Fiction from Bunyan to Beckett* (Baltimore: Johns Hopkins University Press, 1974); S. E. Fish, *Is There a Text in this Class? The Authority of Interpretative Communities* (Cambridge, Mass.: Harvard University Press, 1980); and U. Eco, *The Role of the Reader: Explorations in the Semiotics of Texts* (Hutchinson, 1981).

critics do when they read a text and write about it (*a fortiori* what they should and should not do) is a subject of intense debate. One of the strengths of a rhetorical approach to critical reading is precisely that it attends to observable phenomena in a text; but how these phenomena relate to each other and how they work on a text's varied readers and audiences is usually a delicate matter for the critic to judge. Rhetoric does not throw a strait-jacket around the literary critic. It offers a set of tools, which different critics will apply in different ways. Even less does rhetoric throw a strait-jacket around the text. Frequently in this book rhetoric helps to highlight ambiguities and subtleties in the texts discussed, and points the way to plural readings.

For detailed rhetorical analysis, some understanding of both the overall framework of rhetoric and its individual devices is essential. That is the purpose of Chapter 1, which constitutes a practical guide to rhetorical theory, illustrated with wide-ranging examples from French texts, mostly, but not exclusively, literary. Specialists of rhetoric should note that I have produced a composite account of traditional rhetorical theory. In a work of this kind it is not possible to trace the different emphases that have been placed on different aspects of rhetoric at different times. Specialists might think that I have sometimes oversimplified or might regret the absence of some favourite devices. There are many rhetorical handbooks to which those who want more detail might be referred.[11]

Non-specialists, on the other hand, might at first be daunted by the technical detail that rhetorical theory entails. To those wary of rhetoric's technicalities I would say that knowledge of the technical terms sensitizes the critic to phenomena that might otherwise go unremarked. It would be possible to write a rhetorical analysis of a text without recourse to rhetoric's often abstruse terminology; but it can be done more expeditiously with the precise technical vocabulary that rhetoric provides. Most academic subjects require specialized technical terms to refer to the phenomena that they observe.

---

[11] The most useful modern guide to rhetorical theory for the student of French is G. Molinié, *Dictionnaire de rhétorique* (Le Livre de Poche, 1992). The fullest modern account of rhetorical theory is H. Lausberg, *Handbuch der literarischen Rhetorik*, 2nd edn. (Munich: Max Hueber Verlag, 1973). Suggestive of the revival of interest in rhetoric are a number of textbooks published in France, though often with a more or less explicit emphasis on *elocution*. See e.g. P. Bacry, *Les Figures de style et autres procédés stylistiques* (Belin, 1992); C. Fromilhague, *Les Figures de style* (Nathan, 1995); J. Gardes-Tamine, *La Rhétorique* (Armand Colin, 1996).

There is no reason why, in this respect, literary study should be different. Of course, merely labelling devices in a text with a rhetorical term is of little interest. Rhetorical analysis should seek always to understand the ways in which the devices identified might operate in the communicative situation in which readers find themselves. I have sought to encourage familiarity with rhetorical terminology by putting it in italics throughout the book. To benefit most from the analyses in Chapters 2–6, readers will need to have a working knowledge of at least the outlines of Chapter 1. I have, however, tried to write my analyses in such a way that they are comprehensible to readers who cannot remember all the terms presented in Chapter 1. The outline of this chapter in the appendix is intended to serve as a visual *aide-mémoire* of the theory.

All these considerations raise the question as to how the book as a whole is to be read. It can be read from beginning to end. Indeed, its arguments and its illustrations make best sense when read consecutively, moving from theory to practice, and from apparently more to apparently less overtly rhetorical kinds of writing. The flow of the book is designed to make a compelling case for the rhetorical analysis of writings of very varied kinds, written at different times from the sixteenth century to the twentieth.

Though I take pleasure in rhetorical analysis because it allows multiple means of access to a text, I confess that it is an austere pleasure, and perhaps an acquired taste. Readers might want to read this book selectively, therefore, concentrating on those genres or texts in which they are interested. Within each of Chapters 2–6, three texts are discussed in detail, and these are arranged chronologically. This is purely for the sake of neatness, not because I have a primary interest in demonstrating the historical evolution in the relationship between rhetoric and literary practice. Notwithstanding, I do make some comments of a historical nature; but a history of rhetoric in French literature would require a vast multivolume work.

The principles I have adopted in choosing texts for inclusion are simple. I wanted to cover a range of genres, and to represent each century from the sixteenth onwards, with a slight bias towards the modern period, partly because this is the period with which most readers are likely to be more familiar, and partly because it seemed more of a challenge to attempt rhetorical analyses of authors who have so far remained relatively immune to the efforts of rhetorical critics.[12] I also wanted to select texts that are generally well known, or that have an obvious significance beyond the pages of this book. I regret that other genres (like the dialogue, the pamphlet, the essay, satire, pulpit oratory) are absent, and that the medieval period is not represented (for no better reason than that I am not a medievalist). Exhaustiveness would have been impossible. One result of these various considerations is that I discuss texts and authors on which the critical bibliography is usually enormous. In order to keep the focus on rhetorical analysis, I have chosen not to engage explicitly in my text with the work of other critics, but to mention in notes and in the bibliography at the end of the book those critical works which attend most obviously to my chosen texts as rhetorical constructs.

Writing about rhetoric is a perilous task. Rhetoric claims to foster an effective relationship between writer and reader. Rhetoricians themselves, however, as the desiccated pages of their treatises may remind us, have sometimes been oblivious of the requirements of their own readers. I hope I have not been as insensitive to mine.

---

[12] There is a tendency, exemplified by P. H. Nurse, to assume that rhetorical criticism can be really helpful only for pre-Romantic texts. He writes: 'This method of approach [*explication de textes*] is more suitable for literature which is above all designed to *persuade*, and such a view of the writer's function was predominant in the pre-Romantic era. It is reflected in the stock divisions of the old treatises on rhetoric [. . .]. Provided the critic gave due place in his analysis to [the] third element, style, he was not radically failing in his task' (P. H. Nurse (ed.), *The Art of Criticism: Essays in French Literary Analysis* (Edinburgh: Edinburgh University Press, 1969), 5).

RHETORICAL THEORY: A PRACTICAL GUIDE

Rhetoric teaches the art of speaking or writing persuasively and pleasingly. Most rhetoricians have repeated Cicero's famous statement of the three main duties of the orator: to move, to instruct, and to delight ('movere', 'docere', 'delectare'). Rhetoricians tend not to combine these three elements successfully in their theoretical treatises. Few subjects lend themselves as well as rhetoric to unappealing presentation. Rhetoricians display their skill by identifying as many verbal and argumentational devices as they can: this makes for long lists. They give names to all the devices they find, and, whatever language they are in, the names are usually strange in both sound and appearance. Rhetoricians distinguish themselves from each other by arranging the devices they are presenting in new ways. This significantly complicates the task of modern readers trying to understand the ground plan of rhetorical theory. But for all its taxonomic complexity, and for all the technical terms it uses, rhetoric offers the opportunity for a probing and extended analysis of the persuasive strategies operating in written and spoken discourse. The critical insights and new levels of appreciation that rhetorical analysis promises make the acquisition of some familiarity with rhetorical theory well worth while. The purpose of this chapter is to encourage such familiarity.

The account of rhetorical theory given here is a composite one. Any reader who subsequently compares it with Quintilian's *Institutio Oratoria* or Pierre Fontanier's *Les Figures du discours* will find much that is similar, but a good deal that is different. I have tried to present many, though by no means all, of the recurrent features of traditional rhetorical theory over many centuries, and my choice has been determined by what I have found most fruitful in my own critical practice. If the account is selective, the selection is a wide one. In arranging the material, I have been keen to make the outlines of rhetorical theory memorable. When the outlines are clear, the detail falls into place. Yet it is less important that critics master the enormous battery of technical terms than that they are aware of the kinds of device to which rhetoric attends. Naming a device is much less important than observing it at work.

This chapter will serve as a point of reference throughout the rest of the book. But the chapter is more than just a reference grid. By illustrating many of the technical terms from French writers of different periods, the chapter implicitly launches one of the arguments that will be pursued all through the book: that rhetoric is not only useful for the critic approaching texts written in a self-consciously rhetorical style in a period when all educated writers would have been taught the skills of rhetoric, but that all aspects of French culture, of whatever period, can be illuminated to some degree by reference to rhetorical theory.

I have chosen to use English terms whenever possible, but sometimes risk of confusion between a term's rhetorical connotation and other connotations (e.g. *correctio*) has led me to prefer a non-English term. For the convenience of readers I have given, in this chapter only, the French equivalent of all the terms presented.

1. KINDS OF ORATORY (LES GENRES (M.) ORATOIRES)

Rhetoric traditionally caters for three kinds of discourse relating to real-life situations in which orators had to perform in the ancient world. The first kind is *judicial oratory* (*le genre judiciaire*), which belongs primarily in courts of law. *Judicial* oratory incorporates speeches of accusation or defence, and deals above all with events in the past. The second kind is *deliberative oratory* (*le genre délibératif*), which was originally associated with political assemblies. *Deliberative* oratory embraces speeches of persuasion and dissuasion, speeches in which a particular course of action is urged or discouraged. It looks to the future. Both *judicial* and *deliberative* oratory entail a certain dynamism: the orator tries to influence people's minds as they prepare to reach a decision. The third kind, *demonstrative oratory* (*le genre démonstratif*), typically lacks this dynamism, as no decision likely to affect the future in an immediate way rests upon the orator's performance. *Demonstrative* oratory involves speeches of praise or blame.

As such, it can perform the interesting function of inviting an audience to confirm a decision already reached or a view already held. The three kinds of oratory have a far wider application than their origins might suggest.

1.1 Judicial Discourse

Judicial discourse is that of barristers in courts of law, but it can also be directly relevant to the study of literature and culture. When *Madame Bovary* was put on trial for its alleged immorality, there was a speech attacking the novel (*le réquisitoire*) and a speech in defence of it (*la plaidoirie*). Fictional writing often explicitly depicts *judicial* discourse at work. The second part of Camus's *L'Etranger* shows how a prosecuting barrister can use (or rather misuse) the facts of Meursault's life (presented in the first part) to persuade a jury that he was guilty of murder. The central character of Camus's *La Chute* is a retired barrister who is shown to continue practising adversarial techniques on an individual he has met in a bar. *Judicial* discourse, however, can be found in situations quite removed from courts of law and barristers. It is the kind adopted by Zola when he defends himself against those critics who object to his use of vulgar language:

La forme, là est le grand crime [. . .]. Je ne me défends pas d'ailleurs. Mon livre me défendra. (Zola, preface to *L'Assommoir*)

1.2 Deliberative Discourse

Deliberative discourse is used by politicians when they debate whether or not to bring back the death penalty, for example. It is also used by advertisers, as in the French government slogan 'Boire ou conduire. Il faut choisir', which aimed to persuade people not to drink and drive. *Deliberative* discourse of a strictly political nature can be found in works of literature. In *L'Éducation sentimentale* Flaubert depicts Frédéric as a candidate for election to the National Assembly, though Frédéric is comically unable to make a *deliberative* speech in support of his candidature. Rousseau writes his *Discours sur l'origine et les fondements de l'inégalité parmi les hommes* in order to persuade readers that inequality between human beings is due to the growth of ownership in primitive societies and to the consequential development of civilization and moral corruption of its members.

Deliberative discourse does not need to have a political dimension, however. It is central to human relationships, both sexual and emotional. Tartuffe uses *deliberative* discourse in his attempt to persuade Elmire to grant him sexual favours:

> En vous est mon espoir, mon bien, ma quiétude:
> De vous dépend ma peine ou ma béatitude:
> Et je vais être enfin, par votre seul arrêt,
> Heureux, si vous voulez, malheureux, s'il vous plaît.
>
> (Molière, *Tartuffe*)

1.3 Demonstrative Discourse

Speeches of welcome or funeral orations are characteristic examples of *demonstrative* discourse in which individuals are praised (or, much less commonly, blamed). These forms are still practised today in obituary notices or in speeches made at the Académie Française by new members in praise of the previous occupant of their chair or by existing members in praise of a newly elected member. Like the other two kinds of discourse, it lends itself to incorporation into literary contexts. The speech made by L'Exempt at the end of *Tartuffe* is a hymn of praise to the king, who has seen through the criminal Tartuffe and ordered his arrest:

> Nous vivons sous un prince ennemi de la fraude,
> Un prince dont les yeux se font jour dans les cœurs,
> Et que ne peut tromper tout l'art des imposteurs.
> D'un fin discernement sa grande âme pourvue
> Sur les choses toujours jette une droite vue;
> Chez elle jamais rien ne surprend trop d'accès,
> Et sa ferme raison ne tombe en nul excès.
>
> (Molière, *Tartuffe*)

The other characters, as well as the theatre audience, are being persuaded to share this flattering view of the king.

2. INVENTION (L'INVENTION (F.))

Invention is the first step in composing a text. It has to do less with inventiveness than with adopting a variety of strategies that will lead to appropriate material for inclusion. It is about finding something to say. There are four main aspects. *Ethos*, *pathos*, and *logos* all point to various kinds of material. A discussion of forms of reasoning deals with how some of that material might be arranged in the shape of arguments.

✳ 2.1 Ethos (les mœurs (f.))

Ethos concerns the presentation of character, primarily the character of the speaker or the writer. Rhetoricians advise orators to try to impress their audiences as reliable, trustworthy, and sincere characters. It is therefore important to build into a discourse evidence of good character. By extension, orators can evoke the good character of those on whose behalf they are speaking or even the bad character of those against whom they are speaking. In Laclos's *Les Liaisons dangereuses* the scheming Marquise de Merteuil is anxious to come across to some of her correspondents as quite respectable. Having plotted the downfall of Prévan, she gives an account of the event to Mme de Volanges which begins with a carefully engineered fabrication of her own character:

Je vous écris de mon lit, ma chère bonne amie. L'événement le plus désagréable, et le plus impossible à prévoir, m'a rendue malade de saisissement et de chagrin. Ce n'est pas qu'assurément j'aie rien à me reprocher: mais il est toujours si pénible pour une femme honnête et qui conserve la modestie convenable à son sexe, de fixer sur elle l'attention publique, que je donnerais tout au monde pour avoir pu éviter cette malheureuse aventure, et que je ne sais encore, si je ne prendrai pas le parti d'aller à la campagne, attendre qu'elle soit oubliée. (Laclos, *Les Liaisons dangereuses*)

Merteuil tries to make herself seem the unfortunate victim of an event which was of her own making. In addition to the repeated assertions of her modesty and respectability, there is the apparent honesty suggested by her preparedness to admit *some* (unspecified) weaknesses ('Ce n'est pas qu'assurément j'aie rien à me reprocher').

2.2 Pathos (les passions (f.))

Another way of securing the adhesion of an audience is to find appropriate sources of emotive appeal. Orators themselves can feign subjection to certain emotions, and hope to move audiences indirectly by the depiction of emotions. Alternatively, they can appeal directly to the emotional interests of the audience. Emotions most commonly aroused include anger, love, hatred, fear, audacity, shame, shamelessness, benevolence, pity, indignation, envy, emulation, and scorn. Any emotions likely to make an impact on an audience could be considered suitable. In the following quotation, Hermione first exploits *ethos* to suggest that she will not object to Pyrrhus's marriage to her rival (1–2), and then *pathos*, appealing to Pyrrhus's sense of pity, when she asks him to postpone the event (3–4):

> Mais, Seigneur, s'il le faut, si le ciel en colère
> Réserve à d'autres yeux la gloire de vous plaire,
> Achevez votre hymen, j'y consens; mais du moins
> Ne forcez pas mes yeux d'en être les témoins.
>
> (Racine, *Andromaque*)

✳2.3 Logos (les preuves (f.))

The third way of securing adhesion is to exploit what rhetoric calls *logos*, or also proofs or arguments. What is in question here is not proofs or arguments in the sense of reasoning or logic. Rather, *logos* embraces three different strategies which aim to help the orator to find relevant subject-matter: *external proofs*, *internal proofs*, and *topics*.

External proofs (les lieux extrinsèques (m.))

External proofs are not the product of the orator's imagination, but exist externally, and can be incorporated into a text when they are relevant. They may, but need not, be verbal in nature. Statements of witnesses, statements extracted under torture, oaths, accounts of dreams, quotations from recognized authorities are all common examples of *external proofs*. So are daggers bearing fingerprints, blood-stained clothing, lipstick-smeared collars. Thésée is persuaded by Œnone that Hippolyte attempted to violate his stepmother Phèdre. It is her production of Hippolyte's sword that secures conviction, as Thésée admits:

> Pour parvenir au but de ces noires amours,
> L'insolent de la force empruntait le secours!
> J'ai reconnu le fer, instrument de sa rage,
> Ce fer dont je l'armai pour un plus noble usage.
>
> (Racine, *Phèdre*)

Internal proofs (les lieux intrinsèques (m.)) or places (les lieux (m.))

By contrast, *internal proofs* are the result of the orator's own mind at work on the subject in hand. Rhetoricians recommend a number of mental strategies that can be applied to any subject, in order to find something worthwhile to say about it. The technical term for these strategies is *places* (translation of the Latin *loci*). It is as if orators have mentally to visit a number of places to see what they can find there. The most common can be summed up as follows:

1. *definition (la définition)*: defining or describing a term or an idea, or also considering its etymology and words related to it;
2. *division (la division)*: considering the different elements of which something is constituted;
3. *genus (le genre)* and *species (l'espèce* (f.))*: considering how a term or idea relates to a larger group of which it is a member (*genus*), or assessing the particular qualities of a word or idea within that larger group (*species*);
4. *cause (la cause)* and *effect (l'effet* (m.))*: considering what has given, or might give, rise to the term or idea (*cause*), or what the term or idea has given, or might give, rise to (*effect*);
5. *comparison (la comparaison)*: comparing a term or an idea to another which is of the same, or greater, or lesser importance;
6. *opposites (les contraires* (m.))*: exploring a term or an idea that is opposite, or nearly opposite, to the main subject of interest;
7. *circumstances (les circonstances* (f.))*: exploring things that are associated with the subject of interest by asking and answering the questions who? what? where? by what means? why? how? when? (more memorably expressed in a line of Latin verse repeated by many rhetoricians: 'Quis, quid, ubi, quibus auxiliis, cur, quomodo, quando?').

The use made of the *internal proofs* or *places* can be seen in this extract from Hippolyte's address to Aricie, when he attempts to persuade her to leave Trézène with him:

> Sortez de l'esclavage où vous êtes réduite;
> Osez me suivre, osez accompagner ma fuite;
> Arrachez-vous d'un lieu funeste et profané,
> Où la vertu respire un air empoisonné.
> Profitez pour cacher votre prompte retraite,   5
> De la confusion que ma disgrâce y jette.
> Je vous puis de la fuite assurer les moyens.

Vous n'avez jusqu'ici de gardes que les miens.
De puissants défenseurs prendront notre querelle;
Argos nous tend les bras, et Sparte nous appelle;   10
A nos amis communs portons nos justes cris;
Ne souffrons pas que Phèdre, assemblant nos débris,
Du trône paternel nous chasse l'un et l'autre,
Et promette à mon fils ma dépouille et la vôtre.

(Racine, *Phèdre*)

Hippolyte exploits *definition*, describing Trézène as the kind of place
from which one would want to flee: for Aricie in particular it is a
place of imprisonment; for both of them it is a place of hostility and
deadly danger (3–4). He then exploits *circumstances* showing her that
he has means currently at his disposal to help her flee (his guards),
and future means to take their defence once they have fled (the sup-
portive cities of Argos and Sparta) (7–11). Finally, he considers the
effects of their not fleeing (their murder at Phèdre's hands and her
triumph over them) (12–14).

Topics (les topiques (f.))

A *topic* (or *topos*, pl. *topoi*) differs from an *internal proof* or *place* in
that it is a ready-made body of material. Individual writers or
speakers will adapt the material to suit their purpose; but the core
is given. *Topics* form part of the collective consciousness of all
societies, though some *topics* are more period-specific than others.
Renaissance poets often presented young women as roses.
Ronsard exploits this *topic* in a poem in which the short life span
of the flower is used to urge the young woman to give in
promptly to the speaker's demands:

Donc, si vous me croiés, mignonne:
Tandis que vôtre âge fleuronne
En sa plus verte nouveauté,
Cueillés, cueillés vôtre jeunesse:
Comme à cette fleur, la vieillesse
Fera ternir vôtre beauté.

(Ronsard, 'Ode à Cassandre')

The rose image also figures in a poem by Malherbe, where the
flower's short life span is used to convince Du Périer of the natural
inevitability of his daughter's early death:

> Mais elle estoit du monde, où les plus belles choses
>   Ont le pire destin,
> Et rose elle a vescu ce que vivent les roses,
>   L'espace d'un matin.
>
> (Malherbe, 'Consolation à Monsieur Du Périer')

A *topic* prominent in prefatory material to fictional works in the seventeenth and eighteenth centuries is the claim of moral usefulness. Racine introduces this *topic* in his preface to *Phèdre*, when he evokes the tragedies of the ancients as an achievement to be emulated:

> Il serait à souhaiter que nos ouvrages fussent aussi solides et aussi pleins d'utiles instructions que ceux de ces poètes.

It is the same *topic* that Laclos uses in the 'préface du rédacteur' of *Les Liaisons dangereuses*:

> L'utilité de l'ouvrage, qui peut-être sera encore plus contestée, me paraît pourtant plus facile à établir.

Writers and readers will recognize as *topics* what they have been culturally conditioned to think of as familiar. The success of a *topic* will depend upon the particular use made of it by a given writer in a set context, though the novice reader may not recognize the tradition that lies behind it.

2.4 Forms of Argument (les types (m.) de raisonnement (m.))

When orators have found their material, they usually express at least some of it in the form of an argument or arguments. There are two basic forms of reasoning: deductive and inductive. Rhetoric treats the construction of arguments rather more lightly than formal logic, on the grounds that carefully, systematically constructed arguments are unlikely to be appealing to the majority of audiences or readers.

Deductive reasoning (le raisonnement par déduction)

Deduction begins with the general, and draws conclusions that are either particular or general. Its most rigorous form is the *syllogism* (*le syllogisme*) with its three parts: *major premiss* (*la première prémisse*) (e.g. 'All men are mortal'), *minor premiss* (*la seconde prémisse*) (e.g. 'Socrates is a man'), and *conclusion* (*la conclusion*) (e.g. 'Socrates is mortal'). Its most common rhetorical form, however, is the *enthymeme* (*l'enthymème* (m.)). The *enthymeme* is a reduced form of the *syllogism*. The *major* and *minor premisses* may not be self-evidently true; and one, or even two, of the three parts of the *syllogism* may be missing. In Baudelaire's poem 'L'Invitation au voyage' the speaker is persuading the addressee to consider visiting the Low Countries with him. The main argument is contained in the refrain:

> Là, tout n'est qu'ordre et beauté,
> Luxe, calme et volupté.
>
> (Baudelaire, 'L'Invitation au voyage')

This is an *enthymeme*. It is an argument in which only the *minor premiss* is given (order, beauty, luxury, calm, and voluptuousness are to be found in the Low Countries). The *major premiss* is to be understood (order, beauty, luxury, calm, and voluptuousness are qualities that you should want to seek out); and so is the *conclusion* (therefore you should consider coming to the Low Countries with me). It may seem absurd to attend in this way to the argumentation in a poem known for its exquisite musicality. But the *enthymeme* is none the less a significant part of the speaker's message.

Inductive reasoning (le raisonnement par induction)

Induction begins with the particular, and draws conclusions that are either general or particular. It is based on the use of *examples* (*les exemples* (m.)). From one *example* (or more), conclusions are drawn. Bossuet makes explicit his inductive reasoning at the end of his funeral oration for Henriette d'Angleterre, inviting his audience to draw personal conclusions from her example:

Commencez aujourd'hui à mépriser les faveurs du monde; et toutes les fois que vous serez dans ces lieux augustes, dans ces superbes palais à qui MADAME donnait un éclat que vos yeux recherchent encore, toutes les fois que, regardant cette grande place qu'elle remplissait si bien, vous sentirez qu'elle y manque, songez que cette gloire que vous admiriez faisait son péril en cette vie, et que dans l'autre elle est devenue le sujet d'un examen rigoureux où rien n'a été capable de la rassurer que cette sincère résignation qu'elle a eue aux ordres de Dieu, et les saintes humiliations de la pénitence. (Bossuet, *Oraison funèbre de Henriette d'Angleterre*)

Bossuet urges his congregation to learn from what he has told them about Henriette. Her particular case illustrates the general need for human beings to submit themselves humbly to the will of God.

3. DISPOSITION (LA DISPOSITION)

When the orator has discovered a body of material, it then needs to be arranged or disposed. Rhetoric caters primarily to orators who have to make a single substantial speech in formal surroundings. The tradition over many centuries was for the speech to be composed typically of four main parts, with the possibility of further subsidiary parts being inserted at certain fixed points. The parts might be summed up as follows.

3.1 Exordium (l'exorde (m.))

The *exordium* is the orator's first contact with the audience. Above all, a good impression must be made. This is the part of the speech where *ethos* is crucial. The techniques most associated with the *exordium* are *captatio benevolentiae* (the Latin phrase is used very frequently in both English and French critical writing), in which the speaker says things to secure the good will of the audience, and *insinuation* (*l'insinuation* (f.)), which means adopting a slightly devious route to introduce a particularly delicate subject.

3.1a Proposition (la proposition)

Either as part of the *exordium* or separately, as a *proposition*, the orator might explain how, and in what order, the subject is to be treated.

3.2 Narration (la narration)

The *narration* is where the relevant facts are narrated. It is clearly important in *judicial* and *demonstrative* speeches. It may not be necessary in *deliberative* ones if the facts of the case are well known to all concerned.

3.2a Digression (la digression)

If the speech has already been quite long, this might be the point at which to offer the audience a *digression*, where the focus of interest might change, and, typically, there might be an appeal to the passions (*pathos*).

3.3 Confirmation (la confirmation)

The *confirmation* is often the most substantial part of a *deliberative* speech. This is where arguments are most likely to be constructed and where the bulk of the material found as a result of the processes of *invention* is placed. This is the proper place for the deployment of the *internal* and *external proofs*.

3.3a Refutation (la réfutation)

Either as part of the *confirmation* or separately, as a *refutation*, the orator might anticipate objections to the arguments and attempt to demolish them.

3.4 Peroration (la péroraison)

The *peroration* is the orator's last chance to sway the audience and make an impact. Two techniques are closely associated with the *peroration*: *recapitulation* (*la récapitulation*), in which the major points of the *confirmation* are summarized, and *amplification* (*l'amplification* (f.)), in which, typically, one issue will be dwelt on and exploited for all its emotional appeal. The *peroration* is the privileged place for the emotions (*pathos*). Rhetoricians recognize that, in practice, rational argument is less persuasive than emotional appeal.

It is difficult to illustrate *disposition* fully in a short space. It can best be seen at work in large expanses of text. There are, however, some single persuasive speeches of characters in plays that accurately embody the principles of the four-part *disposition*. In Corneille's *Le Cid*, the hero Rodrigue is tried for murder. His father defends him in this speech which is structured according to the four main divisions:

> Qu'on est digne d'envie
> Lorsqu'en perdant la force on perd aussi la vie,
> Et qu'un long âge apprête aux hommes généreux,
> Au bout de leur carrière, un destin malheureux!
> Moi, dont les longs travaux ont acquis tant de gloire,   5
> Moi, que jadis partout a suivi la victoire,
> Je me vois aujourd'hui pour avoir trop vécu,
> Recevoir un affront et demeurer vaincu.

Ce que n'a pu jamais combat, siège, embuscade,
Ce que n'a pu jamais Aragon ni Grenade,   10
Ni tous vos ennemis, ni tous mes envieux,
Le Comte en votre cour l'a fait presque à vos yeux,
Jaloux de votre choix, et fier de l'avantage
Que lui donnait sur moi l'impuissance de l'âge.
   Sire, ainsi ces cheveux blanchis sous le harnois,   15
Ce sang pour vous servir prodigué tant de fois,
Ce bras, jadis l'effroi d'une armée ennemie,
Descendaient au tombeau tout chargés d'infamie,
Si je n'eusse produit un fils digne de moi,
Digne de son pays et digne de son roi.   20
Il m'a prêté sa main, il a tué le Comte;
Il m'a rendu l'honneur, il a lavé ma honte.
Si montrer du courage et du ressentiment,
Si venger un soufflet mérite un châtiment,
Sur moi seul doit tomber l'éclat de la tempête: 25
Quand le bras a failli, l'on en punit la tête.
Qu'on nomme crime, ou non, ce qui fait nos débats,
Sire, j'en suis la tête, il n'en est que le bras.
Si Chimène se plaint qu'il a tué son père,
Il ne l'eût jamais fait si je l'eusse pu faire.   30
Immolez donc ce chef que les ans vont ravir,
Et conservez pour vous le bras qui peut servir.
Aux dépens de mon sang satisfaites Chimène:
Je n'y résiste point, je consens à ma peine;
Et loin de murmurer d'un rigoureux décret,   35
Mourant sans déshonneur, je mourrai sans regret.

(Corneille, *Le Cid*)

The *exordium* (1–8) exploits *ethos*. Don Diègue presents himself as a
valorous man now in his declining years. The *narration* (9–14) evokes
the key episode which led to the murder: namely, the count's insult
to Don Diègue. The *confirmation* (15–30) argues that Rodrigue was
acting entirely for Don Diègue, and cannot therefore be held
responsible. The *peroration* (31–6) draws the natural and moving conclusion that Don Diègue must now be punished, not his son.

4. ELOCUTION (L'ÉLOCUTION (F.))

Having found and organized material, orators next need to decide
on the precise words they will use to express themselves. The selec-

tion of words is the domain of *elocution*. This is the most celebrated part of rhetoric. It deals with the *ornaments* of style (*les ornements* (m.)). The word '*ornaments*' should not be misunderstood. It does not imply that the devices of *elocution* are designed for purely decorative purposes. These devices may well be decorative and add to the aesthetic impact of a text; but they are primarily functional. The rhetorical term *ornament* is a translation of the Latin *ornatus*, which refers to weapons used in battle. The devices of *elocution* are as persuasive in intent as the features of *invention* and *disposition*: they are meant to sway the minds of audiences or readers. For purposes of clarity, I have divided the devices into four categories: figures of imagery, figures of construction, figures of emotion, and figures of presentation, though these are not watertight. Before discussing specific devices, however, rhetoricians offer general advice on the kinds of style that are available.

4.1 Kinds of Style (les genres (m.) de style)

Traditionally, rhetoric identifies three kinds of style (grand, medium, and low). The styles are characterized by different kinds of lexis and syntax. The style adopted depends upon the subject under discussion and the way in which the audience is to be affected. The styles might be summarized as follows:

Grand style (le style élevé)

This style uses long, balanced sentences with words often removed from the register of ordinary speech. It is the kind of style appropriate to formal political discourse, to solemn occasions, to tragedy. It is particularly linked to the arousal of strong emotions.

Medium style (le style moyen)

This style uses sentences of average length, with less obvious contrivance in their construction and words that are neither elevated nor colloquial. It is the kind of style appropriate to clear explanatory or narrative writing.

Low style (le style simple)

This style uses shorter sentences closer to the patterns of ordinary speech. The words themselves can be colloquial. It is a style that can be used to establish close sympathetic links between speaker and

audience. It is appropriate to comedy and farce, and also to an orator's asides, such as might be found in an *exordium* or a *digression*.

These three styles are comparable to modern notions of register.
Writers, readers, and audiences are aware of which styles are appropriate at which moments. Failure to fulfil expectations can be seen
as comic or iconoclastic. In the sixteenth century Ronsard writes a
sonnet for Pontus de Tyard on the difficulty of choosing the right
style to please one's readers:

> Thiard, chacun disoit à mon commencement
> Que j'estoi trop obscur au simple populaire:
> Aujourd'hui chacun dit que je suis au contraire,
> Et que je me dements parlant trop bassement.

> (Ronsard, *Continuation des amours*, no. 1)

In the seventeenth century Saint-Amant achieves comic effects by
writing about a simple subject (a melon) in an elevated style:

> Baillez-le-moi, je vous en prie,
> Que j'en commette idôlatrie:
> O! quelle odeur! qu'il est pesant!
> Et qu'il me charme en le baisant!

> (Saint-Amant, 'Le Melon')

In the nineteenth century Hugo asserts his stylistic iconoclasm by
claiming no longer to distinguish between different levels of lexis.
He uses the word 'sénateur' to represent the *grand style* and 'roturier'
the *low style*:

> Je fis souffler un vent révolutionnaire.
> Je mis un bonnet rouge au vieux dictionnaire.
> Plus de mot sénateur! Plus de mot roturier!

> (Hugo, 'Réponse à un acte d'accusation')

4.2 Figures of Imagery

Several figures associated with imagery are known as *tropes* (*les tropes*
(m.)) (from the Greek word meaning 'turn'), because they change the
meaning of a word so that it is to be interpreted in a non-literal way.
The two main *tropes* are *metaphor* and *metonymy*; but associated with
them are *simile, personification, allegory, synecdoche, periphrasis,* and *antonomasia. Irony* and its associated figures can also be seen as *tropes*, but
they will be dealt with separately under 'Figures of emotion'. Not

strictly speaking *tropes*, but closely related to imagistic discourse, are the figures of *zeugma*, *hypallage*, and *syllepsis*, which I shall also explain in this section.

➤ Simile (la comparaison) and metaphor (la métaphore)

A *simile* compares one entity (a tenor) with another entity (a vehicle), which in some sense represents it. A *simile* identifies both the tenor and the vehicle, and, in addition, uses semantic markers that make the comparison explicit (words and phrases like 'comme', 'ainsi que', 'ressembler', 'avoir l'air'). For example: A (tenor) is like B (vehicle). A *simile* helps Flaubert to convey the mystery of Salammbô's eyes:

Les yeux de Salammbô, au fond de ses longues draperies, avaient l'air de deux étoiles dans l'ouverture d'un nuage. (Flaubert, *Salammbô*)

A *metaphor* is like a *simile*, except that either (a) the semantic markers indicating comparison are omitted, as in Baudelaire's phrase 'La Nature est un temple' ('Correspondances'); or (b) *both* the semantic markers indicating comparison *and* the tenor are omitted, as in Valéry's line 'Ce toit tranquille, où marchent les colombes' ('Le Cimetière marin'), where 'toit tranquille' can plausibly be interpreted *metaphorically* as a reference to the sea. *Metaphors* like Baudelaire's above, that name both the tenor and the vehicle, are said to be *in praesentia*; *metaphors* like Valéry's, that name only the vehicle, are said to be *in absentia*. Not only nouns, but also verbs and adjectives can be used *metaphorically*. The following passage combines noun and verb *metaphors*, and is an example of an extended *metaphor* (*une métaphore filée* or *continue*). *Metaphors* allow Giono to bring to life a description of the wind:

Tout le jour, le fleuve du vent s'est rué dans les cuvettes de la Drôme. Monté jusqu'aux châtaigneraies, il a fait les cent coups du diable dans les grandes branches; il s'est enflé, peu à peu, jusqu'à déborder les montagnes et, sitôt le bord sauté, pomponné de pelotes de feuilles, il a dévalé sur nous. (Giono, *Colline*)

Here the wind is presented as a river. Words associated with water are applied to wind (e.g. 'fleuve', 'monté', 'déborder').

➤ Personification (la personnification) and allegory (l'allégorie (f.))

Personification, *allegory*, and *metaphor* are closely related figures. *Personification* and *allegory* are special examples of extended *metaphors*. *Allegory* presents one thought or idea as another. It can be read both literally and *metaphorically*, as in Boileau's expression of his preference for gentle streams, which can also be read as a preference for a smooth, flowing style of writing:

> J'aime mieux un ruisseau qui, sur une molle arène,
> Dans un pré plein de fleurs lentement se promène,
> Qu'un torrent débordé qui, d'un cours orageux,
> Roule plein de gravier sur un terrain fangeux.
>
> (Boileau, *L'Art poétique*)

Personification presents an abstract concept or an inanimate object as if it were a person, as Sartre does here with respect to both 'œuvres' and 'roman':

Ces œuvres étranges [. . .] ne témoignent pas de la faiblesse du genre romanesque [. . .] le roman est en train de réfléchir sur lui-même. (Sartre, preface to *Portrait d'un inconnu*)

The *personification* is effected through the use of the verbal *metaphors* 'témoignent' and 'réfléchir'.

> ➤ **Metonymy (la métonymie) and synecdoche (la synec-doque)** Like *metaphor*, *metonymy* and *synecdoche* both present one thing as a substitute for something else. But whereas with *metaphor* the relationship between tenor and vehicle is one of analogy, with *metonymy* and *synecdoche* the relationship can be defined more specifically. *Metonymy* is a subtle device, whereby a particular property, characteristic, or association is substituted for the general concept. Verlaine substitutes the colour of the object (green) for the object itself (grass) in these lines:

> Des arbres et des moulins
> Sont légers sur le vert tendre.
>
> (Verlaine, 'L'Échelonnement des haies')

Synecdoche establishes a relationship between tenor and vehicle in which the part is given instead of the whole, or vice versa, or sometimes the genus for the species, or vice versa. Andromaque refers only to her eyes when she means her whole person, but thereby draws attention to her tears and her distress:

> Quels charmes ont pour vous des yeux infortunés,
> Qu'à des pleurs éternels vous avez condamnés?
>
> (Racine, *Andromaque*)

➤ *Periphrasis (la périphrase) and antonomasia (l'antonomase (f.))* Like *metaphor, periphrasis* and *antonomasia* present one thing in terms of another, but in special ways. *Periphrasis* is an expansive device. It refers to a thing or a concept in more words than would be strictly necessary in prosaic discourse. Hugo uses a phrase to refer unambiguously, but picturesquely, to the simple concept of evening:

> C'était l'heure tranquille où les lions vont boire.
>
> (Hugo, 'Booz endormi')

Antonomasia is the use of a proper name in place of a common name, or vice versa. Alternatively, one proper name can replace another, as in this example of Balzac's evocation of an aged, corpse-like servant, David:

Jamais les os desséchés que le souffle divin doit ranimer dans la vallée de Josaphat, jamais cette image apocalyptique ne fut mieux réalisée que par ce Lazare sans cesse rappelé du sépulcre à la vie par la voix de la jeune fille. (Balzac, *Séraphîta*)

Referring to David as the biblical Lazarus, who was restored to life from death, the narrator suggests the powerful effect the young girl has on the ageing character David.

➤ *Zeugma (le zeugma), hypallage (l'hypallage (f.)) and syllepsis (la syllepse)* The use of *zeugma, hypallage,* and *syllepsis* often contributes to the imagistic force of a writer's language, even though these figures are not strictly *tropes*. Rather, they are devices that depend on syntactic and grammatical structures. *Syllepsis* bridges the figurative and the literal: it is the use of a word in both its figurative and its literal connotations at the same time, as in this line of Corneille:

> Rome n'est plus dans Rome, elle est toute où je suis.
>
> (Corneille, *Sertorius*)

'Rome' here means both the geographical place (the second occurrence) and the qualities of grandeur associated with that place (the first occurrence). The key word does not need to be repeated for the literal and figurative senses to be simultaneously in play. This is the case in Racine's *Bajazet*, when Roxane promises to unite Atalide to her lover 'Par des nœuds éternels'. 'Nœuds' means marriage *metaphorically*; but literally it means the rope with which she will be strangled to death, as her lover was.

Hypallage is the application of one word to another to which it would not normally be applied, typically the application of an adjective to a noun, when there is another noun to which the adjective has to be understood to apply, as in Œnone's attempt to accuse Hippolyte before Thésée:

> Phèdre mourait, seigneur, et sa main meurtrière
> Eteignait de ses yeux l'innocente lumière.
>
> (Racine, *Phèdre*)

The morally charged adjectives ('meurtrière' and 'innocente'), though applied to 'main' and 'lumière', have to be understood as applying to Phèdre herself.

Zeugma makes two (or more) terms dependent on another in such a way that the latter has simultaneously to be understood in different senses, as in Hugo's description:

> Vêtu de probité candide et de lin blanc [. . .] (Hugo, 'Booz endormi')

This is close to *syllepsis*; but the essence of *zeugma* is the playful juxtaposition of two terms lacking in semantic equivalence (here 'probité' and 'lin'). This essential quality of *zeugma* is evident in San Antonio's comic juxtaposition of phrases beginning with 'en' but of very different semantic and syntactic value:

> Vous désirez? me demande-t-elle en souriant et en espagnol. (San Antonio, *Ménage tes méninges*)

4.3 Figures of Construction

A style popularly thought of as rhetorical is one marked by obvious order and pattern. Patterns can be found in the way words are repeated, in the way syntactic units are disposed and in the way phonemes are arranged. But it is misleading to call such a patterned style rhetorical. Rhetoric caters too for the absence of pattern and order (see Figures of emotion). It is true that a text characterized by frequent patterning is sometimes one that is seeking to draw attention to the rhetoric at work within it. It is equally true, however, that patterns can be used subtly and without ostentation.

Word patterns

The following figures dealing with the repetition of words in various configurations are illustrated in this section: *anaphora* and *epistrophe*; *anadiplosis* and *climax*; *symploce*; *reduplicatio* and *geminatio*; *polyptoton*.

➤ **Anaphora (*l'anaphore (f.)*) and epistrophe (*l'épistrophe (f.)*)** *Anaphora* is one of the best-known and most common word patterns. It involves repeating the same word or words at the beginning of successive clauses, sentences, or lines of verse. It yields the following pattern: A . . . . / A . . . . / A . . . . The character Camille expresses her hatred of Rome by repeating the city's name prominently:

> Rome, l'unique objet de mon ressentiment!
> Rome, à qui vient ton bras d'immoler mon amant!
> Rome, qui t'a vu naître, et que ton cœur adore!
> Rome enfin que je hais parce qu'elle t'honore!
>
> (Corneille, *Horace*)

Epistrophe is the twin and opposite of *anaphora*. It involves repeating the same word or words at the end of successive clauses, sentences, or lines of verse. Thus: . . . . A/ . . . . A/ . . . . A. For example:

Mais il n'enseignait rien celui-là, ne savait rien, ne souhaitait rien. (Flaubert, *Madame Bovary*)

➤ **Anadiplosis (*l'anadiplose (f.)*) and climax (*la concaténation*)** *Anadiplosis* involves repeating the word or words that occur at the end of one clause, sentence, or line of verse, at the beginning of the next. Thus: . . . . A/ A . . . . For example:

> [. . .] Et Cérès, que fit-elle?
> Ce qu'elle fit? Un prompt courroux
> L'anima d'abord contre vous.
>
> (La Fontaine, 'Le Pouvoir des fables')

In general usage, a climax is a culminating point. In rhetoric, *climax* has a special meaning. It is a sequence of successive *anadiploses*, exploited to comic effect by Molière when he shows Sganarelle trying to reason with his master:

L'homme est en ce monde ainsi que l'oiseau sur la branche; la branche est attachée à l'arbre; qui s'attache à l'arbre, suit de bons préceptes; les bons préceptes valent mieux que les belles paroles; les belles paroles se trouvent à la cour [. . .]. (Molière, *Dom Juan*)

➤ **Symploce (la symploque)**   *Symploce* is the simultaneous use
of *anaphora* and *epistrophe*. It therefore yields the following pattern:
A . . . . B/ A . . . . B. In this example the repeated
elements are phrases rather than single words:

Il faut que je me dise qu'ils n'ont pas su. Et il faut que je sache pourquoi
ils n'ont pas su. (J. Romains, *Les Hommes de bonne volonté*)

➤ **Reduplicatio (la réduplication) and geminatio (la gémi-
nation)**   *Reduplicatio* is the repetition in immediate or very close
proximity of the same word or words. The pattern is therefore: AA
. . . . There is an example at the beginning of each of the
following lines:

> O triste, triste était mon âme
> A cause, à cause d'une femme.
>
> (Verlaine, 'O triste, triste était mon âme')

More flexible than *reduplicatio*, *geminatio* is the repetition of a word or
words in different places, whether within one sentence or successive
sentences. There is therefore no fixed pattern that might represent
geminatio. Bérénice's use of the figure conveys her deep love for
Titus:

> J'aimais, Seigneur, j'aimais, je voulais être aimée.
>
> (Racine, *Bérénice*)

Geminatio is here combined, for purposes of intensification, with
another *figure* involving the repetition of a word, though in a slightly
modified form (*polyptoton*).

➤ **Polyptoton (le polyptote and la dérivation)**   *Polyptoton*
repeats the same word but in a different morphological form, as
with Bérénice's repetition of 'aimais' in the form 'aimée' in the
example above. La Bruyère conveys his cynical view of society's
hierarchies by using a double *polyptoton* in one sentence, repeating
the verbs 'entourer' and 'saluer' in different forms:

Les grands sont entourés, salués, respectés; les petits entourent, saluent, se
prosternent; et tous sont contents. (La Bruyère, *Les Caractères*)

French rhetoricians distinguish between this kind of *polyptoton*, which
they call *polyptote*, and a more general kind, in which the same root
word is repeated in different parts of speech, and which they call
dérivation. For example:

Je crains Dieu, cher Abner, et n'ai point d'autre crainte.

(Racine, *Athalie*)

Syntax patterns

The patterns created by the repetition of single words have their equivalent on a larger scale in the patterning of words within a clause or in successive clauses. The relevant figures here are *parison* and *isocolon*; *antithesis*; *epitrochasmus*, *gradatio*, and *conglobatio*; rhythmic *gradatio*; *polysyndeton*, *asyndeton*, *hypotaxis*, and *parataxis*; *chiasmus*; *hendiadys* and *metabole*.

➢ **Parison (le parison) and isocolon (l'isocolon (m.))**
Parison and *isocolon* are figures of parallel phrasing, particularly powerful when spoken. *Parison* involves the repetition of similar syntactic constructions in clauses of similar length; *isocolon* is a stricter version of *parison*, in that it is exactly the same syntactic construction that is repeated and in clauses of the same length. Both figures are often combined with other figures of construction, especially *anaphora*. The following two sentences exemplify *parison* and *anaphora*. There is also an example of *polyptoton* in the first ('aimait', 'aimer').

Il lui disait qu'il l'aimait et que personne ne pourrait l'aimer aussi fort. Il lui disait qu'il ne serait rien sans elle, et qu'ils seraient finis l'un sans l'autre. (*Le Monde*, 9 July 1993)

The much closer syntactic repetition in the following sentence qualifies it as an example of *isocolon*:

S'il n'y avait point d'obscurité, l'homme ne sentirait pas sa corruption; s'il n'y avait point de lumière, l'homme n'espérerait point de remède. (Pascal, *Pensées*)

This is also an example of *antithesis*.

➢ **Antithesis (l'antithèse (f.))**   *Antithesis* presents, typically in balanced phrasing, concepts that are in some sense opposite to one another, as light and dark are in the previous example from Pascal. Ocean and granite are presented *antithetically* in the following phrases:

[. . .] une lutte entre l'Océan et le Granit, deux créatures également puissantes: l'une par son inertie, l'autre par sa mobilité. (Balzac, *Séraphîta*)

➢ **Epitrochasmus (l'épitrochasme (m.)), gradatio (la gradation), and conglobatio (la conglobation)**   Both *epitrochas-*

mus and *gradatio* involve lists of words. In the case of *epitrochasmus*, the list is in no particular order, as in these venomous lines of satirical verse:

> Je ne vois rien en vous qu'un lâche, un imposteur,
> Un traître, un scélérat, un perfide, un menteur,
> Un fou dont les accès vont jusqu'à la furie,
> Et d'un tronc fort illustre une branche pourrie.

(Boileau, *Satires*, 5)

By contrast, *gradatio* is a list of words in which there is a clearly significant ascending or descending order of presentation, as in the sequence of verbs suggesting the ebbing away of life in the following sentence:

Je serrais et la vie se fatiguait en elle [la vipère], s'amollissait, se laissait tomber au bout de mon poing. (H. Bazin, *Vipère au poing*)

Conglobatio is a more thoroughgoing and insistent piling up of items, and typically most items in the pile contain more than one word. Hippolyte uses *conglobatio* to evoke fond memories of his father's exploits:

> Tu sais combien mon âme, attentive à sa voix,
> S'échauffait au récit de ses nobles exploits,
> Quand tu me dépeignais ce héros intrépide
> Consolant les mortels de l'absence d'Alcide;
> Les monstres étouffés, et les brigands punis,
> Procuste, Cercyon, et Scyrron, et Sinnis,
> Et les os dispersés du géant d'Epidaure,
> Et la Crète fumant du sang du Minotaure.

(Racine, *Phèdre*)

➤ **Rhythmic gradatio (la gradation)**   *Gradatio* is a figure that can be applied to a broader feature of sentence structure than simply the listing of individual words. It can refer also to a pattern of shortening or lengthening clauses as a sentence progresses. An ascending *gradatio* would apply to a sentence in which the clauses became successively longer. The following sentence illustrates both ascending and descending *gradatio*. The first, longer part contains subordinate clauses of increasing length. But the sentence concludes with a descending *gradatio*, the second part ('après quoi . . .') being much shorter than what precedes it:

Une femme m'ouvrit, à qui je racontai que je m'étais perdu, que d'être sans argent ne m'empêchait pas d'avoir faim et que peut-être on serait assez bon pour me donner à manger et à boire; après quoi je regagnerais mon wagon remisé, où je patienterais jusqu'au lendemain. (Gide, *Si le grain ne meurt*)

The ascending *gradatio* conveys the narrator's needs; the descending *gradatio* his resignation.

➤ **Asyndeton (*l'asyndète (f.)*), polysyndeton (la polysyndète), parataxis (la parataxe), and hypotaxis (*l'hypotaxe (f.)*)** *Parataxis* and *hypotaxis* refer to general types of sentence construction, in which specific examples of *asyndeton* and *polysyndeton* can be found respectively. *Parataxis* is the construction of a sequence of clauses or sentences with no, or very few, explicit links (like conjunctions) between them. Each absence of a link is called an *asyndeton*. The narrator of the following passage recalls her father's semi-literacy without comment, but in a moving paratactic style with several examples of *asyndeton*:

Autre souvenir de honte: chez le notaire, il a dû écrire le premier 'lu et approuvé', il ne savait pas comment orthographier, il a choisi 'à prouver'. Gêne, obsession de cette faute, sur la route du retour. (A. Ernaux, *La Place*)

Parataxis invites the reader's (or listener's) active participation in the creation of links between clauses and sentences. *Hypotaxis*, by contrast, supplies links in abundance. The tendency of La Fontaine's monkey to flatter excessively is conveyed in the following example by the poet's use of *hypotaxis*, or *polysyndeton*:

> Le Singe approuva fort cette sévérité,
> Et flatteur excessif, il loua la colère
> Et la griffe du Prince, et l'antre, et cette odeur.
>
> (La Fontaine, 'La Cour du lion')

➤ **Chiasmus (le chiasme)** *Chiasmus* is the repetition in inverse order of two or more elements. It thus yields the pattern ABBA. Exactly the same words can be repeated in inverse order, as in the favourite saying of Molière's miser, Harpagon:

Il faut manger pour vivre, et non pas vivre pour manger. (Molière, *L'Avare*)

More frequently, however, the repetition is not of exactly the same words but of the same parts of speech, as in the following example, which repeats the pattern noun + adjective in inverse order:

Ces yeux mystérieux ont d'invincibles charmes.

(Baudelaire, 'Les Petites Vieilles')

> ➤ **Hendiadys (l'hendiadyn (m.)) and metabole (la métabole)**   *Hendiadys* is a coupling of, typically, two nouns or two adjectives which are closely related in meaning. There is one example in each of the following lines of verse:

Tonnez, tambours et peaux de bêtes!
Résonnez, cuivres et trompettes!

(P. Ybrak-Piccart, *Inventions*)

Both nouns in the first line signify drums, both in the second signify trumpets. A more general term for this kind of effect, applicable equally to instances where there are more than two synonyms, is *metabole*. For example:

Muse, prête à ma bouche une voix plus sauvage
Pour chanter le dépit, la colère, la rage.

(Boileau, *Le Lutrin*)

Here the final three nouns all signify anger.

Sound patterns

Complex effects can be achieved, particularly in poetry and verse drama by repeating phonemes (individual units of sound) in certain ways. Rhetoric identifies a small number of figures related to sound patterns, but together they embrace many effects. Most prominent among them are *alliteration* and *assonance*; *homoioteleuton*; *paronomasia*; and *onomatopoeia*.

➤ **Alliteration (l'allitération (f.)) and assonance (l'assonance (f.))**   *Alliteration* is the repetition of the same consonants in close proximity, and *assonance* of the same vowels. Verlaine combines both with great concentration in just three short lines:

Les sanglots longs
Des violons
De l'automne.

(Verlaine, 'Chanson d'automne')

The most striking repeated sounds here are /o/, /ɔ̃/, /l/.

➤ **Homoioteleuton (l'homéotéleute (f.))** *Homoioteleuton* is the repetition of words with the same endings, used, for example, by Montaigne when he describes playfully the kind of style he likes:

un parler [. . .] non pédantesque, non fratesque, non plaideresque, mais plutôt soldatesque. (Montaigne, 'De l'institution des enfants')

➤ **Paronomasia (la paronomase)** *Paronomasia* is a generally playful device, bringing into close proximity words that sound very similar, but not quite the same, as in Verlaine's line:

Sans rien en lui qui pèse ou qui pose.

(Verlaine, 'Art poétique')

➤ **Onomatopoeia (l'onomatopée (f.))** *Onomatopoeia* is a very rare device, which occurs in writing or speech that refers to noise or sound. In *onomatopoeia* phonemes combine to suggest the sound being evoked, as the repetition of the /s/ is often taken to conjure up the hiss of snakes in the following line:

Pour qui sont ces serpents qui sifflent sur nos têtes?

(Racine, *Andromaque*)

4.4 Figures of Emotion

I have grouped under the heading 'Figures of emotion' a number of figures which lend themselves to the expression of strong feelings or emotions. There are figures concerned with different kinds of exclaiming and questioning, figures of sarcasm and exaggeration, figures suggesting a loss of syntactic control, and figures of improper language. None of these figures is necessarily and inevitably linked to the expression of emotion. All rhetorical figures are polysemic; they achieve various effects according to their contexts. The figures in this section, however, are the ones most commonly associated with emotion. But to make the point about polysemy, I shall give some examples of the unemotional use of these figures.

Exclaiming and questioning

➤ **Exclamation (l'exclamation (f.)) and apostrophe (l'a-postrophe (f.))** *Exclamations* can indicate different degrees of emotion in the speaker or the writer, and are perceived as arresting by the listener or reader because they constitute a sudden break from the normal flow of discourse. Lamartine's use of *exclamation* brings about a shift in perspective in his description of the effects of spring on the oak-tree:

> Le printemps, de sa tiède ondée,
> L'arrose [le chêne] comme avec la main;
> Cette poussière est fécondée,
> Et la vie y circule enfin.
> La vie! A ce seul mot, tout œil, toute pensée,
> S'inclinent confondus et n'osent pénétrer [. . .].
>
> (Lamartine, 'Le Chêne')

The repetition of 'la vie' (*geminatio*) in exclamatory form introduces into an apparently objective description an unexpected expression of amazement at nature's powers. Even more arresting than *exclamation* is *apostrophe*, when the speaker or writer suddenly addresses his or her words to a person or a thing, who is typically absent. The objects being apostrophized here by Henri Michaux are all the more startling for their being unusual:

Icebergs, Icebergs, Solitaires sans besoin, des pays bouchés, distants et libres de vermine. Parents des îles, parents des sources, comme je vous vois [. . .]. (H. Michaux, 'Icebergs')

➢ *Interrogation (l'interrogation (f.))*   Everyone is familiar with the phrase 'rhetorical question'. Rhetoricians, however, have found the concept of asking questions in the middle of a speech or piece of writing to be more complex than this simple phrase suggests. Different kinds of question can affect audiences in different ways and require a variety of responses. Accordingly, different names have been given to the different types of question. The most basic form of question that can be asked is one to which the reply required is straightforward, usually a 'yes' or a 'no'. This is called *interrogation*. The distressed Andromaque tries to move the haughty Hermione with the question:

> N'est-ce pas à vos yeux un spectacle assez doux,
> Que la veuve d'Hector pleurante à vos genoux?
>
> (Racine, *Andromaque*)

➢ *Subjectio (la subjection)*   In the case of *subjectio*, a question is asked, and the answer is provided. This example does not involve emotion. The figure is used to make an idea come over more clearly to the reader:

Voulez-vous du public mériter les amours?
Sans cesse en écrivant variez vos discours.

(Boileau, *L'Art poétique*)

➤ **Percontatio (*l'épiplexis (f.)*)**   *Percontatio* is asking a question in order to reproach the listener or reader, as Hermione does when she criticizes Oreste for having too readily believed her request that he murder the king:

Ah! fallait-il en croire une amante insensée?
Ne devais-tu pas lire au fond de ma pensée?

(Racine, *Andromaque*)

➤ **Ratiocinatio (*la dubitation*)**   Hermione uses another figure of questioning, *ratiocinatio*, to reveal profound self-doubt and uncertainty. *Ratiocinatio* involves the speaker asking a question of herself:

Où suis-je? qu'ai-je fait? que dois-je faire encore?

(Racine, *Andromaque*)

➤ **Communicatio (*la communication*)**   *Communicatio* is the kind of question to which the answer is not obvious, and which requires thought on the part of the addressee. For example:

Nous aurions pu, pour nous mettre au diapason ordinaire de la grande presse, comparer tout de suite le nouveau professeur à Sainte-Beuve ou à Taine. Mais qu'aurait-il pensé lui-même d'un tel coup d'encensoir?
(J. Fournier, *Mon Encrier*)

Irony

➤ **Irony (*l'ironie (f.)*) and antiphrasis (*l'antiphrase (f.)*)**
Irony is saying the opposite of what one means, or at least something rather different from it. Dorine seems to encourage Mariane to marry Tartuffe, and paints a highly favourable picture of him. Her meaning is the opposite.

Quelle raison aurais-je à combattre vos vœux?
Le parti, de soi-même, est fort avantageux.
Monsieur Tartuffe! Oh! oh! n'est-ce rien qu'on propose?

(Molière, *Tartuffe*)

Although the effect for the theatre audience is comic, the effect on Mariane is emotional: Dorine is trying to bully her, to intimidate her into rejecting Tartfuffe as a husband. *Irony* embraces *antiphrasis*, which is the ironical usage of individual words. In Dorine's lines above, 'fort avantageux' is an *antiphrasis*.

➤ ***Chleuasmos (le chleuasme) and asteismus (l'astéisme (m.))***   *Chleuasmos* and *asteismus* are two special forms of *irony*. *Chleuasmos* is a kind of mock modesty, by means of which the speaker or writer appeals to an interlocutor to reach a favourable character judgement. The device is used to great effect by Tartuffe:

> Oui, mon frère, je suis un méchant, un coupable,
> Un malheureux pécheur, tout plein d'iniquité.
>
> (Molière, Tartuffe)

With *asteismus*, on the other hand, words of reproach are directed at the addressee, but they are intended to be read flatteringly. It is particularly appropriate to expressions of affection, as when Suzanne tells Chérubin:

Oh, dans trois ou quatre ans, je prédis que vous serez le plus grand petit vaurien! (Beaumarchais, *Le Mariage de Figaro*)

➤ ***Hyperbole (l'hyperbole (f.)) and litotes (la litote)*** *Hyperbole* is saying more than is meant. At its simplest, it can be numerical exaggeration. More generally, it refers to exaggeration on any linguistic level, as when Mme de Sévigné introduces an exciting piece of news in this way:

Je m'en vais vous mander la chose la plus étonnante, la plus surprenante, la plus merveilleuse, la plus miraculeuse [. . .]. (Mme de Sévigné, letter of 15 December 1670)

Litotes is the opposite of *hyperbole*. It is saying less than is meant. It can be a way of suggesting great emotion while containing it, as when Chimène tells Rodrigue: 'Va, je ne te hais point' (Corneille, *Le Cid*).

Broken syntax

The following four figures all involve interruptions to the normal flow of speech. Such interruptions sometimes suggest nothing more than the quality of disorder in ordinary speech, but they can also be read as signs of strong emotion.

➤ ***Interruptio (l'interruption (f.))***   *Interruptio* occurs when there is a pause in the discourse. This is sometimes indicated by suspension points or a dash. Sometimes the discourse, when resumed, will take off in a new direction. In dialogue, in the novel, or in drama, an *interruptio* occurs when a second character starts speaking before the first has finished, as in this example:

LE BRET. Ah! dans quels jolis draps . . .
CYRANO. Oh! toi! tu vas grogner.

(E. Rostand, Cyrano de Bergerac)

➤ *Aposiopesis (l'aposiopèse (f.))*   *Aposiopesis* is the kind of silence that occurs when the speaker chooses not to continue, or is unable to do so. When Phèdre refuses to tell Œnone of her secret passion, the effect is to prompt grave and anxious suspicions:

> Je t'en ai dit assez. Epargne-moi le reste.
> Je meurs, pour ne point faire un aveu si funeste.

(Racine, Phèdre)

The effect is quite different when Agnès will not tell Arnolphe what Horace took from her—suspenseful for the increasingly jealous and angry Arnolphe, comic for the theatre audience:

AGNÈS.   Hé! il m'a . . .
ARNOLPHE.   Quoi?
AGNÈS.   Pris . . .
ARNOLPHE.   Euh!
AGNÈS.   Le . . .
ARNOLPHE.   Plaît-il?
AGNÈS.   Je n'ose,
        Et vous vous fâcherez peut-être contre moi.

(Molière, L'École des femmes)

➤ *Correctio (la correction)*   *Correctio* is a pause in the flow that allows the speaker or writer to go back and correct or express differently what he or she has just said. The effect is often emphatic, as in this example:

C'est en effet la première fois dans l'histoire du monde que tout un monde vit et prospère, paraît prospérer contre toute culture. Qu'on m'entende bien. Je ne dis pas que c'est pour toujours. Cette race en a vu bien d'autres. Mais enfin c'est pour le temps présent. (Péguy, *Notre Jeunesse*)

➤ *Parenthesis (la parenthèse)*   A *parenthesis* is typically the insertion of a phrase or sentence into a complete unit of sense. It is usually marked typographically by brackets, commas, or dashes. It can serve a qualificatory or explanatory function. *Parenthesis* is used in this example to provide narratorial comment:

Emma était accoudée à sa fenêtre (elle s'y mettait souvent: la fenêtre, en province, remplace les théâtres et la promenade), et elle s'amusait à considérer la cohue des rustres, lorsqu'elle aperçut un monsieur vêtu d'une redingote de velours vert. (Flaubert, *Madame Bovary*)

The *parenthesis* indicates an ironic comment by the narrator about provincial life and Emma's being irremediably part of it.

Improper language

Discourse can adopt various kinds of improper or unusual language either as a sign of emotion or, quite differently, for comic effect.

➤ **Enallage (l'énallage (f.))** *Enallage* is the substitution of one person, number, or tense for what might be the more expected one. Hermione substitutes the 'tu' for the 'vous' form to express her fury with Pyrrhus:

> Vous ne répondez point? . . . perfide! je le voi,
> Tu comptes les moments que tu perds avec moi.
>
> (Racine, *Andromaque*)

The servant Martine is castigated for her use of *enallage* through ignorance:

> Et je parlons tout droit comme on parle cheux nous.
>
> (Molière, *Les Femmes savantes*)

➤ **Hyperbaton (l'hyperbate (f.))** *Hyperbaton* is the adoption of a different word order from what would normally be expected. The inversion of subject and verb produces a common kind of *hyperbaton*, and can be used for emphasis. *Hyperbaton* is particularly common in poetry, where the order of words has often to adapt itself to requirements of rhythm. In this example, d'Aubigné puts words into the mouth of the Pope to convey the sense of the Pope's self-importance:

> Entre tous les mortels, de Dieu la prevoyance
> M'a du haut ciel choisi, donné sa Lieutenance.
>
> (D'Aubigné, *Les Tragiques*)

The repeated use of *hyperbaton* here has the effect of giving emphasis to some of those words which indicate the Pope's view of himself as God's elect ('de Dieu' coming before, rather than after, 'la prevoyance'; and 'choisi' coming after, rather than before, 'du haut ciel').

➤ **Anacoluthon (*l'anacoluthe (f.)*)** *Anacoluthon* involves the use of what would be perceived conventionally as an incorrect syntactical pattern, as in this famous example from Pascal:

Le nez de Cléopâtre, s'il eût été plus court, toute la face de la terre en eût été changée. (Pascal, *Pensées*)

What looks like the subject of the sentence, 'le nez de Cléopâtre', is unexpectedly displaced by 'toute la face de la terre'.

➤ **Acyrologia (*l'impropriété (f.)*)** Alternatively known in English as a malapropism, *acyrologia* accords a word a meaning which it does not conventionally have. It is often associated with ignorance and comedy. Marotte exclaims to the *précieuses*:

Dame! je n'entends point le latin, je n'ai pas appris, comme vous, la filofie dans *Le Grand Cyre*. (Molière, *Les Précieuses ridicules*)

'Filofie' is her failed attempt to say 'philosophie', and '*Cyre*' is the wrong name of the hero of Mlle de Scudéry's novel *Le Grand Cyrus*.

4.5 Figures of Presentation

In this category I consider a number of figures that might best be described as ideas for presentation. They are distinct from the figures already discussed in that they are not concerned with microstructural detail. They are in some sense closer to the *places* or *topics* of *invention*.

➤ **Concession (*la concession*)** *Concession* involves conceding an argument, either to prepare for a more important argument or as a devious way of attacking an opponent. The device is used repeatedly by Valère in Molière's *L'Avare* when he attempts to persuade Harpagon that Élise should not be forced to marry Anselme. The miser's argument is that Anselme will take his daughter without a dowry. In response to this, Valère uses *concession* before broaching an opposite argument:

Ah! il n'y a pas de réplique à cela: on le sait bien; qui diantre peut aller là contre? Ce n'est pas qu'il n'y ait quantité de pères qui aimeraient mieux ménager la satisfaction de leurs filles que l'argent qu'ils pourraient donner. (Molière, *L'Avare*)

➤ **Ethopoeia (l'éthopée (f.))**   There are two kinds of *ethopoeia*. One is a description of a character's moral and psychological characteristics; in this sense, it is a characteristic feature of portrait writing. *Ethopoeia* is a device used recurrently by La Bruyère in *Les Caractères*. It can also be used as an argumentational strategy. In this sense *ethopoeia* involves putting oneself into someone else's shoes and imagining the feelings of the other person. Valère uses it to comic effect when he represents the views of Élise to her father Harpagon in the same scene from *L'Avare* as that illustrating *concession*:

Cela est vrai. Mais elle pourrait vous dire que c'est un peu précipiter les choses, et qu'il faudrait au moins quelque temps pour voir si son inclination pourra s'accommoder avec . . . (Molière, *L'Avare*)

➤ **Hypotyposis (l'hypotypose (f.))**   *Hypotyposis* is a special kind of description. It paints a scene with such vivid and insistent detail that the audience or readers can almost see it before their eyes. It is sometimes associated with the arousal of emotions. A famous and moving example is Andromaque's evocation of the sack of Troy:

> Songe, songe, Céphise, à cette nuit cruelle
> Qui fut pour tout un peuple une nuit éternelle;
> Figure-toi Pyrrhus, les yeux étincelants,
> Entrant à la lueur de nos palais brûlants,
> Sur tous mes frères morts se faisant un passage,
> Et de sang tout couvert échauffant le carnage;
> Songe aux cris des vainqueurs, songe aux cris des mourants,
> Dans la flamme étouffés, sous le fer expirants.

> (Racine, *Andromaque*)

➤ **Praeteritio (la prétérition)**   *Praeteritio* is the false claim not to mention something while actually mentioning it. The following is an example from a radio broadcast:

A-t-on le droit de signaler ici que cette interprétation est sur disque Decca? Non? Je n'ai pas le droit de dire que c'est le disque Decca n° 2001? Tant pis. Je ne le dirai pas. (Quoted by B. Dupriez, *Gradus*, p. 359)

A literary example is the vision which Hugo doubts he can describe:

> Or, ce que je voyais, je doute que je puisse
> Vous le peindre: c'était comme un grand édifice

> Formé d'entassements de siècles et de lieux;
> On n'en pouvait trouver les bords ni les milieux;
> A toutes les hauteurs, nations, peuples, races,
> Mille ouvriers humains, laissant partout leurs traces,
> Travaillaient nuit et jour.
>
> (Hugo, 'La Pente de la rêverie')

➤ **Prosopopoeia (la prosopopée)** *Prosopopoeia* is a piece of direct speech uttered by someone or something physically unable to speak, typically a *personification* or a dead person. The schoolgirl Gisèle in Proust's *A l'ombre des jeunes filles en fleurs* is asked to write a *prosopopoeia* as an exercise. Her topic is 'Sophocle écrit des Enfers à Racine pour le consoler de l'insuccès d'*Athalie*'. In the following quotation Baudelaire gives direct speech to the soul of wine:

> Un soir, l'âme du vin chantait dans les bouteilles:
> 'Homme, vers toi je pousse, ô cher déshérité,
> Sous ma prison de verre et mes cires vermeilles,
> Un chant plein de lumière et de fraternité.'
>
> (Baudelaire, 'L'Âme du vin')

5. MEMORY (LA MÉMOIRE)

For the orator who has composed a text to be delivered, traditional rhetoricians give advice about how to remember it so that it can be delivered without notes. The orator is encouraged to imagine a physical space divided into a series of compartments (the rooms in a house, for example) and to associate arguments or words with those compartments. Though memory has become an important and fashionable topic in literary criticism, the technicalities of rhetorical *memory* are clearly less useful to the textual critic. Yet writers can have recourse to it in presenting the rhetorical behaviour of their characters. Racine's Titus has often rehearsed the speech of separation he knows he must deliver to Bérénice. When he faces her, it is as if he can name the key ideas he has committed to memory, but he does not have the courage to flesh them out:

BÉRÉNICE.   Parlez.
TITUS.   Rome . . . l'empire . . .
BÉRÉNICE.   Eh bien?
TITUS.   Sortons, Paulin; je ne lui puis rien dire.

> (Racine, *Bérénice*)

The shreds of Titus's *memory*, coupled with the figure of *aposiopesis*, make for a tragic exit from the stage.

6. ACTION (L'ACTION (F.))

The last skill that rhetoricians teach the orator is that of delivery. Rhetoric conventionally considers both the oral and the visual aspects of performance, how voice and gesture can be so controlled as to make the greatest impact on an audience. The interest of *action* is not limited to examples of oratory, however. Writers often incorporate indications about gesture and tone of voice when presenting characters in plays and prose fiction.

6.1 Voice (la voix)

Different tones of voice are required for different effects. Orators wanting to convey and arouse the various passions must change their voice accordingly: for some rhetoricians, anger requires rapid speech and a staccato delivery; pity requires a supple and afflicted voice with distinct pauses; joy requires a confident and effusive delivery. Different tones of voice are also required for the various stages in a speech. The *exordium* requires a gentle tone, which may rise gradually. The *narration* needs a slightly louder voice. For the *confirmation* a distinctly loud voice is required, but there will be modulations according to the passions in play. The *peroration* requires clarity and moderation of tone, with a slower delivery, but without pauses. The Conseiller making the official speech at the agricultural show in *Madame Bovary* finishes his *exordium*, and Flaubert's narrator introduces the Conseiller's *narration* as follows:

Mais, à ce moment, la voix du Conseiller s'éleva d'un ton extraordinaire. Il déclamait: 'Le temps n'est plus, messieurs, où la discorde civile ensanglantait nos places publiques [. . .].' (Flaubert, *Madame Bovary*)

The comic effect for the reader lies partly in the contrast between this and the amorous dialogue between Rodolphe and Emma taking place at the same time and partly in the orator's inappropriate tone of voice: it is far too early in the speech to adopt such a loud tone.

6.2 Gesture (le geste)

Some rhetoricians give detailed advice about the gestures appropriate for certain effects. An *exclamation* will be more successful if accompanied by the raising of open hands into the air, palms out. Horror will be conveyed more effectively if both hands are thrust forwards, palms out. Eyes, eyelids, nose, lips, neck, shoulders, arms, hands, fingers, legs, feet, one's whole posture: nothing should be neglected in determining one's persuasive impact on an audience. Rodolphe is fully aware of the opportunities offered by gestural rhetoric when he is attempting to seduce Emma at the agricultural show:

Et, en achevant ces mots, Rodolphe ajouta la pantomime à sa phrase. Il se passa la main sur le visage, tel qu'un homme pris d'étourdissement; puis il la laissa tomber sur celle d'Emma. (Flaubert, *Madame Bovary*)

Racine's Bérénice too knows that the emperor who has said that she must leave him is most likely to be moved by a dishevelled appearance and a weepy voice. Accordingly, she will not let Phénice restore her regal decorum:

>Laisse, laisse, Phénice, il verra son ouvrage.
>Et que m'importe, hélas! de ces vains ornements?
>Si ma foi, si mes pleurs, si mes gémissements,
>Mais que dis-je mes pleurs? si ma perte certaine,
>Si ma mort toute prête enfin ne le ramène,
>Dis-moi, que produiront tes secours superflus,
>Et tout le faible éclat qui ne le touche plus?
>
>(Racine, *Bérénice*)

For all the vast effort that rhetoricians traditionally expend on the verbal processes of persuasion, the rhetoric of performance, tone of voice, and gesture can have a disproportionately large effect on the target audience. It is therefore unfortunate that, for the three examples of oratory to which we turn in the next chapter, the evidence for the orators' *action* is either non-existent or slight. Yet that is inevitable, because examples of oratory have a short life in performance (unless they are recorded by modern technology); they survive only partially, in printed form. But for the examples of drama and prose fiction in the subsequent chapters there is ample evidence of the characters' *action* for critical analysis.

2

ORATORY

Since its beginnings in the ancient world, rhetoric has catered to those wishing to speak impressively and persuasively on formal public occasions. Whatever transformations rhetoric, or indeed civilization as a whole, has undergone over the centuries, oratory— which might be defined as the live practice of rhetoric—has always been a fact of life. The particular forms of oratory that prevail at any one time are determined by the social and political institutions peculiar to the society at that time. This chapter examines three examples of French oratory since the middle of the nineteenth century. Each constitutes a significant moment in French cultural history. Together they illustrate the three kinds of discourse at which rhetoric is aimed. Flaubert's *Madame Bovary* was put on trial in 1857, its author accused of offending against public and religious morality. The speeches for the prosecution and the defence are examples of *judicial* oratory. In June 1940, after millions had fled from the invading Germans in northern France and when the French Government was on the point of admitting defeat, Charles de Gaulle made the first of many broadcasts from the BBC in London encouraging French people who were still free to continue the struggle. His speeches are examples of *deliberative* oratory. In 1981 Marguerite Yourcenar was formally received into the Académie Française. She was the first woman to be so honoured. Like all newly elected members, she made a speech in praise of her predecessor, in her case, Roger Caillois. One of the existing members, Jean d'Ormesson, replied in praise of her. Such speeches are examples of *demonstrative* oratory. Rhetorical theory offers an excellent tool for analysing the persuasive strategies of all these speakers.

I. THE TRIAL OF *MADAME BOVARY*

Madame Bovary was first published in serial form in *La Revue de Paris* towards the end of 1856.[1] The editor of the journal had been sensitive to possible charges of immorality, and had insisted on a number of cuts, to which Flaubert had very reluctantly agreed. In one instalment a passage was cut without the author's being consulted. Annoyed with this treatment, Flaubert collected from previous issues of *La Revue de Paris* passages written by other authors which some people might have thought immoral. He gave them to a journalist, whose subsequent article about them brought not only *La Revue de Paris* but also Flaubert's own work to the attention of the public prosecutor. As a result, Flaubert, the editor of *La Revue de Paris* (Laurent Pichat), and the printer (Auguste Pillet) were summoned to appear before the 'tribunal correctionnel' on 24 January 1857. They were charged, respectively, with writing, publishing, and printing a work that offended against public and religious morality.

The trial began with the speech of the public prosecutor, Ernest Pinard. His speech is orderly, but his arguments and other aspects of his presentation are weak. His *exordium* does not so much try to win the confidence of the judges on the tribunal as to present them with two problems, which his treatment will, supposedly, render unproblematic. The first is the elasticity of the terms in which the charge is expressed: 'offenses à la morale publique et à la religion' (p. 439). Having admitted that this crucial phrase poses a difficulty, Pinard tries to solve it with suspicious ease. He does so by exploiting *ethos*, and by flattering his audience that they are like him and that he is like them; they must all therefore share the same response to the work: 'quand on parle à des esprits droits et pratiques, il est facile de s'entendre à cet égard, de distinguer si telle page d'un livre

---

[1] Page references to *Madame Bovary* are to the readily accessible edition by B. Ajac (Garnier–Flammarion, 1986), which reproduces, after the text of the novel, the speeches of the public prosecutor, Flaubert's defence lawyer, and the judgment. For an account of the publication and trial, see E. Starkie, *Flaubert: The Making of the Master* (Weidenfeld and Nicolson, 1967), 245–60. A fascinating book interprets the novel in the light of the issues raised by the trial: D. LaCapra, *'Madame Bovary' on Trial* (Ithaca, NY: Cornell University Press, 1982). In chapter 2 LaCapra gives an account of the two speeches delivered at the trial, but with a view to assessing the way in which the lawyers read the novel. My own account examines the rhetorical strategies they employed to persuade the tribunal of the novel's morality or immorality. Quotations from Flaubert's letters are taken from his *Correspondance*, ed. J. Bruneau (2 vols., Gallimard, 1973–80).

porte atteinte à la religion et à la morale' (ibid.). He is almost admitting that his demonstration of Flaubert's immorality will have no
rigorous critical basis. The next problem he raises is that of demonstrating the alleged immorality of a long novel in a short speech. His
solution is to give a summary of the whole novel before selecting
certain passages as proof of the work's immorality. This method of
proceeding determines the structure of the rest of his speech.

He creates the impression that for the *narration* of the plot of
Madame Bovary he will be objective ('raconter d'abord tout le roman
sans en lire, sans en incriminer aucun passage' (ibid.)). His narrative
style, however, tries to steer his audience towards an interpretation
of the novel as immoral by his use of *exclamation* and *hyperbole* at
moments where the text alludes to sexual activity: 'et là il y eut pour
elle comme une initiation à toutes les ardeurs de la volupté!' (p. 441);
'Les amants arrivent jusqu'aux limites extrêmes de la volupté!' (p.
442); 'La chute a lieu dans le fiacre!' (ibid.). These *figures*, which may
seem clumsy on the page, might have been forceful in delivery.

After his *narration* comes the body of his speech, the *confirmation*,
which has two main stages. The first prepares the way for the second, and exploits the *place* of *invention* known as *genus*. Pinard tries to
demonstrate, in general terms, the type of writing that the work
exemplifies: 'il faut savoir à quelle école il appartient, quelle est la
couleur qu'il emploie' (p. 443). It is an example of lascivious writing, and this is supported by *external proofs* in the form of a disparate
sequence of quotations from the text, all of which point to Emma
Bovary's sensuality. Having painted the general picture, Pinard
moves, in the second part of his *confirmation*, to exploit *genus*'s twin
place, *species*. He analyses in some detail four specific instances of
Flaubert's supposedly lascivious writing: Emma's excursion into the
forest with Rodolphe, Emma's interest in the Church and spirituality during her convalescence, her love-affair with Léon in Rouen,
and the scene of her death with the priest in attendance. Together
these examples are supposed to show how Flaubert is guilty of
offending against both public and religious morality. Words in the
novel seem to celebrate adulterous love ('la poésie de l'adultère', as
Pinard says (p. 449)). The novel also juxtaposes the dignified vocabulary of Roman Catholic ritual with terms suggestive of sensuality
('le mélange du sacré au voluptueux' (p. 456)). Throughout the *confirmation* Pinard uses *exclamations* to convey the shock of the text that
he is quoting: 'Voici encore un passage très important—comme

peinture lascive!' (p. 452). He uses *interrogations* which attempt to bludgeon the audience into sharing his viewpoint: 'Connaissez-vous au monde, messieurs, un langage plus expressif? Avez-vous jamais vu un tableau plus lascif?' (p. 449). More particularly, he uses the form of questioning known as *subjectio*, raising questions which his listeners might well wish to ask and answering them immediately in ways which support his case: 'Y a-t-il dans cette femme adultère qui va à la communion quelque chose de la foi de la Madeleine repentante? Non, non, c'est toujours la femme passionnée qui cherche des illusions, et qui les cherche dans les choses les plus saintes, les plus augustes' (p. 450). By deploying inductive reasoning, Pinard closes his *confirmation* with the conclusion that Flaubert is practising 'la peinture réaliste', a mode that was new and controversial in the 1850s—a description, therefore, that might prejudice any reactionary members of the tribunal against Flaubert.

Pinard moves on to the *peroration*, summing up his claims so far, asking that, of the three men on trial, Flaubert be considered 'le principal coupable' (p. 458), and finally introducing a *refutation*. He attempts to refute the possible objection that, despite all his evidence, the novel is moral because it shows immorality punished. To this he replies that a novel showing immorality punished is still immoral if it includes as much lascivious detail as he has found in *Madame Bovary*; and that in any case this novel does not show immorality punished, since Emma dies not because she has been adulterous, but because she wants to die ('elle meurt dans tout le prestige de sa jeunesse et de sa beauté' (pp. 458–9)). The expressions of scandalized horror that recur throughout his speech and the claims of an allegiance to an unargued standard of public and religious morality (not least in his concluding paragraph) may have made Pinard appear to some listeners as the defender of the morals of the age. To others, including the defence lawyer Sénard, he seemed prejudiced, pompous, and officious.

Pinard is deflated by Sénard's superior speech in defence of Flaubert. The pleasure offered by the rhetorical confrontation between Pinard and Sénard and, in particular, by Sénard's deployment of evidently more persuasive strategies is recorded by Flaubert in a letter to his brother of 30 January 1857: 'La plaidoirie de Me Sénard a été splendide. Il a *écrasé* le ministère public, qui se tordait sur son siège et a déclaré qu'il ne répondrait pas' (*Correspondance*, ii. 677). The element of comic theatre suggested by this public humiliation of the public prosecutor must have been a vital factor in Sénard's ability to keep the attention of his audience for some four hours. This long speech begins with a much more extensive *exordium* than Pinard's. He asserts Flaubert's innocence of the crime with which he is charged, and states at the outset an interpretation of the novel which is precisely opposite to the one with which Pinard closed his speech. It is, according to Sénard, a novel that encourages virtue by depicting the horror of vice. In Dominick LaCapra's reading of the trial, Sénard is presented as rather a dull reader of *Madame Bovary*, seeing the text as a 'fully reputable and responsible confirmation of conventional morality' (*'Madame Bovary' on Trial*, 41). LaCapra speculates that Flaubert's eventual dedication of the novel to Sénard might be ironic (ibid. 53). But we should be careful not to suppose that the reading Sénard offers is his own; it is the one he thinks most likely to persuade the no doubt morally conservative judges of Flaubert's innocence. In the circumstances, it does not matter whether or not his interpretation is critically plausible. What matters is whether or not it is expressed persuasively enough for his immediate audience in the tribunal. The remainder of the *exordium* exploits *ethos*, presenting in turn his own character, the character of Flaubert's father, and that of his elder brother (his father had been, and his brother was, a distinguished surgeon in Rouen), as well as Flaubert's own, in order to convince the judges that they are dealing with upright, respectable people. Flaubert particularly noted the way in which Sénard used *ethos* in his speech: 'Tout le temps de la plaidoirie, le père Sénard m'a posé comme un grand homme' (*Correspondance*, ii. 677).

There is no *narration* proper, but a very substantial *confirmation* based on two key, carefully interwoven arguments: that Pinard made improper use of *external proofs*, quoting selectively and thereby falsifying Flaubert's novel; and that comparison with other writers, often distinguished and revered, classic as well as contemporary, shows that *Madame Bovary* cannot possibly be considered immoral (this argument combines *ethos* and *comparison*).[2] Overwhelming his audience with a mass of convincing detail, Sénard returns to those passages which Pinard quoted incriminatingly, and by quoting them

---

[2] The idea of collecting obscene or sensual passages from other writers, and especially religious writers, seems to have been Flaubert's own. See, in his *Correspondance*, his letter to Eugène Crépet of *c.* 26 January 1857. He was advised against it as too risky a manoeuvre by his friend Maxime du Camp. See Starkie, *Flaubert*, 255–6.

more extensively and making sometimes suggestive, sometimes explicit comparisons with other writers, he manages to protest Flaubert's innocence. For instance, he quotes those places in Flaubert's account of Emma's affair with Léon which, to Pinard, both suggested and prompted sensuality: 'elle se déshabillait brutalement (la malheureuse), arrachant le lacet mince de son corset qui sifflait autour de ses hanches, comme une couleuvre qui glisse; et pâle, sans parler, sérieuse, elle s'abattait contre sa poitrine, avec un long frisson' (pp. 491–2). For Sénard, this description of Emma's undressing cannot be interpreted without reference to the narrator's comment, omitted by Pinard in his quotation of the same passage (p. 453), to the effect that there was something inhibitingly lugubrious about their embrace. Sénard's use of *interrogation* invites his audience to agree with him: 'Est-ce que ce n'est pas [. . .] l'excitation à l'horreur du vice que "ce quelque chose de lugubre qui se glisse entre eux pour les séparer"?' (p. 492). He concludes his analysis of the supposedly sensual and provocative descriptions of this affair by quoting an author whom he claims was Flaubert's source of inspiration for such writing. Before revealing the name of the author, he plays with the audience, three times over using the kind of question known as *communicatio* and an ascending *gradatio* to suggest increasing curiosity and excitement (p. 496):

Voilà ce que c'est que la vie des sens. Qui a dit cela? qui a écrit les paroles que vous venez d'entendre, sur ces excitations et ces ardeurs incessantes? Quel est le livre que M. Flaubert feuillette jour et nuit, et dont il s'est inspiré dans les passages qu'incrime M. l'Avocat impérial? C'est Bossuet!

There is, here, substantial food for the judges' thought, if the best-remembered Roman Catholic preacher of the seventeenth century wrote in the same vein as Flaubert. Sénard is of course effecting a sleight of hand, ignoring the enormous differences between Flaubert's novel and Bossuet's religious writing. But it is a trick that he performs repeatedly throughout his *confirmation*, and most triumphantly at the end, when he deals with the death scene, a scandalous mixture of religion and sensuality according to Pinard, but, according to Sénard, a near-translation of the religious service-book known as the *Rituel*, from which learned Latin quotations are drawn that add weight to his claims. Flaubert records the effectiveness with which Sénard deployed this unusual *external proof*: 'Mais le plus beau a été le passage de l'Extrême-Onction. L'avocat général [Pinard] a été couvert de confusion quand Me Sénard a tiré de sous son banc un *Rituel* qu'il a lu; le passage de mon roman n'est que la reproduction *adoucie* de ce qu'il y a dans le *Rituel'* (*Correspondance*, ii. 677). Flaubert shows us a possible response to the confrontation of the two orators: it can be seen almost as a piece of comic theatre.

After so detailed and relentless a *confirmation*, Sénard closes his speech with a brief *peroration*, which recapitulates his main argument and puts the judges in the right frame of mind for reaching a verdict favourable to Flaubert (pp. 514–15):

[1] Permettez-moi de résumer tout ceci.

[2] Je défends un homme qui, s'il avait rencontré une critique littéraire sur la forme de son livre, sur quelques expressions, sur trop de détails, sur un point ou sur un autre, aurait accepté cette critique littéraire du meilleur cœur du monde. [3] Mais se voir accusé d'outrage à la morale et à la religion! [4] M. Flaubert n'en revient pas; et il proteste ici devant vous avec tout l'étonnement et toute l'énergie dont il est capable contre une telle accusation.

[5] Vous n'êtes pas de ceux qui condamnent des livres sur quelques lignes, vous êtes de ceux qui jugent avant tout la pensée, les moyens de mise en œuvre, et qui vous poserez cette question par laquelle j'ai commencé ma plaidoirie, et par laquelle je la finis: [6] La lecture d'un tel livre donne-t-elle l'amour du vice, inspire-t-elle l'horreur du vice? [7] L'expiation si terrible de la faute ne pousse-t-elle pas, n'excite-t-elle pas à la vertu? [8] La lecture de ce livre ne peut pas produire sur vous une impression autre que celle qu'elle a produite sur nous, à savoir: que ce livre est excellent dans son ensemble, et que les détails en sont irréprochables. [9] Toute la littérature classique nous autorisait à des peintures et à des scènes bien autres que celles que nous nous sommes permises. [10] Nous aurions pu, sous ce rapport, la prendre pour modèle, nous ne l'avons pas fait; nous nous sommes imposés une sobriété dont vous nous tiendrez compte. [11] Que s'il était possible que, par un mot ou par un autre, M. Flaubert eût dépassé la mesure qu'il s'était imposée, je n'aurais pas seulement à vous rappeler que c'est une première œuvre, mais j'aurais à vous dire qu'alors même qu'il se serait trompé, son erreur serait sans dommage pour la morale publique. [12] Et le faisant venir en police correctionnelle—lui, que vous connaissez maintenant un peu par son livre, lui que vous aimez déjà un peu, j'en suis sûr, et que vous aimeriez davantage si vous le connaissiez davantage—il est bien assez, il est déjà trop cruellement puni. [13] A vous maintenant de statuer. [14] Vous avez jugé le livre dans son ensemble et dans ses détails; il n'est pas possible que vous hésitiez!

The opening sentence of the *peroration* (1), claiming simply to sum up the foregoing speech, belies the careful rhetorical calculations that have gone into Sénard's closing lines. The *peroration* alludes only fleetingly, but tellingly, to the weight of evidence accumulated in the *confirmation* (9–10). For the most part, Sénard returns cyclically to the issues raised in the *exordium*. In particular, he develops further his earlier exploitation of *ethos*. In addition, for the first time in his speech, he makes use of *pathos*.

His first point is the one that rang out resoundingly at the beginning of the *exordium*, the protestation of Flaubert's innocence (4). But it is more than a simple protestation of innocence. It is reinforced by a combination of *anaphora* and *isocolon* ('tout l'étonnement et toute l'énergie'). And it is located at the climactic point of a structure based on *antithesis* and exploiting *ethos*. Contrasting literary criticism with the charge of immorality, Sénard suggests the disproportionate nature of this public condemnation of Flaubert's novel: by implication, he is claiming that literary criticism would have been a sufficient response. This is the force of the *exclamation* (3). By creating the impression that Flaubert would have been happy to accept points of literary criticism made about his work, Sénard is preparing a favourable picture of him as a writer, which he will develop towards the end of the *peroration*. This favourable portrait is supported by his use of the superlative adjective in the phrase 'du meilleur cœur du monde' in the climactic position at the end of the sentence (2). Another feature of the portrait is the combination of quintuple *anaphora* and *epitrochasmus* in the list 'sur la forme de son livre, sur quelques expressions, sur trop de détails, sur un point ou sur un autre' (2), both devices serving to insist upon the range of criticisms which Flaubert would have been happy to hear. The repetition of the phrase 'critique littéraire' (2) (*geminatio*) is crucial in establishing clearly the point of contrast with 'outrage à la morale et à la religion' (3). This paragraph alerts the judges to the physical presence of Flaubert before them (4). His presence will play a greater role as the *peroration* proceeds.

If the first part of the *peroration* focuses on Flaubert, the next part (5–7) turns to the character of the judges. Sénard tries to flatter them and persuade them to share his view of *Madame Bovary* by drawing a distinction between the kind of people who misread books and those who read carefully and sensitively. The former, 'ceux qui condamnent des livres sur quelques lignes', are implicitly like the public prosecutor. The latter are like the judges on the jury. This *antithesis* is the basis of Sénard's syntax at this point: 'Vous n'êtes pas de ceux qui [. . .], vous êtes de ceux qui [. . .]' (5). But whereas the unfavourable part of the *antithesis* is developed in one single and simple relative clause, the favourable side, with which he wants to impress his audience, is developed in two relative clauses, the second of which is given further weight by a combination of *anaphora*, *isocolon*, and more *antithesis* ('par laquelle j'ai commencé ma plaidoirie, et par laquelle je la finis'). The favourable picture to which Sénard tries to assimilate the judges is developed even further with the questions which he himself poses, but which he suggests the judges will be posing too (6–7). The questions relate to the vitally important matter of the interpretation of the book, and are the kind of questions known as *interrogations*, requiring an obvious 'yes' or 'no' reply. In the case of the first question, its form creates the impression of open-mindedness and choice, using *parison* and *antithesis* ('donne-t-elle l'amour du vice, inspire-t-elle l'horreur du vice?' (6)) to give the appearance of equal weight to the moral and immoral interpretations. But by this point Sénard's listeners cannot opt for the immoral interpretation, because that would consign them to that group of readers who condemn books hastily. The second question capitalizes on the first, inviting listeners to affirm positively the morally uplifting impact of the work. Added emphasis is given to this interpretation by the use of *correctio* ('ne pousse-t-elle pas, n'excite-t-elle pas' (7)), replacing an already forceful verb with an even more forceful one to evoke the alleged transforming power of the novel.

Although the questions do not need a reply, the next stage in the *peroration* (8–11) begins with a reply which asserts unambiguously the unquestionable excellence of the novel, while also making a transition from the focus on the judges to a focus on Sénard and Flaubert together. These few sentences include some cleverly slippery uses of the pronoun 'nous'. The *antithesis* ('vous', 'nous') supported by the *polyptoton* ('produire', 'produite') seems to identify Sénard as the referent of 'nous' and to suggest that he is trying to flatter the judges by inviting them to share his own carefully considered critical judgement. But the respectable 'nous' referring to Sénard soon craftily embraces Flaubert too: 'Toute la littérature classique nous autorisait à des peintures [. . .]' (9). This is an ingenious use of *ethos*, subtly making Flaubert, the accused, appear to share all the respectability of Sénard himself. Moreover, the suggestion of respectability is increased by Sénard's use of *comparison* in his summing up of the author's relationship to earlier writers. Flaubert did less than was permitted by 'Toute la littérature classique', the *hyperbole* and *personification* giving great weight to a revered literary tradition in comparison with which Flaubert, it is claimed, has been very modest. Sénard's use of *parataxis* allows him prominently to pile up the anaphoric pronouns ('nous'), so strengthening the link between himself and Flaubert (10).

Shored up by association with Sénard's respectability, Flaubert is now allowed to stand alone. The focus turns to Flaubert and the judges' response to him (11–12). Sénard adopts here an argument which he has not used so far and which might be thought risky. He draws on the *place* known as *effect*, and contemplates the possible effect of Flaubert's having used one or two unwise words in his novel. The use of *litotes* ('par un mot ou par un autre') is important in diminishing the significance of any imprudence on Flaubert's part. There are two excuses for him. The first is based on an *enthymeme* ('c'est une première œuvre'), whereby the listeners are expected to deduce the conclusion that Flaubert's novel must, by virtue of its being his first published novel, somehow be forgiven any indiscretion. The second is the assertion that the effect of any indiscretion would be harmless. Although it might seem dangerous at this concluding point in the defence to raise even the spectre of Flaubert's having done wrong, Sénard does it in a way which makes use of *pathos*. He is trying to arouse sympathy for a supposedly innocent young writer (though Flaubert was in his mid-30s at the time). He builds on this appeal even more in the subsequent sentence (12), in which he draws the attention of the judges to the physical presence of Flaubert sitting before them. He supposes in the judges a growing interest in and affection for Flaubert, and he plays on this with the anaphoric relative clauses ('lui, que [. . .], lui que [. . .], et que') intricately constructed so that the crucial verbs in the first two clauses ('connaissez', 'aimez') are, by means of *polyptoton* and *chiasmus*, brought together climactically in different forms in the third clause ('aimeriez', 'connaissiez'). This third clause underscores the attractiveness of a better acquaintance with the author by the use of *epistrophe* ('[. . .] davantage [. . .] davantage'). This accumulation of clauses, however, is simply the preparation for the climax of the sentence, an even more intense appeal for the sympathy of the judges:

'il est bien assez, il est déjà trop cruellement puni'. The use of *correctio* allows Sénard to stress how cruelly Flaubert has already been treated. The contrast between the affection stirred up in the longer relative clauses and the cruelty stated starkly in the main clause contributes to the emotional appeal.

An even greater contrast is that between the combination of *pathos* and *hypotaxis* in the sentences dealing directly with Flaubert and the judges' reaction to him (11–12) and the *parataxis* of the closing sentences (13–14), which now focus dramatically on the judges: 'A vous maintenant de statuer'. When Sénard tells the judges 'Vous avez jugé le livre dans son ensemble et dans ses détails', he is again playing cleverly with the personal pronoun. He is referring to the analysis of the novel that he himself has conducted in the course of his speech, but he is subtly transferring responsibility for his analysis and its conclusions to the judges. Although his closing sentences are not expressed in interrogative form, they explicitly invite the judges to consider their verdict, and the very last sentence suggests that only one verdict, a favourable one, is conceivable.

Flaubert was delighted with Sénard's performance. The letter he wrote to his brother on 30 January 1857 rings with words and phrases that convey his relish for Sénard's superior oratorical display. Observing rhetorical strategies in action is fun: 'La salle était comble. C'était chouette et j'avais une fière balle. [. . .] En somme, ç'a été une crâne journée et tu te serais amusé si tu avais été là' (*Correspondance*, ii. 677). There is almost a dissociation between the fun of the performance and the seriousness of its implications. In the very next sentence Flaubert wrote: 'Ne dis rien, tais-toi: après le jugement, si je perds, j'en appellerai en cour d'appel, et si je perds en cour d'appel, en cassation.' It mattered very much to Flaubert that the judges found in his favour. Fortunately, no appeal was necessary. When the judgment was delivered, he and his co-accused were acquitted. They were not, however, awarded damages. And though Flaubert was found innocent, the judges commented unfavourably on the 'réalisme vulgaire et souvent choquant' (p. 519) that characterized some of his writing. The trial of *Madame Bovary* demonstrated a tension between, on the one hand, writing that raised questions about the conventions governing society and, on the other hand, the state's suspicion of any work of art that might bring into doubt a *status quo* with which it is comfortable. Flaubert was neither wrong nor immodest when he wrote to Champfleury on

4 February 1857: 'Vous avez compris que ma cause était celle de la littérature contemporaine tout entière. Ce n'est pas mon roman qu'on attaque, mais tous les romans, et avec eux le droit d'en faire' (*Correspondance*, ii. 678).

2. GENERAL DE GAULLE AT THE BBC, 18 JUNE 1940

The French nation was in disarray when General de Gaulle spoke on BBC radio in London on 18 June 1940. The Germans had invaded France on 10 May, and had taken the French generals by surprise with their rapidly effective combination of air and tank forces. British and French troops had been cornered in Dunkirk, and had escaped by boat to England. Millions had fled the north and headed south. The 84-year-old Marshall Pétain was negotiating with the Germans for an armistice, which took effect on 25 June. France was to be a divided nation: the north and west under German control, the south under Pétain's Vichy government. General de Gaulle, who was, for a few weeks in May and June, junior war minister, firmly believed that France should not give up the struggle against the German invader. He arrived in London on 17 June, and asked Winston Churchill if he might use the only weapon now available to him, the BBC.

The speech he eventually delivered live in the evening of 18 June was simple in appearance. It was a *deliberative* speech seeking to persuade any French people with military or technical skills, who were already in, or who were coming to, Britain, to contact him so that they could plan resistance. The circumstances in which the speech came to be delivered, however, were far from simple, and the speech itself, for all its apparent simplicity, is, as one of De Gaulle's biographers has called it, 'a suberb piece of craftsmanship, full of Jesuitical subtlety and cunning'.[3] Although Churchill was keen to help de Gaulle and to allow him to speak, the other members of the War Cabinet took some persuading. In effect, de Gaulle was appointing himself as the leader of the Free French, but the British Government was still negotiating with Pétain's government and was

---

[3] C. Williams, *The Last Great Frenchman: A Life of General de Gaulle*, 2nd edn. (Abacus, 1995), 113. Williams gives a clear account of the problems facing de Gaulle as he composed this speech (pp. 109–13). For the text of de Gaulle's speech see C. de Gaulle, *Discours et messages: Pendant la guerre, juin 1940–janvier 1946* (Plon, 1970), 3–4.

afraid of allowing de Gaulle to say anything which might jeopardize their negotiations. De Gaulle's message might also be thought to be disloyal to the Pétain government, constituting, as it does, a direct appeal to the French armed forces. De Gaulle might have encouraged the French to fight under British command, but his aim was to identify an undefeated France that could act independently. His greatest audacity was to think of making the speech in the first place: he had no authority whatsoever to speak for anyone. Nor was it obvious who would be listening to him. His intended primary audience was French people in Britain, including, of course, those who had come over from Dunkirk. But it was far from clear that such people would be spending their evenings listening to the BBC.

De Gaulle's triumph as an orator is to have hidden these tensions beneath a clear, impassioned appeal. It took him four minutes to deliver it, but several hours to write it. As befits a radio speech, with the speaker unseen by his audience and the reception sometimes poor, it is characterized by short sentences and an artful use of balanced phrasing and repetition. This is the speech in its entirety:

[1] Les chefs qui, depuis de nombreuses années, sont à la tête des armées françaises, ont formé un gouvernement.

[2] Ce gouvernement, alléguant la défaite de nos armées, s'est mis en rapport avec l'ennemi pour cesser le combat.

[3] Certes, nous avons été, nous sommes, submergés par la force mécanique, terrestre et aérienne, de l'ennemi.

[4] Infiniment plus que leur nombre, ce sont les chars, les avions, la tactique des Allemands qui nous font reculer. [5] Ce sont les chars, les avions, la tactique des Allemands qui ont surpris nos chefs au point de les amener là où ils en sont aujourd'hui.

[6] Mais le dernier mot est-il dit? [7] L'espérance doit-elle disparaître? [8] La défaite est-elle définitive? [9] Non!

[10] Croyez-moi, moi qui vous parle en connaissance de cause et vous dis que rien n'est perdu pour la France. [11] Les mêmes moyens qui nous ont vaincus peuvent faire venir un jour la victoire.

[12] Car la France n'est pas seule! [13] Elle n'est pas seule! [14] Elle n'est pas seule! [15] Elle a un vaste Empire derrière elle. [16] Elle peut faire bloc avec l'Empire britannique qui tient la mer et continue la lutte. [17] Elle peut, comme l'Angleterre, utiliser sans limites l'immense industrie des États-Unis.

[18] Cette guerre n'est pas limitée au territoire malheureux de notre pays. [19] Cette guerre n'est pas tranchée par la bataille de France. [20] Cette guerre est une guerre mondiale. [21] Toutes les fautes, tous les

retards, toutes les souffrances, n'empêchent pas qu'il y a, dans l'univers, tous les moyens nécessaires pour écraser un jour nos ennemis. [22] Foudroyés aujourd'hui par la force mécanique, nous pourrons vaincre dans l'avenir par une force mécanique supérieure. [23] Le destin du monde est là.

[24] Moi, Général de Gaulle, actuellement à Londres, j'invite les officiers et les soldats français qui se trouvent en territoire britannique ou qui viendraient à s'y trouver, avec leurs armes ou sans leurs armes, j'invite les ingénieurs et les ouvriers spécialistes des industries d'armement qui se trouvent en territoire britannique ou qui viendraient à s'y trouver, à se mettre en rapport avec moi.

[25] Quoi qu'il arrive, la flamme de la résistance française ne doit pas s'éteindre et ne s'éteindra pas.

[26] Demain, comme aujourd'hui, je parlerai à la Radio de Londres.

There is no *exordium*. De Gaulle begins with a *narration* (1–5), which lays bare the present state of affairs. He proceeds with proposals about what might be done, the *confirmation* (6–24), and concludes with a brief and punchy *peroration* (25–6).

A conventional *exordium* would have been difficult. Exploiting *ethos*, it would have had to address the question of the speaker's identity. As de Gaulle was not a well-known figure at the time, this could have constituted an unnecessary diversion from the real topic, the state of France. De Gaulle chooses only to identify himself at a point when his credentials as a patriotic Frenchman have been established and when he needs to tell his listeners whom they should contact (24). The first two sentences are primarily factual, narrating the formation of the new French Government and its negotiations for an armistice. But they are designed to provoke indignation in the hearts of his French listeners. The indignation is directed against the leaders of the French Government, and in particular Marshall Pétain: the phrase 'Les chefs qui [. . .] sont à la tête des armées françaises' is in effect a *synecdoche* referring primarily to Pétain himself. The indignation comes from the combined effect of the two sentences: the specific verbal links between the two are the *geminatio* ('des armées françaises' (1), 'de nos armées' (2)) and the *anadiplosis* ('un gouvernement.// Ce gouvernement'). The emergent *antithesis* invites scorn for those leaders who, for all their military reputation, are so ready to admit defeat. The word 'alléguant' (2) carries a force which anticipates de Gaulle's defiant message of hope in the *confirmation*. It is significant that the first mention of the Germans is an example of

antonomasia, identifying them as 'l'ennemi', a forceful way of implying the treachery of Pétain, who was negotiating with them.

The next part of the *narration* and the beginning of the *confirmation*
use the device of *concession* ('Certes' (3), 'Mais' (6)). De Gaulle admits
to the appearance of defeat, but not to defeat as an inescapable fact.
The *narration* paints an apparently wretched picture of French military defeat. The use of *correctio* emphasizes the continuing weakness
of the French position ('nous avons été, nous sommes, submergés'
(3)), as does the *metaphor* of submergence. This statement of French
weakness is expanded in the next two sentences (4–5), where the
generalization 'la force mécanique, terrestre et aérienne, de l'ennemi' (3) is explained specifically with reference to tanks and planes.
These two sentences work cumulatively. They represent an ascending *gradatio*, the effect of which is to highlight the unpreparedness of
France's military leaders. The shape of the ascending *gradatio* is
made all the clearer by the use of *parison* and multiple *geminatio*: 'ce
sont les chars, les avions, la tactique des Allemands qui [. . .]' (4),
repeated in the next sentence with its longer relative clause. De
Gaulle is known to have previously discouraged the French generals from assuming that a war with the Germans would be a trench
war, and to have urged a preference for combined tank and air
forces. But he was not believed. He is not of course explicitly promoting himself in the *narration*. He is evoking the miserable incompetence and defeatism of the current leaders. He is, however,
preparing for the moment when he will say 'Moi, Général de
Gaulle, actuellement à Londres'. He is starting to imply that he will
offer the kind of leadership that the *narration* shows France does not
now have.

The transition to the *confirmation* is made by way of three *interrogations* (6–8), examples of *parison*. All three questions mean the same
thing, though they use different words to express it. They contemplate the bleak facts sketched in the *narration*, but invite the listeners
not to see the current state of affairs as the end of the French struggle against the enemy. *Alliteration* makes de Gaulle's questioning of
his audience more emphatic, by creating a firm rhythm within each
question. The *alliterative* phoneme is /d/: 'dernier [. . .] dit' (6), 'doit
[. . .] disparaître' (7), 'défaite [. . .] définitive' (8). There is specially
forceful *alliterative* emphasis in the third question, with its four
repeated phonemes in the key words: /d/, /e/, /f/, /t/. An *interrogation* is the kind of question to which the answer is so simple and

so obvious that it does not need to be supplied. But de Gaulle spells out the *exclamatory* answer 'Non!' (9) as a sign of his determination, resolution, and hope.

The body of the *confirmation* has two parts: the first and longer part tries to make a convincing argument for continued French resistance (10–23); the second part is the consequent appeal to French listeners to respond to de Gaulle by contacting him in London (24). The argument for continuing the French struggle is based on the *place* known as *circumstances*, and specifically tackles the question of the means that the French will have at their disposal to help them. De Gaulle begins his argument with an introductory sentence (10), in which he exploits *ethos* and refers to himself, though without yet giving his name. His main strategy is to establish himself as an authoritative speaker on military matters. He does so in the most direct way possible, by bold assertion: 'moi, qui vous parle en connaissance de cause'. It is here more than anywhere else in his speech that he attempts to create a relationship of trust between himself and his audience, referring to both parties in close proximity at three moments within this one sentence: 'Croyez-moi', 'moi qui vous parle', 'et vous dis' (10). His own patriotic credentials are bolstered by his statement of the argument that he will go on to support: 'rien n'est perdu pour la France'. This also appeals to the patriotic emotions of his listeners and to their desire for hope (*pathos*). The supporting argument, that France has relevant means at its disposal, is summed up in general terms (11) before being elaborated. This summing up constitutes a further appeal to the emotions, in particular to the desire for vengeance or, at the very least, table turning. The phrase 'Les mêmes moyens' refers to the combination of air and tank forces which the Germans had used to subdue the French. De Gaulle suggests that the same means can be used in reverse. It is a reversal that is underscored by a combination of rhythm, *alliteration*, and that kind of *polyptoton* which the French call *dérivation*: 'vaincus' is converted into 'victoire', both words falling in stressed positions, and 'victoire' falling significantly at the end of the sentence (11).

What de Gaulle lacks in tangible promises of help, he makes up for in terms of rhetorically elaborate assertions. The six sentences that follow (12–17) are neatly symmetrical. The first three (12–14) are to all intents and purposes the same exclamatory sentence spoken three times over. This repeated assertion that France, now

personified, is not alone is backed up by three specific examples of support in the following three sentences (15–17). These too gain added
force from their use of *anaphora*: 'Elle' is repeated three times.
Although the examples appear specific, they do not in fact refer to
actual offers of help. Far from it. His audience, however, cannot be
expected to know that. He aims instead to sweep listeners along with
his vision of patriotic hope. The help of what he refers to as the
French Empire was, at this time, far from certain. The Empire's
allegiance to Pétain was greater than de Gaulle had thought. It is
true that he does not explicitly state that he is assured of help from
such quarters. But he gestures broadly and promisingly. The adjective 'vaste', qualifying 'Empire', is less an indication of size than an
evocation of the possibility of very extensive help (15). He does not
actually claim that he has the help of Britain and its empire (16), but
rather that the Free French could make common cause with the
British. This suggestion constitutes a dramatic distortion, the aim of
which is to flatter his listeners into thinking that somehow he and
they can be considered equal partners to Britain. This suggestion of
an equal partnership with Britain is also contained in the *comparison*
with England in the next sentence (17), which addresses their relationship to the United States. The vision he offers of France and
England drawing communally on the resources of the United States
is a fleeting example of *hypotyposis*, exploiting descriptive detail for
persuasive effect ('sans limites', 'immense'). Again, de Gaulle is
speaking without authority. The American Government would continue to support Pétain for some time to come.

The next six sentences (18–23) broaden the perspective, playing
on an *antithesis* between France and the whole world: the first of
these sentences paints the 'territoire malheureux de notre pays', the
last conjures up the 'destin du monde'. But this broadened perspective is merely a pretext for a repetition, in different words, of
some of the points he has already made. The first three sentences
emphatically make the point that what is happening is a world conflict. They have a cumulative effect. They constitute a descending
gradatio. They exploit what has already proved a favourite device of
de Gaulle's, *anaphora*: 'Cette guerre' occurs three times in initial position. The first two sentences express de Gaulle's view negatively.
The last uses *geminatio* to underscore its positive expression of de
Gaulle's view: 'Cette guerre est une guerre mondiale' (20). There is
an element of prophetic insight in de Gaulle's vision of a world war.

Most people had no reason to think of the conflict as a world war until somewhat later. If the listing of sources of help earlier in the speech (French Empire, British Empire, USA) operates like a *gradatio* (15–17), the logical extension and climax of this list and of de Gaulle's vision of help in support of the French cause comes now in his evocation of universal support (21). This assertion of world support accompanies an implicit *refutation* contained in the *anaphoric epitrochasmus* 'Toutes les fautes, tous les retards, toutes les souffrances' (21). Again he is suggestive rather than specific. His listeners may well feel that the human behaviour which they have witnessed has been faulty or criminal (a reference to the invading Germans? or, more probably, to the Pétain Government?), that the responses to the situation have been too slow (surely a critical reference to the French generals?), and that the suffering they have seen has been extensive. But de Gaulle asserts that none of these things implies that world resources would be inadequate to defeat the enemy. Again, as he has done earlier (11), he offers his listeners the emotional satisfaction of feeling that they will be able to turn the tables on their conqueror (22). Again there is an *antithesis* between present defeat ('Foudroyés aujourd'hui') and promised victory ('vaincre dans l'avenir'). Instead of the earlier *polyptoton*, there is now a *geminatio* using, in stressed positions, the words 'force mécanique', the second occurrence significantly qualified by the further adjective 'supérieure'. Every detail contributes to de Gaulle's vision of hope for the future. His claims are extensive and apocalyptic. It is as if the fate of the world hung on the technical resources of the Free French (23). De Gaulle has led his listeners compellingly from the beginnings of his argument which took France as its starting-point ('la France n'est pas seule' (12)) to a tersely expressed conclusion about the whole world's involvement ('Le destin du monde est là' (23)).

The remainder of the *confirmation* returns the focus to the practical situation of the speaker and his audience (24). The juxtaposition between 'destin du monde' (23) and 'Moi' (24) might seem abrupt. Its effect is to create confidence in the speaker's competence to deal with matters of world significance. The mention of his name is a practical necessity. His listeners need to know whom they should contact. But, rhetorically, it is almost a *parenthesis*. What should matter to the audience most about the speaker is the picture he has drawn of himself: as confident, informed, visionary, and authoritative. By pure coincidence, however, his name does help his persuasive strategy. For it echoes the ancient name of the region now known as France ('la Gaule'), and thereby hints at the spirit of opposition with which the Gauls had once met the invading Romans. Of practical importance also at this point is his location ('actuellement à Londres'). After these identifying details have been given, de Gaulle makes a direct appeal. The appeal is the first step towards accomplishing the ambitious aims sketched out in the earlier part of the *confirmation*. This is an uncharacteristically long sentence. But its structure, based on *isocolon*, continues to make the message very clear for the radio audience. The *isocolon* allows de Gaulle to identify two sharply distinct but equally essential groups of people: those with military and those with technical skills. The invitation is simple: they should contact him. This crucial part of the message is delayed until the end of this long sentence, which closes with the same emphatic pronoun with which it began: 'moi'.

The request made, de Gaulle delivers a very brief *peroration* which fulfils two clearly delineated functions. The first is what all rhetoricians identified as proper to a *peroration*, an appeal to the listeners' emotions. It is an appeal to patriotism, to hope, and to determination, summing up the mood of the whole speech (25). De Gaulle expresses himself here with a greater concentration of metaphorical language than he has used previously. The *metaphor* of the French resistance as an undying flame, suggestive of elemental power, is made all the more vigorous by its association with *polyptoton*: 'ne doit pas s'éteindre et ne s'éteindra pas'. The second, and very different, function of the *peroration* is expressed in contrastingly different language (26). It is a return to the practicalities of the present and an offer of support for all his French listeners, whether or not they are able to respond to his appeal. They will all be able to listen to him again tomorrow. This practical information is of more than practical importance, however. It is of rhetorical importance too. For it helps to arouse interest in his listeners to know the outcome of the appeal. It tells them that this is a man who will report back and who will continue to appeal until his aim is achieved. It is entirely consonant with his message of steadfast hope.

His audience could not have known that his final sentence was also an extraordinary indication of his audacity. When he announced his intention to speak the following day, he had asked nobody's permission, and it came as a great surprise to the BBC producers. In his speech on 19 June, he did not report the immediate response to his first appeal. A few French people had turned up to see him on the morning of 19 June, but they were very few, and they were not especially helpful. In his speech that evening, he went much further than in his visionary but cautiously worded first speech. He identified himself explicitly as the leader of the Free French: 'moi, Général de Gaulle, soldat et chef français, j'ai conscience de parler au nom de la France' (p. 4). And he gave any listening French soldiers a clear command: 'Soldats de France, où que vous soyez, debout!' (p. 5). De Gaulle was deploying a language of political persuasion that was to serve him well for many years ahead.

3. MARGUERITE YOURCENAR AT THE ACADÉMIE FRANÇAISE

Despite, or perhaps because of, its élitism and traditional ways, the Académie Française attracts enormous public interest in France. Founded by Cardinal Richelieu in 1635, its aims have remained constant. It seeks to establish the correct usage of the French language, to maintain its character and principles. The main task of its forty distinguished members is the production of the dictionary of the Académie, the ninth edition of which has been in preparation for most of the twentieth century. Never is public interest in the Académie greater than when a new member is being elected. The cause of various candidates is championed by members of the Académie or by other individuals in the public eye, before the members take a vote. The newly elected member is received into the Académie during a formal ceremony, which unfolds with great pomp. Traditionally, members wear their green and gold embroidered uniform with cocked hat and personalized sword. The new member is required to make a speech in which the Académie is thanked and, above all, the deceased predecessor is praised. In response, an existing member delivers a speech welcoming and praising the new member. Both speeches can last up to one hour. They are rehearsed privately in front of a small committee of members before being delivered in public beneath the cupola of the Institut de France.[4]

---

[4] For an informed and witty account of these proceedings, see F. Fossier, *Au Pays des immortels: L'Institut de France hier et aujourd'hui* (Fayard–Mazarine, 1987), 180–98. There is a succinct account of Yourcenar's election in P. L. Horn, *Marguerite Yourcenar* (Boston,

Speeches of praise are standard examples of *demonstrative* oratory. Because they focus on the past and no decision hangs on them, they can seem less dynamic than *judicial* and *deliberative* speeches, both of which seek to sway the minds of listeners in such a way as significantly to affect a future course of action, like the publication of *Madame Bovary* or the conduct of the Second World War. In the case of *demonstrative* speeches, the interesting decisions have already been taken. This does not mean, however, that such speeches may not fulfil a vital persuasive function. They may, for instance, reassure an audience that the right decisions have been taken. A new member of the Académie Française must somehow contrive both to confirm the glorious status of the deceased predecessor as Academician and to imply the wisdom of the Académie's decision to elect this particular new member. Rhetorically, therefore, *demonstrative* speeches can perform fascinatingly delicate operations.

The speech delivered by Marguerite Yourcenar on the occasion of her reception into the Académie on 22 January 1981 was uniquely delicate. Her election had been specially fraught with anxiety, as she was the first woman candidate to be elected. The usual arguments about candidates were, in this case, complicated and embittered by gender issues. There were those who objected to her candidacy on the grounds that she was of non-French birth (she was born in Belgium, and from 1947 held American citizenship), forgetting that this had not stood in the way of male Academicians Eugène Ionesco and Julien Green. In her reception speech, she would need to thank those who had battled on behalf of the first woman member, in particular Jean d'Ormesson, who was to make the speech in reply. She would need also to be conciliatory with respect to those members, now colleagues, who had opposed her candidature on more or less explicitly gender grounds. However, she would not wish to betray former generations of women who had suffered the exclusionary prejudices not only of the Académie but of society as a whole. Her speech, it is true, would focus on her praise of Roger Caillois, her predecessor, who had died in 1978, noted for his diverse writings on sociological, zoological, botanical, and geological topics and his early interest in Surrealism. But when she stood before the assem-

---

Mass.: Twayne Publishers, 1985), 5. For the text of her speech see M. Yourcenar, *Discours de réception de Mme Marguerite Yourcenar à l'Académie Française et réponse de M. Jean d'Ormesson* (Gallimard, 1981).

bled Academicians and other members of the public, she had to walk a slippery tightrope.

In terms of *action*, her physical appearance said much. She did not pretend to be like other Academicians by wearing the green costume, hat, and sword. She marked her difference by wearing a black velvet skirt and a white blouse, the creation of Yves Saint Laurent. For her the most crucial, and for us the most interesting, part of her speech is the *exordium*, her first verbal contact with her audience, the point at which she most needs to reconcile, or at least to juggle, the conflicting issues facing her. The *exordium* intertwines her three major concerns, all of which are treated both explicitly and implicitly: an expression of gratitude, in particular to her supporters; an attempt to seek conciliation with those members who had opposed her candidature; and an evocation of worthy, but neglected, women writers of the past. The result is an *exordium* which is not nearly as transparent as an *exordium* in a *demonstrative* speech might normally be expected to be (*Discours de réception*, pp. 9–12):

[1] Messieurs,
Comme il convient, je commence par vous remercier de m'avoir, honneur sans précédent, accueillie parmi vous. [2] Je n'insiste pas—ils savent déjà tout cela—sur la gratitude que je dois aux amis qui, dans votre Compagnie, ont tenu à m'élire, sans que j'en eusse fait, comme l'usage m'y eût obligée, la demande, mais en me contentant de dire que je ne découragerais pas leur effort. [3] Ils savent à quel point je suis sensible aux admirables dons de l'amitié, et plus sensible peut-être à cette occasion que jamais, puisque ces amis, pour la plupart, sont ceux de mes livres, et ne m'avaient jamais, ou que très brièvement, rencontrée dans la vie.

[4] D'autre part, j'ai trop le respect de la tradition, là où elle est encore vivante, puissante et, si j'ose dire, susceptible, pour ne pas comprendre ceux qui résistent aux innovations vers lesquelles les pousse ce qu'on appelle l'esprit du temps, qui n'est souvent, je le leur concède, que la mode du temps. [5] *Sint ut sunt: Qu'ils demeurent tels qu'ils sont*, est une formule qui se justifie par l'inquiétude qu'on ressent toujours en ne changeant qu'une seule pierre à un bel édifice debout depuis quelques siècles.

[6] Vous m'avez accueillie, disais-je. [7] Ce moi incertain et flottant, cette entité dont j'ai contesté moi-même l'existence, et que je ne sens vraiment délimité que par les quelques ouvrages qu'il m'est arrivé d'écrire, le voici, tel qu'il est, entouré, accompagné d'une troupe invisible de femmes qui auraient dû, peut-être, recevoir beaucoup plus tôt cet honneur, au point que je suis tentée de m'effacer pour laisser passer leurs ombres.

[8] Toutefois, n'oublions pas que c'est seulement il y a un peu plus ou

un peu moins d'un siècle que la question de la présence de femmes dans cette assemblée a pu se poser. [9] En d'autres termes c'est vers le milieu du XIXᵉ siècle que la littérature est devenue en France pour quelques femmes tout ensemble une vocation et une profession, et cet état de choses était encore trop nouveau peut-être pour attirer l'attention d'une Compagnie comme la vôtre. [10] Mme de Staël eût été sans doute inéligible de par son ascendance suisse et son mariage suédois: elle se contentait d'être un des meilleurs esprits du siècle. [11] George Sand eût fait scandale par la turbulence de sa vie, par la générosité même de ses émotions qui font d'elle une femme si admirablement femme; la personne encore plus que l'écrivain devançait son temps. [12] Colette elle-même pensait qu'une femme ne rend pas visite à des hommes pour solliciter leur voix, et je ne puis qu'être de son avis, ne l'ayant pas fait moi-même. [13] Mais remontons plus haut: les femmes de l'Ancien Régime, reines des salons, et, plus tôt, des ruelles, n'avaient pas songé à franchir votre seuil, et peut-être eussent-elles cru déchoir, en le faisant, de leur souveraineté féminine. [14] Elles inspiraient les écrivains, les régentaient parfois et, fréquemment, ont réussi à faire entrer l'un de leurs protégés dans votre Compagnie, coutume qui, m'assure-t-on, a duré jusqu'à nos jours; elles se souciaient fort peu d'être elles-mêmes candidates. [15] On ne peut donc prétendre que, dans cette société française si imprégnée d'influences féminines, l'Académie ait été particulièrement misogyne; elle s'est simplement conformée aux usages qui volontiers plaçaient la femme sur un piédestal, mais ne permettaient pas encore de lui avancer officiellement un fauteuil. [16] Je n'ai donc pas lieu de m'enorgueillir de l'honneur si grand certes, mais quasi fortuit et de ma part quasi involontaire, qui m'est fait; je n'en ai d'ailleurs que plus de raisons de remercier ceux qui m'ont tendu la main pour franchir un seuil.

Her first paragraph weaves a path between the comfortably conventional and the provocatively unconventional. There is the conventional opening address to the fellow members, 'Messieurs'. There is the immediate recourse to *ethos* in the picture of her gratitude to the whole of the assembled membership. And there is a further more subtle recourse to *ethos*, suggesting her modesty, in the statement that she did not herself ask to be a candidate for membership of the Académie (2). The subtlety here lies in the way she is already preparing for the conciliatory tone of her second paragraph, which will be addressed to those who favoured another candidate (Jean Dorst). As she will do throughout her speech, she cultivates the *grand style*, using intricately constructed sentences and the pluperfect subjunctive in the phrase 'comme l'usage m'y eût obligée'

(2), thereby establishing, by her choice of syntax and lexis, her solid credentials as an Academician.

The opening word 'Messieurs', however, spoken by a woman, immediately evokes the gender issues that are the subtext of this *exordium*. It is true that she alludes to the conventional nature of her first sentence ('comme il convient'). But the parenthesis ('honneur sans précédent'), made prominent by its location between the two parts of the verb, draws attention to the break in convention that her situation represents. Moreover, her use of *praeteritio* (2–3), whereby she claims not to mention something while actually mentioning it, puts the focus precisely on the controversial nature of her election by singling out those members who supported her and whom she thanks vigorously by means of *geminatio* ('amis' (2), and again (3)). Her gratitude to these particular supporters is expressed also by her careful choice of epithet ('admirables dons de l'amitié') and her use of *dérivation* ('amis', 'amitié'). Without doing so explicitly, she is foregrounding the crucial issue of her sex. The reference to her not having made the customary request to be considered for election may appear to be a conventional suggestion of modesty; but it is also an allusion to the exceptional nature of her candidature. This uniqueness is made more explicit in the next sentence: 'plus sensible peut-être à cette occasion que jamais' (3). In the following clause she glosses this reference to the extraordinary nature of the occasion, perhaps wittily, since she refers not to her being a woman (the obvious point she might be thought to be making), but to her not being well known to her supporters. In theory, this further use of *ethos* should have the conciliatory effect of not alienating her opponents from her supporters, whose judgement, she claims, was based purely on what she wrote, not on her personal qualities (and not, therefore, on her being a woman).

Conciliation dominates the second paragraph, at least on the surface. Here she expresses sympathy with the views of her opponents. She is careful, however, not to sympathize explicitly with their anxiety about the admission of a woman to membership of the Académie. Exploitation of *genus* allows her to talk more generally about the competing claims of tradition and innovation, rather than more specifically about her own innovatory status. She talks in an explicitly concessionary way about the demands for innovation, making playful use of *epistrophe* to redefine 'l'esprit du temps' as 'la mode du temps' (4). Her concessionary mode is part of her

continued deployment of *ethos*, offering an image of herself as understanding and unthreatening. The refusal at this point to discuss the
gender issue explicitly contributes to this image. This aspect of *ethos*
is developed further with her use of the *metaphor* of a fine and ancient
building easily spoilt by the displacement of a single stone (5). But
this point also helpfully promotes the other aspect of her use of *ethos*,
the view of her as a great and cultivated writer. She shows that she
can use an appropriate image, the revered building being the vehicle whereby the tenor, the generations of Academicians, is conjured
up. It is a particularly appropriate image, because it can be taken
to refer simultaneously to the architecturally splendid building in
which the ceremonies of the Académie take place. Reinforcing the
sense of the image and also the picture of Yourcenar as a learned
woman is the Latin phrase '*Sint ut sunt*', which she translates. It is
not a well-known Latin quotation. Rather it demonstrates her ability to sum up a point in phonetically memorable Latin, a good
example of *paronomasia* and *polyptoton* working together.

Despite the expression of sympathy for those who are suspicious
of change, there are two features of this second paragraph which
suggest a limit to her sympathy. The first is present in the way in
which adjectives are used to *personify* tradition (4). 'Vivante' and
'puissante' certainly offer a positive view of tradition, but 'susceptible', thrown into prominence by the preceding phrase 'si j'ose
dire', can only be interpreted negatively as suggestive of the prickli-
ness of some sticklers for tradition. There is a certain kind of traditionalism which she can understand, but not condone. This same
suggestion of a limit to her sympathy might be present at a subtextual level in her Latin phrase. Although it is not a direct quotation
from any Latin work, this collocation of words can be found, in
almost the same form, in Cicero's *Philippics* (IV. 4. 9), where the
Roman orator is attacking those who think of Mark Antony as con-
sul. Cicero says of them: 'nec ab iudicio omnium mortalium,
quamvis impii nefariique *sint, sicut sunt*, dissentire possunt' ('although
they may be disloyal and criminal, *as they are*, they cannot dissent from
the judgement of everybody alive'; my italics). The syntactic and
semantic context of the relevant phrase is so different in the Cicero
and Yourcenar speeches that the literal meaning of the phrase is
inevitably different in both cases. But if the Ciceronian context is
borne in mind, the Yourcenar phrase gains in associative power. For
whilst, on the surface, it seems to sympathize with the traditionalists

by suggesting that things should stay as they are, subtextually it refers to a group of men who are disapproved of and who are inclined to disagree with a majority view, such men as those who might have opposed Yourcenar's election. We cannot know if Yourcenar intended this subtextual meaning, so much at variance with the literal meaning. She can certainly not have intended it to be obvious; for it would have been too impolite and too discordant with her careful manipulation of *ethos* at other points in the *exordium*. We do know, however, that she had an excellent knowledge of Roman history and Latin literature.

The third paragraph tackles the gender issue explicitly, but uses the technique of *insinuation* to lead up to it in an unexpected way. To begin with, Yourcenar performs the trick of making all that she has said since her first sentence seem digressive, by returning self-consciously to the subject of that sentence: 'Vous m'avez accueillie, disais-je' (6). This also fulfils the function of making the subject she is about to tackle now seem more important than what she has already said. The way she develops this apparently innocent and incontrovertible phrase is to pick out the object pronoun 'me' and to exploit the two *places* of *definition* and *circumstances*, defining her self and considering the unusual circumstances of her presence in the Académie.

The first half of the sentence (7) in which she broaches the topic of the self creates the impression that her line of thought is a philosophical or a literary-critical one. The indeterminacy of the self is the message of the adjectives ('incertain et flottant') and of the relative clauses. This first part of the sentence deploys a descending *gradatio*, as longer phrases give way to a very short one when 'Ce moi' is identified tersely in the words 'le voici'. Yourcenar is here using wit, playing on the contrast between the serious reflections on the difficulty of knowing and identifying the self and the very physical allusion to her bodily presence as she stands before her audience. This wit, however, serves a persuasive function, securing the interest and approval of her audience at the very point in her sentence when she will change tack and address the tricky issue of gender.

The second half of the sentence is, in terms of structure, a mirror image of the first half, an ascending *gradatio*, in which she presents herself as a woman. Or rather, she associates herself with a tradition of women who deserved to be Academicians but who were overlooked. The use of the word 'troupe' to refer to these women is perhaps both an ironic gesture towards the deprecatory tone adopted by some men when discussing the claims of women and a *hyperbolic* allusion to the number of women who have been passed over. Their invisibility is a *metaphor* for their death or their neglect. It is true that, in conciliatory mode, the implied criticism of the Académie is attenuated by the use of the phrase 'peut-être' in the claim that other women should have been honoured like her. The criticism is intensified, however, in the phrase 'beaucoup plus tôt' and in the dramatic imagery which concludes the sentence. Moving aside to leave room for the ghosts of the neglected could allude to a verbal device, whereby she might intend to exploit *prosopopoeia* and give voice to those who had suffered the gender prejudices of the Académie. The same image could also refer to a physical movement, whereby she might be suggesting that she could step back to create space for all the slighted ghosts.

The subject of the exclusion of women from the Académie is now pursued in the fourth paragraph. Yourcenar, aware of her audience and the occasion, combines attack and attenuation. She continues to use wit in a way which might both niggle and command approval for her intellectual skill. Having just launched a direct attack (7), the fourth paragraph opens with an attempt to attenuate it, and adopts a conciliatory tone. The attenuation of criticism is evident in the way she draws arguments from the *place* of *circumstances* (8–9). Whereas she has just evoked the possibility of there being many generations of women who might have been members of the Académie (7), she now considers the historical circumstances in which the election of women might first have become a serious issue. By locating the key moment in the mid-nineteenth century, when women first became professional writers, she appears to be removing any blame from the Académie for not electing women before then. The blame for not electing women from the mid-nineteenth century onwards, however, might still be thought to attach to them. To deal with this question, she finds an argument based on the character of the Académie (*ethos*), but it is spectacularly double-edged and daringly witty. The Académie's traditionalism and inability to deal with a new phenomenon until a century or more after its occurrence is offered as an excuse for its members' failure to take on board the professional status of women writers; but it is an excuse which is also a criticism, a caricatural representation of the Académie's backwoods conservatism. The words 'trop nouveau' are heavily ironic, since they are meant to refer to a period starting in the nineteenth century and ending in the late twentieth century.

Yourcenar offers three examples of *external proofs* to support this line of argument which, on the surface, makes excuses for the Académie, but, not far beneath the surface, suggests criticism of its attitude to the cause of women (10–12). She devotes one sentence to each of three women writers, two from the nineteenth century and one from the early twentieth. In each case, she suggests a reason why it might seem proper for these major figures not to have been elected to the Académie; but in the first two she also indicates a striking personal quality which contributes to their greatness and makes it seem the Académie's loss not to have had them among its number. The sentences gain in effect by their cumulative, repetitive nature. Each begins with the name of the woman writer, and each is an example of a descending *gradatio*. In the first and longer part of each sentence, Yourcenar gives the reason which might be cited to explain why the woman in question could have been thought an inappropriate candidate for election to the Académie. In the second and shorter (and hence punchier) part, she suggests the woman's real quality.

The possible objections to Mme de Staël's election have a certain piquancy, since one of them, her Swiss origins, resembles the objection of non-French birth that some members had raised against Yourcenar's own election. There is wit in the way Yourcenar expresses Mme de Staël's positive qualities: 'elle se contentait d'être un des meilleurs esprits du siècle' (10). The contrast between the anticipation of an ordinary, unexceptional quality (such as would normally follow the phrase 'elle se contentait de') and the actual statement about her superlative intellect points an accusing, and perhaps even a mocking, finger at the members of the Académie.

In the case of George Sand, there is bold defiance in the way Yourcenar turns even her supposedly negative quality (her morally unconventional life-style) to her advantage. Sand's emotional life makes her 'une femme si admirablement femme' (11). The use of *syllepsis* allows Yourcenar to let the crucial word 'femme' ring out before her predominantly male audience, its effect increased by its juxtaposition with the positive adverb 'admirablement' and the intensifying 'si'. Yourcenar herself adopted an unconventional life-style, her main relationship being with another woman, Grace Frick. The last clause sums up Sand's supreme quality as a pioneer.

Again there is a suggestion of criticism that the Académie is unable to cope with novelty.

The treatment of Colette is slightly different. The first half of the sentence (12) follows the previous pattern of giving the reason why she might not have been elected. She would not follow the convention whereby would-be members must ask for the support of existing members. Yourcenar's expression of this, however, has special implications. Expressing Colette's reluctance to follow convention makes it clear that the convention could not have been the same in the case of a woman as in that of a man. It would have required a woman to ask a favour from a group of men. Yourcenar tries to alert her audience to the sexual politics of seeking membership of the Académie. And lest they think it no longer an issue in the light of her own election, she concludes her treatment of Colette by associating herself closely with her. It is true that Yourcenar has already made the point that she did not seek election in the normal way (2). The report of this occasion that appeared in *Le Nouvel Observateur* on 26 January 1981 (p. 30) adopts a slightly mocking attitude to Yourcenar's insistence on this point: 'La récipiendaire [. . .] insista bien sur le fait qu'elle ne demandait, pour sa part, rien du tout et qu'on était allé la chercher dans sa petite île américaine.' Her passivity in the election process was stated earlier, however, to indicate her lack of aggression during her candidacy. Restated here, it acquires new vigour, suggesting that the sexual politics of candidacies for election is still a problematic issue which deserves the members' attention. The association established between Yourcenar and Colette also has the effect of strengthening the case that earlier women writers were unjustly neglected by the Académie.

Her argument apparently justifying the Académie's failure to have elected a woman before her has so far been based on the special historical circumstances since the mid-nineteenth century. The justification turns out to be rather dubious, and to give the Académie reason to ponder its past. Yourcenar now extends the argument back in time, considering the position in the seventeenth and eighteenth centuries and again exploiting the *place* known as *circumstances* (13–14). Ostensibly she is on safer ground if her wish is to defend the Académie's position and to appease its members. She is dealing now with a period when there were very few professional women writers (a period, in fact, when the concept of the professional writer was only just taking shape). Women would simply not have thought of being members of the Académie, so the Académie cannot be blamed for not electing them.

Her wit operates differently in dealing with women in the *ancien régime*. She promotes their virtues in writing and the arts not so much by suggesting their oppression in a patriarchal society, but rather by conjuring up, in a picturesque way, a particular domain dominated by women. A host of devices of *elocution* stresses the prominent role they played in the literary circles of the *ancien régime*. *Metaphor* transforms them into queens or potentates ('reines' (13), 'souveraineté' (13), 'régentaient' (14)), suggesting their control of literary life. Yourcenar's own *grand style* evokes their linguistic refinement, particularly the collocation of inversion, the pluperfect subjunctive, the rare use of 'déchoir de' and the intercalated participial clause in the phrase 'peut-être eussent-elles cru déchoir, en le faisant, de leur souveraineté féminine' (13). The female literary and social space of the seventeenth century is identified with the archaic word 'ruelles' (originally the space between the wall and the bed where the Marquise de Rambouillet received her guests as she lay in bed; later the term designated any salon assembly). The nature of women's involvement is conveyed in the verbal *gradatio* 'inspiraient', 'régentaient', 'ont réussi à faire entrer' (14), and in the *antithesis* between their enthusiasm for literary life and the lack of interest in their own candidacy for the Académie ('elles se souciaient fort peu d'être elles-mêmes candidates' (14)). Yourcenar's wit plays on the contrast she creates between her picture of the distant world of salon life and her *parenthetical* allusion to the present-day practice of women promoting male candidates (14). The effect is to create surprise that the Académie should provide this link between the role of women in the apparently long-vanished days of the *ancien régime* and their role in the late twentieth century. Whatever the superficial differences of historical age, the role of women seems always to have been primarily to support male candidates for election.

At the end of this fourth paragraph Yourcenar draws conclusions from the glimpses into history that she has just given (15–16). The first conclusion is the conciliatory one that was implied at the beginning of the paragraph (15). The Académie cannot be singled out on account of its misogyny. The evidence of women's involvement in the literary life of the *ancien régime* shows how male writers were receptive to female influence. This exoneration of the Académie could hardly be called decisive, however. The presentation of her material and views has all along been ambiguous. Now Yourcenar's use of adverbs is crucial in defining a limit to the extent of her exoneration of the Académie. She says that it has not been 'particulièrement misogyne' (15): yet her discussion of nineteenth- and twentieth-century women writers pointed precisely to areas in which the Académie had been blind to the qualities of women or the problems facing them in seeking election. The adverb with which she describes the conformist ways of the Académie can also be read critically: the Académie is simply conformist ('simplement' (15)). The Académie has certainly conformed to society's norms, but the word 'simplement' might well raise the question as to whether that is too comfortable an attitude for an élite body of writers and intellectuals to have adopted. To convey the Académie's submission to convention, Yourcenar uses a conventional *topic*, referring to the 'usages qui volontiers plaçaient la femme sur un piédestal'. She further demonstrates her wit by contrasting this conventional pedestal image of woman with her own image of woman being offered an armchair: 'mais ne permettaient pas encore de lui avancer officiellement un fauteuil' (15). Since the members of the Académie sit in 'fauteuils', this is a peculiarly suitable image with which to convey their reluctance to elect women.

The second conclusion she draws pertains to Yourcenar herself. It is based on a further exploitation of *ethos*, insisting on her own modesty and lack of pride. The conclusion might seem somewhat elliptical. It is that, given the Académie's recognition of women's literary role in the past, Yourcenar has no special reason to feel pride. She suggests, therefore, that she accepts the superficially specious reasons she has offered in defence of the Académie. She also reminds her audience, for the third time in this *exordium*, that she did not seek election. She recapitulates her opening expression of thanks to those who encouraged and supported her candidature. By all these means, she cultivates an appropriate *ethos* with which to appeal to her audience. But her final image sounds a different note. The people she thanks are identified as 'ceux qui m'ont tendu la main pour franchir un seuil' (16). It is a note of progress. The threshold she has crossed is invested with symbolic significance. She is the first woman to have entered a world peopled only by men since 1635. Crossing the threshold is a step she takes in her own right, but also on behalf of other women. If some aspects of her speech so far have suggested the Académie's reluctance to accept change, this image makes the progressive step it has just taken very plain. For Yourcenar has just used the same image when presenting the women of the *ancien régime*, who 'n'avaient pas songé à franchir votre seuil' (13). Ending her *exordium* with the image of her stepping across that same threshold marks the advance which it took the Académie 346 years to accomplish. Her choice, however, of the indefinite article ('un seuil') rather than the alternative demonstrative adjective ('ce seuil') implies that there are other thresholds that women have yet to cross.

The rest of her speech is devoted to an eloquent account of the achievements of Roger Caillois. Her triumph in the *exordium* is to have cultivated a rich multiplicity of meaning. She thanks all those to whom thanks are due. She presents herself as a grateful and unassuming recipient of a prestigious honour. She does not overtly blame the Académie for its earlier attitude to the election of women; on the contrary, she tries to understand and explain it. Yet, some of those thanked especially are precisely those who had to fight hard for her election because she is a woman. Her sympathy with traditions seems to incorporate a critique of blinkered traditionalism. Her reflections on earlier women writers include praise of their neglected achievements. The frequent and fleeting shifts in perspective, the elegant and elevated syntax, the constant recourse to wit ensures that Marguerite Yourcenar seems to say, in the *exordium*, the right thing for everybody. What exactly she thought on the issues raised here is hidden from view, as befits the occasion.

The question of progress, treated tentatively by Yourcenar, is fully foregrounded in the *exordium* of Jean d'Ormesson's reply to her speech. His *exordium* is addressed to the existing male members of the Académie. He is conciliatory in his celebration of progress tempered by tradition: 'La plus haute tâche de la tradition est de rendre au progrès la politesse qu'elle lui doit' (p. 56). The remainder of his speech will, following convention, be addressed to the new member, whose writings will be praised. But he effects a stylistically clever and thematically telling transition between *exordium* and *narration* (p. 56):

Ce sont, j'imagine, des réflexions de cet ordre qui vous ont incités, Messieurs, à me permettre de prononcer devant vous—sans que le ciel me tombe sur la tête, sans que s'écroule cette Coupole, sans que viennent m'arracher de mon fauteuil les ombres indignées de ceux qui nous ont précédés dans cette lignée conservatrice d'un patrimoine culturel où, fidèles à l'étymologie, nos pères semblent s'être livrés depuis toujours et tout seuls à une espèce d'équivalent masculin et paradoxal de la parthénogenèse—un mot inouï et prodigieusement singulier: Madame.

In addition to the witty reference to the Académie's tradition of male self-perpetuation ('espèce d'équivalent masculin et paradoxal de la parthénogenèse'), there is the astonishing *parenthesis* with its complex syntax and *anaphoric* subordinate clauses ('sans que', 'sans que', 'sans que'), deliberately delaying the object of the verb 'prononcer'. When the object is given, there is further adjectival and adverbial delay: 'un mot inouï et prodigieusement singulier'. *Hyperbole* helps to create suspense, and an ingenious *syllepsis* gives 'singulier' not only its obvious meaning ('unusual') but also its grammatical meaning ('singular' as opposed to 'plural', she being the only woman member). When the word 'Madame' is finally pronounced, the contrast between its stark ordinariness and brevity and the preceding lexical, syntactic, and stylistic intricacy is massive. The effect is humorous. He has his audience on his side. He can now address the Académie's first woman member. He too has crossed a threshold, and he has helped the Académie to cross it with him.

As diverse as the texts considered in this chapter may seem, they all have in common the fact that they were prepared in advance to be spoken to, and to impress, an audience. They are not literary texts in the conventional sense of the word. Yet all the texts repay close study. They work complex effects on their audience by exploiting the resources of *invention, disposition,* and *elocution.* All these texts live on in print. But they were most alive at the moment of delivery. We may speculate that the *action* with which they were delivered must have counted for something. The *action,* however, cannot easily be recovered. De Gaulle's radio broadcast might normally have been recorded, but on 18 June 1940 the BBC's equipment was busy recording a speech by Winston Churchill. All the devices employed by orators, including *action,* are used in yet richer ways by writers of fictions, to which the next three chapters now turn.

3

DRAMA

The orator and the actor have much in common. The link between
rhetoric and drama, particularly in the early modern period, is a
strong one. Tragedy and comedy emerged in France in the mid-
sixteenth century, not out of any dramatic impulse to write plays for
entertainment, but out of a rhetorical impulse to increase the range
of writing in the French language by imitating the genres practised
by the ancient Greeks and Romans. Plays were performed before
select court or school audiences. What was on offer was less an
exciting plot based on compelling conflicts than a succession of
speeches and set-piece dialogues, each to be admired as a description, a narration, or the evocation of a mood or an emotion. Since
the sixteenth century and the subsequent emphasis placed on plot,
excitement, and conflict by dramatists writing for the public theatre,
Renaissance drama, especially tragedy, has been dismissed as static
and 'rhetorical'. This view is as unfair to the poetic qualities of
Renaissance tragedians as it is to the proteiform nature of rhetoric
and its importance in drama.[1] If sixteenth-century plays were
rhetorical, so were their seventeenth- and eighteenth-century successors, but in a different way.

Throughout the seventeenth and eighteenth centuries, schoolboys
educated at Jesuit schools performed plays, usually in Latin, as part
of their curriculum. Their teachers were not interested in turning
them into actors. Far from it. What performance gave them was an
opportunity to practise those skills of public deportment and speaking that they would need as preachers or lawyers. The plays, composed by their teachers, also brought them into contact with

---

[1] On the significance of rhetoric in Renaissance tragedy, see R. Griffiths, *The Dramatic
Technique of Antoine de Montchrestien: Rhetoric and Style in French Renaissance Tragedy* (Oxford:
Clarendon Press, 1970), and G. Jondorf, *French Renaissance Tragedy: The Dramatic Word*
(Cambridge: Cambridge University Press, 1990), esp. ch. 3, 'The Rhetor', which suggests
that characters in Renaissance tragedies employ rhetoric to communicate the dramatist's
moral message to the theatre audience or readership rather than to communicate with
each other.

examples of written exercises of the kind that they themselves were expected to produce for their lessons. Drama was therefore a good way of teaching and practising rhetoric.

But the opposite was also true. Throughout the period, rhetoric was an essential acquisition for the dramatist and the actor. The dramatic theorist d'Aubignac, whose *Pratique du théâtre* appeared in 1657, repeatedly wrote, at the beginning of successive chapters on dramatic speech, that the dramatist needed a knowledge of rhetoric:[2]

Je présuppose icy d'abord un Poëte instruit en la Rhetorique, et en tout ce que les excellens Autheurs de cét art ont écrit de la Narration.

Mon dessein n'est pas icy d'enseigner cette partie de la Rhetorique, qu'on nomme le *Genre deliberatif*, où l'on traitte les adresses dont il faut se servir pour dire son avis avec art et ornement, touchant les matieres sur lesquelles on demande son conseil. Nostre Poëte ne doit pas attendre qu'il soit monté sur le Theatre, pour prendre la connoissance de ces principes.

Je ne croy pas non plus qu'il soit necessaire de monstrer l'art [de se servir des passions] pour bien persuader, après ce qu'en a dit Aristote au 2. Livre de sa Rhetorique, et ceux qui l'ont suivi.

Le meilleur avis qu'on puisse donner aux Poëtes, est de se rendre tres-sça-vans en la connoissance des Figures par l'étude de ce qu'en ont écrit les Rhetoriciens.

D'Aubignac alludes to some key elements of rhetorical theory for the dramatist: *deliberative oratory*, the narrative part of a speech (*narration*), emotional arguments (*pathos*), and the *figures of speech*. For him at least, it is clear that rhetorical theory underpins dramatic dialogue.

Rhetoric is also important for the actor. According to Grimarest, who wrote a life of Molière as well as a treatise on declamation, 'le Comédien doit se considérer comme un Orateur, qui prononce en public un discours fait pour toucher l'auditeur'.[3] The analogy between the actor and the orator is obvious. Both speak in public so as to compel attention, and both are aware of the importance of tone of voice and gesture (*actio*). But Grimarest's evocation of the similarities between actor and orator raises a crucial issue. The ora-

---

[2] D'Aubignac, *La Pratique du théâtre*, ed. P. Martino (Champion, 1927; Geneva: Slatkine Reprints, 1996), 288, 304, 332, 346.
[3] J.-L. Grimarest, *La Vie de M. de Molière*, ed. G. Mongrédien (Brient, 1955), 162.

tor speaks directly to a single audience. However invisible and
diverse de Gaulle's BBC audiences may have been, his speeches
were addressed directly by him to them. And the critic can look
back at his speeches and assess how his rhetoric was constructed to
work on them. But when actors speak, what is their audience? It is
true that the ultimate aim of the dramatist who has written the dialogue and the actors who deliver it must be to grip, stir, and entertain the spectators in the auditorium. But it is very rare that the
words spoken by the actors are addressed directly to the spectators;
they are most frequently addressed to other actors in their guise as
characters.

The implications of this are significant for the student of rhetoric.
In drama, rhetoric is deployed by one character to influence
another. It is by showing characters in rhetorical interactions that
the dramatist seeks to engage the attention of the spectators. When
we judge the rhetoric of an orator, we may or may not know the
actual response of his audience, but we can assess how successfully
his rhetoric has been chosen and deployed. In a play, on the other
hand, the success or failure of a character's rhetoric is made plain
to us by the response of the other characters. The interest for the
critic lies in observing how the rhetorical interaction has been constructed so as to maximize (or not) the interest of the spectators.

This approach is especially fruitful for French drama in the seventeenth century, owing to the conventions according to which
plays in the period were conceived.[4] The dominant dramatic theory
was illusionistic. Dramatists were supposed to conjure up an illusion
of real life on the stage. It was accepted that this could best be done
if there was little discrepancy between the time over which the dramatic action elapsed and the actual time of performance: hence the
unity of time, which determined that the action should take place
in less than twenty-four hours. A spatial restriction, the unity of
place, followed from the temporal one. The action should evolve in
one place. This also avoided the need for different scenery, which
would further have compromised the illusion of reality. Given the
temporal and spatial constraints, the action typically involved a
small number of characters, usually well known to each other. From

---

[4] On the conventions of seventeenth-century drama, see J. Scherer, *La Dramaturgie classique en France* (Nizet, 1950). The most interesting seventeenth-century theorist (along with
d'Aubignac) is Pierre Corneille. See his *Writings on the Theatre*, ed. H. T. Barnwell (Oxford:
Blackwell, 1965).

these conventions it flowed that drama dealt with a crisis coming to a head and depicted the efforts of a few individuals to ensure that their point of view prevailed. It also flowed that the characters should never seem to be too much like orators or poets; otherwise the illusion would again be broken. Pierre Corneille insisted on this: 'Ceux que [l'orateur] fait parler ne sont pas des orateurs' (*Writings on the Theatre*, 19). None the less, persuasive interaction was the key concept that lay beneath dramatic dialogue. This is one way of interpreting d'Aubignac's claim that in these plays '*Parler*, c'est *Agir*' (*Pratique*, 282), or, in Corneille's version: 'Les actions sont l'âme de la tragédie, où l'on ne doit parler qu'en agissant et pour agir' (*Writings*, 19).

This chapter looks at rhetoric at work in two plays from the seventeenth century, Molière's *Tartuffe* (1669) and Racine's *Britannicus* (1669). It then turns to a play of a seemingly very different kind, written almost three centuries later, in which the role of rhetoric will need to be reassessed, Beckett's *En attendant Godot* (1952).

I. RHETORIC AND HYPOCRISY: MOLIÈRE'S *TARTUFFE*

The interlocking skills of the orator and the actor are explicitly the subject of Molière's *Tartuffe*.[5] The title character deliberately abuses his rhetorical and theatrical skills in order to deceive those around him by a false display of religious behaviour, which is what made the play so controversial in the 1660s. By way of defence, Molière suggests that he wrote the play in such a way as to prevent any confusion in the spectators' minds: it would be clear to them all along that Tartuffe was a hypocrite, even if some of the characters in the play believed him to be sincere. Molière's comment conveys the care he took in writing the role: 'j'ai mis tout l'art et tout le soin qu'il m'a été possible pour bien distinguer le personnage de l'hypocrite d'avec celui du vrai dévot [. . .] il ne dit pas un mot, il ne fait

---

[5] I refer to the edition of the play in vol. i of Molière's *Œuvres complètes*, ed. G. Couton, Bibliothèque de la Pléiade, (2 vols., Gallimard, 1971). This edition includes the anonymous *Lettre sur la comédie de l'Imposteur* (pp. 1147–81), which suggests how the play's rhetoric worked on one particular individual in performance in 1667. The play was first performed in 1664 and banned. Molière rewrote it for public performance in 1667, when it was banned again. He was finally allowed to perform his third version, the only one extant today, in 1669. The edition of *Tartuffe* by R. Parish (Bristol Classical Press, 1994) can be recommended for its commentary, which is particularly sensitive to *elocution*.

pas une action, qui ne peigne aux spectateurs le caractère d'un
méchant homme' (preface, *Œuvres complètes*, i. 884). This comment
implicitly conveys one of the crucial sources of comic pleasure in the
play, the entertainingly ambiguous nature of Tartuffe's role, which
depends on his portrayal as a skilled orator. His rhetorical skills are
evoked explicitly by Elmire, the married woman whom he tries to
seduce: 'Je vous écoute dire, et votre rhétorique / En termes assez
forts à mon âme s'explique' (1001–2). Elmire's comment highlights
the impact of Tartuffe's rhetorical skills on her.

Tartuffe immediately strikes the theatre audience as an actor and
an orator, but the structure of the play requires that the other characters too engage in rhetorical interaction with each other, and their
varying degrees of success contribute to the comedy that arises from
an array of conflicts. Conflict arises from the different reactions to
Tartuffe in Orgon's household, into which he has been welcomed in
the guise of an impoverished but devout Christian by the gullible
Orgon. The master of the house and his mother, Mme Pernelle, are
besotted with the pious newcomer, and take every opportunity to
defend him. Mme Pernelle delivers a devastating series of critical
portraits, attacking those who claim he is a hypocrite (I. i). She
returns later and tries to persuade Orgon of Tartuffe's sincerity, even
though by that time even Orgon has been disabused (v. iii). Mme
Pernelle is a comically incompetent orator, uncompromising, author-
itarian, and irrelevant. Orgon's rhetorical skills are also comically
undeveloped. Whilst he tries to persuade his brother-in-law Cléante
of Tartuffe's sincerity (I. v) and his daughter Mariane and the servant Dorine of the desirability of the wedding he proposes between
Mariane and Tartuffe (II. i–ii), his preferred mode of discourse is
peremptory assertion and even threats of violence.

Other characters oppose Tartuffe and try to disabuse Orgon,
showing, on the whole, much greater rhetorical skill than Tartuffe's
supporters. Cléante's careful argument about the need to distinguish
true from false piety goes unheeded by Orgon, but Cléante has spoken well, and the audience laughs at Orgon's foolish inattentiveness
(I. v). Orgon's wife Elmire tries to persuade Tartuffe to decline the
proposed marriage to Mariane by cleverly exploiting the feelings
that she knows he has for her (III. iii). But her strategy is foiled by
the interruption of her son Damis, who has heard Tartuffe's
attempted seduction of Elmire and thinks that this *external proof* is
sure to persuade Orgon of Tartuffe's hypocrisy (III. iv–v), but it does

not. Tartuffe is a better orator than Damis, and defends himself superbly well (III. vi). The limits of Tartuffe's skills are seen in Act IV. He argues Jesuitically with Cléante, who attempts to persuade him to relinquish the right to all the wealth which Orgon has decided to transfer from Damis to Tartuffe, but Cléante is persistent, and Tartuffe simply makes his excuses and leaves (IV. i). Finally, Elmire furnishes Orgon with the most compelling *external proof* of Tartuffe's hypocrisy by making him witness Tartuffe's second attempt to seduce her (IV. v), as a result of which Orgon turns against him.

If Orgon takes a long time to be persuaded of the truth, and Mme Pernelle takes even longer, the king, by contrast, needs no persuasion. He has the power immediately to distinguish truth from falsehood (lines 1906–8):

> Nous vivons sous un Prince ennemi de la fraude,
> Un Prince dont les yeux se font jour dans les cœurs,
> Et que ne peut tromper tout l'art des imposteurs.

According to this report, when Tartuffe approached the king and accused Orgon of keeping documents belonging to an enemy of the crown, the king was not in the least persuaded by Tartuffe's *judicial* oratory. On the contrary, he recognized him immediately as a criminal. The king's critical ability to distinguish the abuse of rhetoric creates the happy ending: his official comes on stage and arrests not Orgon, as Tartuffe was expecting, but Tartuffe himself (V. vii). The same official also makes a speech explaining what has happened, which constitutes an example of *demonstrative* oratory in praise of the king.

Read in this perspective, the play not only relies on the depiction of successive rhetorical encounters for the fundamental structure of the dialogue; it also exploits one of the perennial thematic concerns of rhetorical theorists: the danger of rhetoric in the wrong hands, used to persuade people of falsehood. Rhetoricians always took the view that the orator had to be a good person. In that way, nothing could come amiss. But Molière shows what can happen when the orator is a criminal with the ability to dupe a figure of authority like Orgon. It takes an even greater authority to prevent catastrophe. Molière maintains a comic perspective by depicting Orgon as a ridiculous figure, and showing how most of the other characters easily see through Tartuffe's rhetorical skills. Presenting Tartuffe as a good, but not quite good enough, orator requires considerable rhetorical skill on Molière's own part. Three passages taken from different scenes demonstrate how Molière maintains comic and dramatic interest by engaging the audience in Tartuffe's delicately ambiguous rhetorical performance.

Tartuffe and Elmire

Elmire meets Tartuffe in Act III, scene iii, especially to persuade him not to marry Mariane. But Tartuffe sees the meeting as an opportunity to make progress in his lustful designs on Elmire. Molière works on two levels of ambiguity in his depiction of Tartuffe. On the one hand, there is a discrepancy between what he says and how he acts, between his verbal and his gestural rhetoric. The words he speaks are respectable, but his actions betray comically crude lust: he clasps Elmire's hand, he touches her knee, he moves his chair closer to hers. On the other hand, there is a subtler discrepancy between the outwardly respectable words and the immoral message which they cloak. Tartuffe is trying to persuade a married woman to grant him sexual favours, but he does so in the most devoutly Christian terms (lines 933–60):

L'amour qui nous attache aux beautés éternelles
N'étouffe pas en nous l'amour des temporelles;
Nos sens facilement peuvent être charmés
Des ouvrages parfaits que le Ciel a formés.
Ses attraits réfléchis brillent dans vos pareilles; 5
Mais il étale en vous ses plus rares merveilles:
Il a sur votre face épanché des beautés
Dont les yeux sont surpris, et les cœurs transportés,
Et je n'ai pu vous voir, parfaite créature,
Sans admirer en vous l'auteur de la nature, 10
Et d'une ardente amour sentir mon cœur atteint,
Au plus beau des portraits où lui-même il s'est peint.
D'abord j'appréhendai que cette ardeur secrète
Ne fût du noir esprit une surprise adroite;
Et même à fuir vos yeux mon cœur se résolut, 15
Vous croyant un obstacle à faire mon salut.
Mais enfin je connus, ô beauté toute aimable,
Que cette passion peut n'être point coupable,
Que je puis l'ajuster avecque la pudeur,
Et c'est ce qui m'y fait abandonner mon cœur. 20

Ce m'est, je le confesse, une audace bien grande
Que d'oser de ce cœur vous adresser l'offrande;
Mais j'attends en mes vœux tout de votre bonté,
Et rien des vains efforts de mon infirmité;
En vous est mon espoir, mon bien, ma quiétude,   25
De vous dépend ma peine ou ma béatitude,
Et je vais être enfin, par votre seul arrêt,
Heureux, si vous voulez, malheureux, s'il vous plaît.

This speech is Tartuffe's opportunistic response to Elmire's attempt to argue that he should not be interested in a marriage with Mariane, since his claims to devotion should direct all his love heavenwards: 'Pour moi, je crois qu'au Ciel tendent tous vos soupirs, / Et que rien ici-bas n'arrête vos désirs' (931–2). Tartuffe takes up, on the one hand, Elmire's sharp *antithesis* between heaven and earth and, on the other, her reference to his amorous intentions expressed both literally ('désirs') and *metonymically* ('soupirs'), and he responds by combining these different elements to create a Neoplatonic argument about the way human love is an image of divine love and can show the way to it. But his refutation of Elmire changes the course of the argument drastically. He does not deploy the Neoplatonic argument to justify his proposed marriage to Mariane, which would have been the logical step in the exchange. He uses it to justify his love of Elmire.

The *disposition* of Tartuffe's speech is strikingly formal. Whilst speakers engaging in formal oratory tend to structure their speeches according to the *disposition* recommended by rhetoricians, characters engaged in a dialogue in a play might normally be expected to demonstrate more informality in the structure of even fairly long speeches. Yet Tartuffe begins with an *exordium* (1–4) which introduces the Neoplatonic argument with which he will refute Elmire, and does so in general terms. The *narration* (5–12) applies the argument specifically to the case of Tartuffe and Elmire by recounting his alleged admiration for God through her. A *refutation* follows (13–20), in which he attempts to dispense with any doubts about the morality of his feelings. It is only in the *peroration* (21–8) that he makes the request for which all that precedes has prepared the ground: he wants sexual satisfaction. This is expressed in *metaphorical* terms. The formal structure of Tartuffe's speech is a sign to the audience of the degree of calculation with which he operates. In other words, the very skilfulness of the *disposition* gives him away as a schemer. Yet, in choice of vocabulary, he gives nothing away, and is impressively controlled. Throughout he adopts the *grand style*, using abstract words expressing religious emotion. The words themselves are entirely praiseworthy in moral and religious terms, but the intention behind them is entirely reprehensible. Molière's talents as a highly subtle comic writer are fully in evidence here: Tartuffe's carefully crafted ambiguity is sustained through the whole of this speech and most of his next one.

Given the new and rather risky direction in which Tartuffe intends to move the dialogue, he uses the best possible technique, which dominates the *exordium* and the *narration*. He does not immediately declare love and demand sexual satisfaction: he uses the technique of *insinuation*. In the *exordium* it is not at all clear that Tartuffe is changing the subject from Mariane to Elmire. He remains general in his assertion of the Neoplatonic argument, and the 'nous' to which he refers is the whole of humanity. The argument is stated first negatively, as a refutation of Elmire's claim (1–2), then positively (3–4). The way in which Tartuffe speaks establishes a certain moral authority for his views, as rhetoricians recommend for the beginning of a speech (*ethos*). Elmire speaks of 'Ciel' and 'ici-bas', but Tartuffe transmutes this *antithesis* into something more abstract and hence more learned ('beautés éternelles' / 'temporelles'). Elmire uses different terminology to refer to divine love ('soupirs') and human love ('désirs'), but it suits Tartuffe's argument about the coincidence of these two kinds of love to use the same word for both ('amour'), and he underscores this point by using the same word twice within the first two lines (*geminatio*). Indeed, the whole structure of the first two lines is based on an impressive-seeming combination of parallels, contrasts, and repetitions: 'amour' / 'amour'; 'nous' / 'nous'; 'attache' / 'étouffe'; 'éternelles' / 'temporelles'. Having refuted Elmire so quickly and so authoritatively, but basically by means of a calculated choice of *elocution*, Tartuffe states the argument positively. His terminology remains general and abstract: 'Nos sens' refers to humanity in general; 'Des ouvrages parfaits' is a *metaphor* referring to all that is best in God's creation; 'charmés' is a common *metaphor* evoking the pleasure we feel on seeing beautiful things. Yet these lines (3–4) give the actor the opportunity to indicate by his *action* (at the very least, desirous looks) the particular application of the argument that his words will soon explain. For 'Nos sens' refers of course to his own sexual susceptibility; 'Des ouvrages parfaits' can be interpreted as a *synecdoche*, referring not to all God's beautiful creatures, but just to Elmire; and 'charmés' can be read as a *metaphor* suggestive of sexual arousal.

The extent to which the levels of meaning in the *exordium* emerge in performance depends on the acting technique deployed (perhaps on Elmire's as well as Tartuffe's). Verbally, it is only in the *narration* that the application of the Neoplatonic argument to the case of Tartuffe and Elmire is made explicit. But even here *insinuation* is at work. In the first part of the *narration* (5–8), Tartuffe gradually reveals the application of the argument to Elmire. This measured revelation is based on the *places* of *genus* and *species*. Tartuffe becomes increasingly specific: from all God's perfect creations in the *exordium* (4), to that part of his creation that is female ('vos pareilles' (5)), and finally to that most perfect example of his female creation, Elmire (6). Tartuffe conveys his sensitivity to God's dazzling creation by means of *metaphor* and *hyperbole*: 'brillent' (5), 'ses plus rares merveilles' (6). And he begins to suggest the effect of Elmire's beauty on those who see her; but he still employs the technique of *insinuation*, so does not at first mention himself. The effect is generalized: 'Dont les yeux sont surpris, et les cœurs transportés' (8). The balanced phrasing and repeated syntactical construction (*isocolon*) coupled with the *synecdoches* 'yeux' and 'cœurs', referring to all the men who behold Elmire, suggest the powerful physicality of her beauty. This flattering praise is no doubt intended by Tartuffe to appeal to Elmire's vanity (*pathos*) and to prepare her for his final revelation: namely, that he himself is affected by her in this way.

This revelation occupies the remainder of the *narration* (9–12). For the first time in this speech he uses a first-person singular pronoun. But even now, this account of his admiration for Elmire is couched in words which, on the surface, express above all his supposed devotion to God. The balance between the expression of Christian devotion and the suggestion of sexual desire shifts minutely in teasing ways. Twice he begins by evoking the pleasure she arouses in him (9, 11); twice he attempts to justify it with reference to religious devotion (10, 12). This account of his love exploits the *places* of *cause* and *effect*: the cause seems to be Elmire's beauty, and the effect his admiration for her; but Tartuffe would have his listener believe that the ultimate cause is God's power of creation, and the ultimate effect devotion to God. He conveys strong emotion in his combination of *apostrophe*, *hyperbole*, *metaphor*, and *parenthesis* when he interrupts his sentence to call Elmire 'parfaite créature'. But the admiration he at first seems to be expressing for her ('Sans admirer en vous') is swiftly presented as a sign of his admiration for God ('l'auteur de la nature'). The rhythm of the line, divided into two by these phrases, supports Tartuffe's deliberate ambiguity. The next two lines deploy a similarly ambiguous structure, but even more daringly. Tartuffe draws on the imagery of sexual arousal. His admiration has now become explicitly love ('amour'), and stirring passion is suggested by the combination of the *metonymy* 'cœur' and the *metaphors* 'ardente' and 'atteint' (11). Once again, the following line exploits a rhythmic division into two equal halves to imply, initially, that Elmire is the cause of these strong feelings ('Au plus beau des portraits'), her power further underscored by the *metaphor* drawn from art and by the *hyperbole*. Yet again, however, the second half of the line interprets these strong sexual desires as deep religious devotion: Elmire's beautiful portrait is really an image of God himself, his self-portrait.

By the end of his *narration*, Tartuffe's words have made his adulterous passion plain, even while retaining the veneer of Christian respectability. The orator's next step would normally be to argue his position positively in a *confirmation*. Tartuffe does not do that. Instead, he attempts to counter any shock Elmire may feel in a *refutation* (13–20). The first four lines of the *refutation* raise the possibility that Tartuffe's feelings are evil, the last four lines counter it. The main rhetorical strategy at work here is his exploitation of *ethos*. The *refutation* is presented not as a generalized argument, nor as an argument that Elmire might put, but as an account of Tartuffe's own alleged response to his feelings. He attempts to appear respectable by claiming to have had doubts about the propriety of his feelings. More than that, he claims to have acted on those doubts by deciding to avoid Elmire's presence. He creates an *antithesis* between his fears of the devil at work, *personified* in the expressions 'noir esprit' and 'surprise adroite' (14), and his preoccupation with his own salvation (16). The dissolution of his doubts is expressed, once again, not as an argument, but as an account of his conviction that his feelings are justified, and again his primary concern is with *ethos*. He begins tentatively, expressing his attitude in a paradoxical combination of understated *litotes* and overstated *alliteration*: 'cette passion peut n'être point coupable' (18) (the /p/ is repeated four times, three times in initial position). His confidence is then expressed more positively: 'je puis l'ajuster avecque la pudeur' (19). The final line of the *refutation* looks like a triumphant logical conclusion: 'Et c'est ce qui m'y fait abandonner mon cœur' (20). But it is nothing of the sort, whence its humour. The *refutation* has consisted of Tartuffe's feelings and assertions. By suggesting a contrast between feelings of doubt and assertions of propriety, followed by a line expressing a conclusion in support of the latter, he has created the illusion of a logical argument. What he has singularly failed to do is to explain by what arguments he can reconcile adulterous passion with modesty and religious devotion. He has offered the conclusion of a *syllogism* without any prior reasoning. He has adopted possibly the best strategy in his unusual circumstances, but one which is evidently flawed. The weakness is exemplified by his inability, in this part of his speech when he is claiming to be modest, to resist a further passionate *apostrophe* and flattering *metaphor* addressed to Elmire: 'ô beauté toute aimable' (17).

Finally, in his *peroration*, Tartuffe makes his request for sexual satisfaction in his most patterned and highly wrought language. He begins with studied modesty and anxiety: 'je le confesse', presented *parenthetically*, suggests uncertainty about the appropriateness of what he is about to say (21), but is also a comically ironical perversion of the concept of Christian confession. Tartuffe is not confessing a sin and repenting; he is asking Elmire to participate with him in a sinful act. But before the request proper, he restates his declaration of love in a continued combination of gallant *synecdoche* ('ce cœur') and religious *metaphor* ('l'offrande') (22). The implicit argument is that, as he is offering something to her, she must be kind enough to reciprocate. The nature of the reciprocation is spelt out in a heady climax of *antitheses*, *parison*, *isocolon*, and religious *metaphors*. It is a language of religious and sexual ecstasy. The first *antithesis* contrasts her envisaged kindness with his own feebleness (22–3): he has done all he can to persuade her; she now has to satisfy his wishes. His *hyperbolic* request for everything ('tout' (23)) is sexually suggestive, and prepares the way for the ecstatic linguistic patterning that follows. Lines 25 and 26 are an example of *parison*, a near-repetition of the same grammatical construction: 'En vous est mon espoir, mon bien, ma quiétude, / De vous dépend ma peine ou ma béatitude.' Both lines exploit the *place* known as *effects*, listing the effects Elmire's response might produce in him. But whereas the *gradatio* in the first of these lines lists increasingly intense degrees of simultaneous religious devotion and sexual satisfaction with the excitedly *anaphoric* repetition of the possessive adjective ('mon', 'ma'), the second line begins to play on her pity for him. Two possible effects are contrasted in an *antithesis*: 'béatitude' is the ultimate joy that he wants, but 'peine' is what he will suffer if she rejects him. This *antithesis* is restated in the final *isocolonic* line, which spells out her crucial role in determining his fate. 'Heureux' contrasts with, and balances, 'malheureux', as 'si vous voulez' balances 's'il vous plaît'. It is interesting that Tartuffe reserves the more pessimistic phrase for the very end of his speech, appealing to her sense of pity.

Tartuffe's speech is a *tour de force* on Molière's part, a sustained piece of rhetorical wit, the particular piquancy of which derives from the *risqué* combination of religion and lust. Molière manages to suggest sufficient linguistic skill in Tartuffe to entertain the audience, and also to make it plausible for Tartuffe to think that he has spoken well and persuasively. This contributes to the comic effect when Elmire replies, briskly undermining his delicate balancing act by commenting on it simply as a declaration of love, surprising in a man who claims to be devout: 'La déclaration est tout à fait galante, / Mais elle est, à vrai dire, un peu bien surprenante' (961–2). Elmire's refusal to be swayed by his insinuating language does not deter him. He attempts once again to seduce her with words of devotion (966–1000). It is this next speech that prompts her explicit comment on his rhetorical skill: 'Je vous écoute dire, et votre rhétorique / En termes assez forts à mon âme s'explique' (1001–2). Unfortunately for Tartuffe, rhetoric is effective only when its audience is so taken in by it as not to notice it. Elmire is too good at reading him rhetorically to succumb to his linguistic powers.

Some of Molière's contemporaries, however, were quick to condemn Tartuffe's language in this scene as the author's own blasphemy. The anonymous *Lettre sur la comédie de l'Imposteur*, describing the 1667 version of the play, suggests that this is the wrong way to read Tartuffe's rhetoric in this scene, and strongly implies that those spectators are right who read Tartuffe's rhetoric on the character axis and not on the writer–audience axis (i. 1157):

Bien des gens prétendent que l'usage de ces termes de dévotion que l'hypocrite emploie dans cette occasion est une profanation blâmable que le poète en fait. D'autres disent qu'on ne peut l'en accuser qu'avec injustice, parce que ce n'est pas lui qui parle, mais l'acteur qu'il introduit; de sorte qu'on ne saurait lui imputer cela, non plus qu'on ne doit pas lui imputer toutes les impertinences qu'avancent les personnages ridicules des comédies.

This is a basic lesson in the rhetorical interpretation of fictional dialogue.

Tartuffe and Orgon

Unlike Elmire, Orgon is not a good interpreter of Tartuffe's rhetoric. The hypocrite employs his rhetorical skills on Orgon to devastating effect in Act III, scene vi, when he has been accused rightly by Damis of attempting to seduce Elmire. This news ought to shock Orgon and make him question his trust in Tartuffe, the allegedly devout Christian. Orgon is indeed suitably shaken, as suggested by a powerful *apostrophe* and *communicatio*, the kind of question which requires some thought: 'Ce que je viens d'entendre, ô Ciel! est-il croyable?' (line 1073). Tartuffe's response is richly ironic, and demonstrates the extent of his rhetorical resourcefulness, the extent of Orgon's gullibility, and above all Molière's ability to apply *judicial* oratory in an unusually comic way. Tartuffe's simple strategy is to tell Orgon the truth, but to tell it in a way that constitutes a highly successful exploitation of *ethos* (1074–86):

> Oui, mon frère, je suis un méchant, un coupable,
> Un malheureux pécheur, tout plein d'iniquité,
> Le plus grand scélérat qui jamais ait été;
> Chaque instant de ma vie est chargée de souillures;
> Elle n'est qu'un amas de crimes et d'ordures;   5
> Et je vois que le Ciel, pour ma punition,
> Me veut mortifier en cette occasion.
> De quelque grand forfait qu'on me puisse reprendre,
> Je n'ai garde d'avoir l'orgueil de m'en défendre.
> Croyez ce qu'on vous dit, armez votre courroux,   10
> Et comme un criminel chassez-moi de chez vous:
> Je ne saurois avoir tant de honte en partage,
> Que je n'en aie encor mérité davantage.

Without actually admitting the specific offence of which Damis has accused him (and without explicitly defending himself against it), he tells the truth about himself in the most general terms by using the device of *chleuasmos*, mock modesty. The theatre audience will find fun in his *hyperbolic gradatio* (1–3), four increasingly detailed descriptions of himself as an unambiguously wicked man. There is fun too in the *hyperbolic metaphors* with which he describes his life (4–5). The verbal form is *hyperbolic*, but the audience knows the truth of these statements. The conclusion he draws with mock stoicism is that the occasion of this accusation is in itself just punishment for all his wickedness. The greatest fun of all, though provocative in its implications, is that Tartuffe's self-accusation works on Orgon as a brilliant self-defence. On the surface, Tartuffe's language aims to persuade Orgon to condemn him and expel him, but by accusing himself in words that resonate with Christian overtones of sin, confession, and mortification, he presents himself to Orgon as an honest and pitiable Christian. Moreover, Damis's accusation is so much at odds with the image Orgon has of Tartuffe that his gullible response is immediately to be persuaded by Tartuffe's *hyperbolic* rhetoric and to condemn Damis as a liar. By the end of the encounter, Orgon has dismissed and disinherited Damis, and made Tartuffe his sole heir. Rhetoric of the kind deployed here by Tartuffe might potentially seem seriously frightening to the audience, were it not for the fact that it works only on Orgon; the conventions of comedy make the audience feel distant from, and superior to, Orgon, and so better able to enjoy Tartuffe's rhetorical wit and Orgon's incapacity to read it as the tissue of clever lies that it is.

Tartuffe and Cléante

Tartuffe meets his match in Cléante, who proves to be the more skilled and persistent orator (IV. i). But by the time of their encounter, Tartuffe has already got the upper hand in that he knows he is now Orgon's heir. Cléante's superior words can do little about that. Yet Molière creates interest by depicting the manœuvres of two practised orators, one trying to outwit the other. Cléante's purpose is to engage in *deliberative* oratory, persuading Tartuffe to forgive Damis and to reconcile father and son. He sets about his task by manipulating *ethos* carefully, so as not to appear threatening. He pretends, for instance, that Damis's accusation was false, but argues that forgiveness is Tartuffe's Christian duty. In other words, Cléante begins by arguing on the very terms that Tartuffe himself always adopts.

Tartuffe responds with the superficial Christian unctuousness which the audience has come to expect: 'Je lui pardonne tout, de rien je ne le blâme, / Et voudrais le servir du meilleur de mon âme' (1205–6). But he draws the line at reconciling father and son. The audience knows that this is for financial reasons: Tartuffe does not want to give up his unexpectedly acquired inheritance. Instead, he gives two false reasons. The first is impressive-sounding but vague and ill-explained: 'l'intérêt du Ciel n'y saurait consentir' (1207). The implication is that heaven must punish Damis for his wrongdoing. The second argument is more fully explained, but highly specious: Tartuffe's intervention on Damis's behalf could look as if he was simply trying to silence the youth and prevent him from making further accusations.

Unlike Orgon, Cléante is not taken in by Tartuffe's rhetoric. Like Elmire, he sees Tartuffe's speech as weasel words. But he goes further than Elmire. He dissects and hence undermines Tartuffe's rhetorical strategy, demonstrating the inadequacy of both the reasons given: 'Vous nous payez ici d'excuses colorées, / Et toutes vos raisons, Monsieur, sont trop tirées' (1217–18). His reply is a kind of *refutation*: he systematically refutes the arguments advanced by Tartuffe. It is not up to Tartuffe to look after the interests of heaven by punishing Damis; and concern with what people might think is dismissed as a 'faible intérêt' (1225). The audience will assume that Cléante, like them, knows the real self-interested reason preventing Tartuffe from reconciling father and son, and will be amused by the way he has so far skirted around it, tackling Tartuffe on his own ground. At the climax of this speech Cléante once again uses religion to support his own view, and takes a sideswipe at Tartuffe for his attempt to befuddle his interlocutor with unsubstantiated assertions and specious argument: 'Non, non: faisons toujours ce que le Ciel prescrit, / Et d'aucun autre soin ne nous brouillons l'esprit' (1227–8). Tartuffe's reply suggests a certain frustration in the face of Cléante's persistent rhetoric: 'Je vous ai déjà dit que mon cœur lui pardonne' (1229), and he tetchily claims that he should not be expected to live under the same roof as Damis, naming heaven in support: 'Le Ciel n'ordonne pas que je vive avec lui' (1232). In self-consciously rhetorical mode, Tartuffe usually speaks at length; but this reply has been only four lines long. When pared down in this way, what has been Tartuffe's basic strategy throughout is reduced to its bare essentials: he states what he personally wants, but tacks on some religious terminology (here 'le Ciel') which is meant to add respectability. Cléante then introduces a new argument, making Tartuffe confront the real point at issue (1233–6):

Et vous ordonne-t-il, Monsieur, d'ouvrir l'oreille
A ce qu'un pur caprice à son père conseille,
Et d'accepter le don qui vous est fait d'un bien
Où le droit vous oblige à ne prétendre rien?

Cléante is becoming aggressive. He shifts the argument in a way that probes explicitly beneath Tartuffe's religious rhetoric, and he suggests the correct course that ought to flow from Tartuffe's professed Christian principles. Framing the argument in a *percontatio*, he challenges Tartuffe to justify a financial gain to which Cléante claims he has no real right.

Tartuffe takes up the challenge and continues, resourcefully, to deploy a religious rhetoric, despite Cléante's explicit effort to probe his profiteering (1237–48):

Ceux qui me connaîtront n'auront pas la pensée
Que ce soit un effet d'une âme intéressée.
Tous les biens de ce monde ont pour moi peu d'appas,
De leur éclat trompeur je ne m'éblouis pas;
Et si je me résous à recevoir du père   5
Cette donation qu'il a voulu me faire,
Ce n'est, à dire vrai, que parce que je crains
Que tout ce bien ne tombe en de méchantes mains,
Qu'il ne trouve des gens qui, l'ayant en partage,
En fassent dans le monde un criminel usage,   10
Et ne s'en servent pas, ainsi que j'ai dessein,
Pour la gloire du Ciel et le bien du prochain.

There are basically two lines of argument here. The first (1–4) is based on *ethos*, and attempts to reorientate the mercenary picture Cléante had started to sketch of Tartuffe towards the image of a man unimpressed by worldly goods. In support of this self-portrait, he gestures vaguely towards possible *external proofs*, 'Ceux qui me connaîtront' (1). The second argument (5–12) is based on the *place* of *effects*, and attempts to justify his determination to receive Orgon's wealth in spite of his alleged personal disinterest in it. He would use the money for Christian and charitable ends, whereas others would not. The *antithesis* he implicitly draws between himself and Damis is almost the opposite of the truth: it is Tartuffe, not Damis, who is the criminal, and Damis, if he would not use the money 'Pour la gloire du Ciel et le bien du prochain', would at least have the right to use it as he pleased. Such a studied and erroneous *antithesis* allows the audience to savour fully Tartuffe's wilfully perverted rhetoric.

Cléante continues to argue, painstakingly explaining the weakness of Tartuffe's position: what Damis does with money that is his by right is none of Tartuffe's business. And he develops a further, threatening argument expressed *syllogistically* in the form of a *percontatio* (1259–64):

> Et s'il faut que le Ciel dans votre cœur ait mis
> Un invincible obstacle à vivre avec Damis
> Ne vaudrait-il pas mieux qu'en personne discrète
> Vous fissiez de céans une honnête retraite,
> Que de souffrir ainsi, contre toute raison,
> Qu'on en chasse pour vous le fils de la maison?

God does not require Tartuffe to live in the same house as Damis (a point already made by Tartuffe); Tartuffe lives in the house as Orgon's son; therefore Tartuffe should leave. It is a compelling argument, for which Tartuffe himself had supplied the initial premiss. The question form in which it is expressed drives Tartuffe into a corner, and requires him to think and reply. However, Cléante has opposed to Tartuffe's rhetoric, which is based primarily on *ethos* and unsubstantiated argument, a rhetoric of his own which systematically lays bare the weaknesses of Tartuffe's claims and proposes significantly more solid counter-arguments in their place. Tartuffe knows he has been beaten, verbally at least, and his answer makes this comically plain. He interrupts Cléante, and retreats from the rhetorical battlefield with the lamest of excuses, though characteristically hypocritical (1265–7):

> Il est, Monsieur, trois heures et demie:
> Certain devoir pieux me demande là-haut,
> Et vous m'excuserez de vous quitter sitôt.

Critics often recall that Molière was a master of performance techniques, and that his comedy is highly visual. It is true that some of the key comic and dramatic moments in *Tartuffe* are engineered visually. The disillusionment of Orgon occurs when he is made to hide under a table and witness Tartuffe's second attempt to seduce Elmire (IV. v). But Molière is also a master of verbal comedy, building interest out of the constantly shifting and crafty rhetorical manoeuvres of his main characters. The character of the hypocrite is particularly well suited to this kind of comic rhetoric. Empty assertions based on allusions to heaven, an overwhelmingly Christian

vocabulary with profane overtones, and blantantly specious arguments are the religious hypocrite's stock-in-trade.

2. RHETORIC AT COURT: RACINE'S *BRITANNICUS*

Throughout most of the early modern period, comedy and tragedy
were distinct genres. Comedy depicts ordinary characters in a contemporary setting, whereas tragedy depicts nobles in a historical or
mythological setting. Comedy portrays an action of domestic significance, tragedy an action of national or international political significance. Comedy aims to make spectators laugh, tragedy to make
them feel pity and fear for the characters on stage. Rhetoric, however, shows what the two genres have in common. Dramatic
momentum comes from the rhetorical interaction of a limited number of characters pursuing opposing aims. For all their generic differences, Molière's *Tartuffe* and Racine's tragedy *Britannicus* both
depict a central authority figure (Orgon and Néron, respectively)
whose rhetorical skills are poor and who attempts to prevail by mere
command. In both plays other characters attempt to influence this
figure for better or worse. But whereas in the comedy there is a clear
dividing line between wrong-headed persuaders (Tartuffe and Mme
Pernelle) and right-headed ones (the rest), in the tragedy the influences on Néron are morally more mixed. His adviser Burrhus wants
him to be a well-liked emperor, and urges him against the tyrannical assassination of his half-brother (and rival in love) Britannicus.
A different adviser, Narcisse, seems determined that he should rule
by fear and by diktat, and argues for Britannicus's murder. His
mother Agrippine defends Britannicus and clearly wants her son to
be a successful emperor; but, above all, she wants him to be her
puppet. Racine creates a complex interplay of influences and a tense
drama in which human life is at stake.

In his comedy Molière deploys rhetoric wittily, for the audience's
amusement. That is the point of Tartuffe's daring use of religious
language with sexual and criminal connotations. Molière's rhetorical encounters are funny, because they show the fool being gulled
by the rhetorical trickster, and the trickster being fenced into a corner by the superior orator. In tragedy the tense interaction as characters attempt to persuade and influence each other is linked to
issues of life and death. The spectators listen with alternating hope

and fear as the encounters proceed. Act IV of *Britannicus* demonstrates how well rhetoric can suit the ends of tragic drama. Irked by
his mother's support for Britannicus, Néron has taken the extraordinary step of arresting her. By the end of Act III it looks as if Néron
is set upon a course of ill-calculated, power-crazed atrocities. Act IV
depicts the final skirmishes in the battle for Néron's soul, and it is
fought rhetorically. Racine creates drama of high tension out of
three lengthy interviews in which Agrippine, Burrhus, and Narcisse
try in turn to prevail upon the emperor.[6]

Agrippine and Néron

The importance of rhetorical strategies to the characters for the success of their plans, and to the spectators as a source of theatrical
pleasure, is made plain at the very beginning of Act IV in a short
scene in which Burrhus prepares Agrippine for the audience she is
about to have with her son. Orators need ideally to have an intimate knowledge of the psychology of the person they wish to persuade. Burrhus's advice suggests his own deep knowledge of the
emperor, as well as of Agrippine, and he proposes an appropriate
rhetorical strategy (1104–6):

> Ne vous souvenez plus qu'il vous ait offensée:
> Préparez-vous plutôt à lui tendre les bras;
> Défendez-vous, Madame, et ne l'accusez pas.

Though Agrippine is Néron's mother, she is also now his prisoner.
He has agreed to see her, and the confrontation will therefore be
suggestive of *judicial* oratory. Aware of her tendency to browbeat her
son, Burrhus advises her that Néron will be sitting in judgement on
her, and that she must defend herself. Sensitive to Néron's fear of
his mother's overbearing personality and to his newly demonstrated

---

[6] References are to Racine's *Théâtre complet*, ed. J. Morel and A. Viala (Garnier, 1980;
Dunod, 1995). Much has been written specifically on rhetoric in Racine. See especially
P. France, *Racine's Rhetoric* (Oxford: Clarendon Press, 1965); D. Maskell, *Racine: A Theatrical
Reading* (Oxford: Clarendon Press, 1991), ch. 4, 'Verbal Action'; and M. Hawcroft, *Word
as Action: Racine, Rhetoric, and Theatrical Language* (Oxford: Clarendon Press, 1992). On
Néron's verbal impotence, see C. Venesoen, 'Le Néron de Racine: Un Cas curieux d'im-
puissance verbale', *L'Information littéraire*, 33 (1981), 130–6; and R. Parish, *Racine: The Limits
of Tragedy*, Papers on French Seventeenth-Century Literature, (Paris, Seattle, Tübingen:
Biblio 17, 1993), 193–9. On the argumentational strategies deployed by Narcisse in IV. iv,
see G. Declercq, 'Crime et argument: La Persuasion dans *Britannicus* acte IV, scène 4', in
Lalies: Actes des sessions de linguistique et de littérature (Aussois, 1ᵉʳ–6 septembre 1981) (1984), 165–75.

willingness to resort to physical violence in order to silence those he
does not wish to hear, he spells out precisely that she must not
accuse her son. Burrhus urges a rhetoric of conciliation and defence,
not one of aggression and accusation.

These expectations are crucial in focusing the audience's pleasure
during Agrippine's long speeches to her son (IV. ii). Meticulously and
systematically, she ignores Burrhus's advice. From her opening *action*
of sitting down before the emperor and beckoning him to sit next
to her, contrary to seventeenth-century etiquette, she shows an
attacking spirit. Her first (and very long) speech is predominantly a
detailed *narration* of everything she has done to secure Néron's
emperorship, followed by examples of his own recent disrespect
towards her. She overwhelms him with *external proofs*, beneath all of
which lies the argument that he is guilty of ingratitude, for which
he should atone. He attempts feebly to respond, and manages to
clarify one of his anxieties: namely, that she has transferred her loy-
alties to Britannicus. To the suggestion that she might be conspiring against him, she replies with devastating force, besieging him
with *interrogations*, so that he is reduced almost to silence. He appears
to give in, and asks her to make her demands. She tells him what
she wants with the full force of *anaphora* and *parison* (1288–94):

> De mes accusateurs qu'on punisse l'audace;
> Que de Britannicus on calme le courroux;
> Que Junie à son choix puisse prendre un époux;
> Qu'ils soient libres tous deux, et que Pallas demeure;
> Que vous me permettiez de vous voir à toute heure;
> Que ce même Burrhus, qui nous vient écouter,
> A votre porte enfin n'ose plus m'arrêter.

Néron agrees readily. Racine has filled the spectators with fear and
trepidation as we watch Agrippine making one ill-advised rhetorical
choice after another, and then he surprises us with her apparent success in achieving her objectives. She was supposed to speak defensively. But she speaks accusingly, before veering away from *judicial*
towards *deliberative* oratory, persuading Néron to accede to her
demands. But her apparent success is won not by rhetorical skill, but
by her domineering personality and her son's fear of it. Moreover,
it is no success at all. It is a miserable failure.

Burrhus and Néron

Some spectators might be taken in by Néron's easy consent; others
will find it suspect. But the beginning of the next scene (IV. iii), after
Agrippine's triumphal exit and Burrhus's happy entrance, shows
Néron turning the tables again, and making the situation even more
desperate than it was before Agrippine's catastrophic rhetoric. The
result of her misguided efforts has been to persuade Néron to
despatch Britannicus forthwith and in doing so, he thinks, to loosen
his mother's hold over him. He had expressed consent to his
mother's demands only to be rid of her. Spectators share Burrhus's
horror at the blood that Néron seems prepared to shed so arbitrar-
ily, and despair at an action that would alter his image in the public's eye from popular to tyrannical ruler. Burrhus makes a speech,
by the end of which he has persuaded Néron to change his mind,
to cancel the assassination attempt (1337–85):

> Et ne suffit-il pas, Seigneur, à vos souhaits
> Que le bonheur public soit un de vos bienfaits?
> C'est à vous à choisir, vous êtes encor maître.
> Vertueux jusqu'ici, vous pouvez toujours l'être:
> Le chemin est tracé, rien ne vous retient plus;   5
> Vous n'avez qu'à marcher de vertus en vertus.
> Mais si de vos flatteurs vous suivez la maxime,
> Il vous faudra, Seigneur, courir de crime en crime,
> Soutenir vos rigueurs par d'autres cruautés,
> Et laver dans le sang vos bras ensanglantés.   10
> Britannicus mourant excitera le zèle
> De ses amis, tout prêts à prendre sa querelle.
> Ces vengeurs trouveront de nouveaux défenseurs,
> Qui, même après leur mort, auront des successeurs.
> Vous allumez un feu qui ne pourra s'éteindre.   15
> Craint de tout l'univers, il vous faudra tout craindre,
> Toujours punir, toujours trembler dans vos projets,
> Et pour vos ennemis compter tous vos sujets.
> Ah! de vos premiers ans l'heureuse expérience
> Vous fait-elle, Seigneur, haïr votre innocence?   20
> Songez-vous au bonheur qui les a signalés?
> Dans quel repos, ô ciel! les avez-vous coulés!
> Quel plaisir de penser et de dire en vous-même:
> 'Partout, en ce moment, on me bénit, on m'aime;
> On ne voit point le peuple à mon nom s'alarmer;   25
> Le ciel dans tous leurs pleurs ne m'entend point nommer;

Leur sombre inimitié ne fuit point mon visage;
Je vois voler partout les cœurs à mon passage!'
Tels étaient vos plaisirs. Quel changement, ô dieux!
Le sang le plus abject vous était précieux.   30
Un jour, il m'en souvient, le sénat équitable
Vous pressait de souscrire à la mort d'un coupable;
Vous résistiez, Seigneur, à leur sévérité:
Votre cœur s'accusait de trop de cruauté,
Et, plaignant les malheurs attachés à l'empire: 35
'Je voudrais, disiez-vous, ne savoir pas écrire'.
Non, ou vous me croirez, ou bien de ce malheur
Ma mort m'épargnera la vue et la douleur:
On ne me verra point survivre à votre gloire;
Si vous allez commettre une action si noire,   40
    (*Il se jette à genoux.*)
Me voilà prêt, Seigneur: avant que de partir,
Faites percer ce cœur qui n'y peut consentir;
Appelez les cruels qui vous l'ont inspirée,
Qu'ils viennent essayer leur main mal assurée. . .
Mais je vois que mes pleurs touchent mon empereur.   45
Je vois que sa vertu frémit de leur fureur.
Ne perdez point de temps, nommez-moi les perfides
Qui vous osent donner ces conseils parricides;
Appelez votre frère, oubliez dans ses bras. . .

This *deliberative* speech succeeds spectacularly well where Agrippine's had failed. The pleasure for the theatre audience lies in the contrast between Agrippine's rhetorical incompetence and Burrhus's carefully controlled skill. Burrhus's speech does not have the conventional four-part *disposition* of a formal speech: it begins with a reply to Néron, and ends with an interruption from him. Burrhus avoids *deductive reasoning*, but he deploys *ethos* and *pathos* to excellent effect, artfully combining flattery of Néron's self-image with intimations of fears for the future.

He begins with an *interrogation*, a response to Néron's chilling claim that he does not want to be emperor only to have to satisfy the public (1–2). The question invites Néron's assent to its proposition that procuring the public good should make him happy. When he does not reply, Burrhus continues. Potentially the question could be answered by a yes or a no: an emperor concerned about his public image, or indifferent to it. Burrhus invites Néron to decide: 'C'est à vous à choisir' (3). His presentation of the two options determines

the structure of the rest of the speech. He describes the virtuous path
(2–6), then the vicious path (7–18); he offers evidence from Néron's
past about the desirability of the virtuous course (19–36), then
graphically conjures up the immediate implications of Néron choosing the course of vice, Burrhus's own suicide (37–42). Finally he
comments on the visible success of his rhetoric, and urges Néron to
practical virtuous action (45–9). The bulk of the speech is based on
the development of two successive *antitheses*: virtue/vice; virtue/vice.
The imbalance between them, in terms of number of lines, and the
placing of them are strategic.

The first *antithesis* is between a brief evocation of Néron's virtuous
path and a fuller, more detailed account of the vicious path, and is
underscored by the use of *reduplicatio* in each of the two elements:
'de vertus en vertus' (6), 'de crime en crime' (8). Virtue is made to
appear the simpler, more obvious and more attractive option.
Burrhus makes it appear so partly by recourse to *ethos*: he presents
Néron as an emperor who has been, and still is, virtuous; it is therefore easy for him to continue along the same route. The *metaphors* of
movement and travel also contribute to the more inviting presentation of virtue: 'Le chemin est tracé' (5), 'Vous n'avez qu'à marcher'
(6). Virtue, traditionally presented by philosophers as difficult of
access, is here made to seem the path best adopted by someone
wishing to make little effort. The obviousness of this choice is also
implied by Burrhus's syntax, in particular his use of *parataxis*: no
connectives link any of the seven short phrases or sentences in lines
2–6.

Syntax and imagery change substantially for the evocation of the
vicious life (7–18). Another *metaphor* of movement makes the contrast
explicit. Vice will require more haste: the verb 'marcher' associated
with virtue becomes 'courir' when associated with vice. *Ethos* is used
subtly to deter Néron from this path. Burrhus's rival adviser
Narcisse and his associates are referred to by means of an unflattering *antonomasia*, 'flatteurs' (7). Whereas the sentences recommending virtue were short and to the point, the sentence introducing vice
begins with a conditional clause and contains a long main clause
with three dependent infinitives, which produce a *gradatio* (7–10).
The first infinitive clause ('courir de crime en crime' (8)) reinforces
the equation between haste and criminality by the *alliteration* of its
expression (/k/, /ʀ/). The second clause ('Soutenir vos rigueurs par
d'autres cruautés' (9)) introduces a specific instance of the type of

criminality that will be necessary: Néron will have to carry out acts of cruelty. This appeal to *pathos*, as Burrhus attempts to play upon Néron's fears of committing physical violence, is maximized in the third and final infinitive clause ('Et laver dans le sang vos bras ensanglantés' (10)) with the introduction of *hyperbolic* blood imagery. The picture Burrhus sketches is meant to be graphic and frightening for Néron: his own involvement is suggested by the personalized *synecdoche* 'vos bras', the image of cleansing is horribly undermined by the suggestion that blood will be the only cleaning liquid available, and the image is strengthened by the use of *dérivation* ('sang', 'ensanglantés', both words falling in stressed positions in the line).

Burrhus's argumentational strategy is to consider the *effects* of vice. He continues to do this in an even more specific way, using the form of argument known as *climax* (11–14). He turns to the immediate issue that would set Néron on a course of criminality, the murder of Britannicus. The relentless succession of avengers gives rise to the climactic argument: 'Britannicus'/'ses amis'; 'Ces vengeurs'/'de nouveaux défenseurs'; 'Qui'/'des successeurs'. This endlessly fertile source of opponents is meant to intimidate Néron. Burrhus then makes the point succinctly with a new *metaphor*: 'Vous allumez un feu qui ne pourra s'éteindre' (15). Burrhus encapsulates key aspects of his vision in this line: Néron's responsibility for the future, the devastation that might ensue, and the loss of control. In an attempt to make the fullest possible impact on the emperor, Burrhus restates the same points, underscoring them heavily with devices of *elocution*, and appealing particularly to Néron's anxieties (16–18). A combination of *polyptoton* and *chiasmus* suggests the stifling, inescapable atmosphere of reciprocal fear between emperor and subjects: 'Craint de tout l'univers, il vous faudra tout craindre' (16). This line is also *antithetical*: the first half conveys the fear that superficially Néron might want his people to feel; but the second half hits back, stating the universal fear that he would have to feel as a consequence. The sentence as a whole is constructed around four infinitives dependent on the verb *falloir*. The sense of the *antithesis* 'Craint'/'craindre' is more or less repeated in the second and third infinitives, with supporting *anaphora* and *isocolon* ('Toujours punir, toujours trembler'). None of the devices is gratuitous. They are all calculated to make a persuasive impact on Néron. The *anaphora* here contributes to the frightening impression of an eternally hostile environment in which Néron would have to live. Similarly, the use of *hyperbaton* in the last infinitive clause ('Et pour vos ennemis compter tous vos sujets' (18)) allows the word 'ennemis' to fall in a stressed position, and so heightens the effect of the *antithesis* between 'ennemis' and 'sujets'. Making the wrong choice, Néron would live in a world of enemies. This part of Burrhus's speech has consisted in repeatedly stated and re-emphasized visions of Néron's terrifying future. He says far more than he needs to say to make his point; but he needs to persuade Néron and his technique is to arouse, and to maintain, a simmering fear.

This lengthy play on Néron's fears lets Burrhus create a striking contrast when he starts the next section of his speech, returning to the path of virtue and depicting a terror-free environment (19–36). *Pathos* dominated the previous section; *ethos* dominates this one. Two *interrogations* (19–21) followed by two *exclamations* (22) seek to engage Néron's interest in the happy picture Burrhus paints of Néron's early years as emperor. Once again the argumentation is built around the *place* of *effects*. But this time, it is the effects of Néron's innocence, rather than his potential crimes, and they are summed up in four abstract terms each intensified by featuring in its own *interrogative* or *exclamatory* sentence: 'l'heureuse expérience', 'bonheur', 'repos', and 'plaisir'. The *apostrophe* to heaven (22) provides further intensification of the pleasures associated with virtuous rule. Whereas Burrhus's evocation of the miseries of criminal rule were merely hypothetical, he can rely on *external proofs* to support his claims about virtue. He does so by means of *prosopopoeia*, putting into Néron's mouth words expressing his happiness with the kind of rule he has so far embodied and presenting them like a quotation (24–8). *Prosopopoeia* is usually used to conjure up vividly the words of someone absent or deceased. Its use here is all the more forceful, given that the words are those of Burrhus's interlocutor. Burrhus's aim is to offer Néron as attractive an image as possible of himself, and this device allows him to do just that. The opening and closing lines here suggest, almost ecstatically, the degree of adoration that Néron inspires in his public. The *isocolonic* 'on me bénit, on m'aime' (24) is echoed more forcefully in the *hyperbolic metaphor* 'Je vois voler [. . .] les cœurs à mon passage' (28), both lines linked by repeated *hyperbole* 'partout' (*geminatio*). In between these lines that express the pleasures of imperial innocence in positive terms, there are three lines that suggest the same qualities by means of negative expressions, which themselves serve as a reminder of the fears and anxieties attendant upon any criminal behaviour Néron might engage in. The parallel syntax of these three lines with the emphatic repetition of the negative particles 'ne [. . .] point', linked in turn with alarm, tears, and hostility, suggests the certainty of the happiness Burrhus is holding out to Néron if only he chooses the path of virtue.

So far in this section of his speech, Burrhus has used the present tense or the virtual present tense (the perfect), contriving to imply that Néron's happy innocence is still current. But of course it is not. Néron has just revealed his intention to murder Britannicus. So at this stage, when Burrhus hopes to have made his interlocutor afraid of the criminal course and desirous of his continued happiness, he introduces a past tense in a short stark statement: 'Tels étaient vos plaisirs' (29): the imperfect tense perhaps suggests that the pleasures are not necessarily over for good in the way that the past historic would have done. Burrhus's fears for Néron are summed up in the following *exclamation* and *apostrophe*: 'Quel changement, ô dieux!' (29). A further *external proof*, related in a *narration* and including another quotation from Néron, makes plain the distance between the innocent emperor and the one now standing before Burrhus. Just as Burrhus had finished enticing Néron with an attractive image of himself, he shocks him by making it clear that this image is a thing of the past. Imperfect tenses dominate the rest of this section. The planned assassination of Britannicus is not mentioned explicitly, but it is the constant point of contrasting reference, as Burrhus narrates an episode that illustrates Néron's former revulsion at the prospect of bloodshed. The *place* being exploited here to convey the degree to which Néron has changed is that of *comparison*. He is now proposing the murder of an innocent man, his brother; in the past he had been reluctant to sanction the execution of even a guilty man. The point is introduced in general terms (30) before being fleshed out in the anecdote. Burrhus's language is designed to imply an extraordinary sensitivity in Néron. When making the point generally, and by means of *synecdoche*, Burrhus insists on Néron's attachment to 'le sang le plus abject' (30), the superlative suggesting the emperor's all-reaching compassion. The senate had wanted the guilty man to die, and is described as 'équitable' (31). Néron's sympathy is seen in his alleged perception of the senate as severe and its intention as cruel (33–4). Burrhus's story has an emotional climax (*pathos*). Néron was so reluctant to sign the warrant for the execution that he is supposed to have said: 'Je voudrais [. . .] ne savoir pas écrire' (36). The naïve simplicity of this sentence and its presentation as direct speech are surely meant to tug at whatever heart-strings Burrhus thinks Néron has left.

The emotional appeal is intensified much further, however, in what is basically the last part of Burrhus's speech (37–44). The 'Non' introducing it is not a logical response to a preceding point, but a sign of the resolution Burrhus has taken and is about to express. He returns explicitly to the two options facing Néron that were sketched out at the start of the speech and underpin its whole structure. If Néron follows Burrhus's advice and chooses virtue, the implication is that all will be well. For his final words Burrhus dwells on the *effects* on himself, should Néron opt for the criminal course. Burrhus plays the ultimate card that *pathos* offers, the threat of suicide. First he presents it in the future, and does so twice over (37–8, 39–40). The phrases 'ce malheur' and 'une action si noire' are both *periphrases* for the assassination of Britannicus. A forcefully *chiastic* pattern results from the way in which 'ce malheur' is followed by the statement of its effect ('Ma mort m'épargnera la vue et la douleur') and 'une action si noire' is preceded by a *periphrastic* evocation of the same effect ('On ne me verra point survivre à votre gloire'). The final stage of his address, however, now maximizes his emotional appeal by making the threat of suicide immediate. The threat is accompanied by rhetorically significant *action*: he kneels before Néron, both a gesture of supplication and, here, an invitation for Néron to call on those of his advisers whom Burrhus wishes to be his own assassins. Burrhus's speech so far has toyed with Néron's emotions: frightening him, appealing to his desire for pleasure and peace, flattering his self-image. But now he presents him with a crisis: how to deal with Burrhus. The words strongly suggest that Néron makes as if to leave ('avant que de partir'), presumably in distress. But three one-line imperatives hold him back (42–4). He is also moved by the tears Burrhus is now weeping (45). Burrhus's *deliberative* speech is over.

The remaining lines constitute Burrhus's response to Néron's silent reaction. The emperor is visibly moved and shaken by what he has seen and heard (45–6). In the course of one speech, Burrhus has stopped in his tracks a man who was about to instigate a murder. After his determination at the beginning of the scene, Néron is reduced to shuddering silence. In the remaining lines Burrhus's tone changes to one of brisk efficiency, as he sees he can capitalize on the successful outcome of his rhetoric. He urgently requests the names of Néron's evil counsellors and urges reconciliation with Britannicus. Néron is momentarily shocked at this thought, but quickly yields. By focusing on Néron, dwelling on his good points, and terrifying him with his bad points, Burrhus has succeeded where Agrippine and her self-centred rhetoric failed. Having dashed spectators' hopes at the beginning of the scene, Racine has engaged them in a piece of intelligent rhetorical manipulation, the upshot of which has been to see their hopes raised: Britannicus, it seems, will be saved.

Narcisse and Néron

Unfortunately for Burrhus, just as he has left the stage, the rival adviser Narcisse walks on (IV. iv). On learning that the plan to assassinate Britannicus has been abandoned, he brings his rhetorical skills to bear to persuade Néron to change his mind once again. His first step to shake Néron in his resolve is to appeal to his fear of his mother (*pathos*) and his desire to be free of her constraint. Narcisse's statement that 'Elle a repris sur vous son souverain empire' reawakens all the fears of the scene in which Agrippine was browbeating him (IV. ii). This prepares Néron for the next stages of Narcisse's strategy.

It is eloquent testimony to Néron's own rhetorical incompetence and to the ease with which he can be manipulated by the rhetorically skilled that Narcisse manages finally to reverse the emperor's decision by using arguments similar to those that Burrhus had used. The two compelling arguments that send Néron on his murderous way are both based on *ethos*. Narcisse undermines Burrhus by portraying him as a cunning manipulator anxious to look after his own interests: 'Burrhus ne pense pas, Seigneur, tout ce qu'il dit: / Son adroite vertu ménage son crédit' (1461–2). He then turns craftily to Néron's own image and, just as Burrhus had done, he employs quotation, the imagined words of hypothetical observers of the emperor. The picture is a very unflattering one. Néron is presented as a feeble puppet: 'Néron, s'ils en sont crus, n'est point né pour l'empire; / Il ne dit, il ne fait que ce qu'on lui prescrit' (1468–9). This picture plays on Néron's fears and insecurities even more tellingly than Burrhus's favourable picture had affected him. Burrhus had assured him that he was liked and that he would endanger his image if he

acted violently now. More deviously, Narcisse presents him as a
weak-minded individual, whose image can be improved only by resolute action to show his independence. It is a sign of Narcisse's
rhetorical skill, and confirmation of the emperor's rhetorical incompetence, that he persuades Néron that he will be acting independently in murdering Britannicus, when he will in fact be depending
entirely on the strategically calculated words, plans, and desires of
his wicked adviser. Once again Racine has dashed the audience's
hopes as a result of tensely executed rhetorical manipulation. The
catastrophe of Britannicus's murder in Act V is the direct result of
the rhetorical confrontations in Act IV.

3. RHETORIC IN A VOID: BECKETT'S *EN ATTENDANT GODOT*

Although the effects of tragedy and comedy are diametrically
opposed—pity and fear on the one hand, laughter on the other—a
rhetorical approach to *Tartuffe* and *Britannicus* shows how dramatic
momentum can be maintained in both genres by securing the audience's interest in the rhetorical behaviour of the characters.
Moreover, the way the dramatist makes his characters deploy their
rhetoric, as well as the situations in which it is deployed, determines
the effect on the theatre audience. Writing *En attendant Godot* more
than 150 years after the sharp distinction between tragedy and comedy had disappeared, Beckett subtitled it, in the French version,
'pièce en deux actes', and, in the English version, 'tragicomedy in
two acts'. The English subtitle nicely conjures up the mixture of
reactions which spectators and critics have had to the play. It is very
funny, but also very sad. It is a celebration of comic theatre and performance, but it offers a vision of humankind leading purposeless
lives with little room for hope.[7]

The play's generic peculiarity can be observed at close quarters
if we scrutinize its dialogue. Traditionally, plays have shown a number of characters pursuing related, but usually conflicting, aims.
Dramatic dialogue of this kind lends itself especially well to appre-

---

[7] Page references will be to the edition of *En attendant Godot* by C. Duckworth (Walton-
on-Thames: Nelson, 1985). There has been an attempt to infer Beckett's attitude towards
rhetoric from an examination of his entire *œuvre*: B. Clément, *L'Œuvre sans qualités:
Rhétorique de Samuel Beckett* (Seuil, 1994). An introductory study of *Godot* includes generously
detailed discussions of Beckett's verbal art: J.-P. Ryngaert, *Lire 'En attendant Godot'* (Dunod,
1993), 95–114.

ciation along rhetorical lines, because characters so often speak to
persuade or to manipulate. But in Beckett's play the two main characters, Vladimir and Estragon, share one aim, to wait for the arrival
of Godot, who never comes. Whatever interpretation one gives of
the play, this basic situation establishes conditions of language usage
that would, on the surface, seem unfavourable to the deployment of
rhetoric. Since Vladimir and Estragon have no compelling and conflicting aims to debate, they often have nothing to say to each other
and fall silent: the text of the play is punctuated by the frequently
repeated stage direction '*silence*'. To break the silences, they search
feebly for things to do or to say. Estragon asks: 'Tu voulais me parler? [. . .] Tu avais quelque chose à me dire?' Vladimir replies: 'Je
n'ai rien à te dire' (pp. 10–11). Estragon spurs himself and Vladimir
to conversational effort: 'En attendant, essayons de converser sans
nous exalter, puisque nous sommes incapables de nous taire' (p. 54).
But just afterwards, the difficulty of finding topics is made clear
(p. 55):

Long silence.
VLADIMIR. Dis quelque chose.
ESTRAGON. Je cherche.
Long silence.

Possible topics of conversation quickly slip from their minds, especially from Estragon's. Vladimir: 'Qu'est-ce que tu voulais savoir?'
Estragon: 'Je ne me rappelle plus' (p. 15). Dialogue is impeded by
inattention and misunderstanding. Estragon cannot remember
Lucky, and Vladimir's attempt to explain only confuses him further
(p. 70):

ESTRAGON. Lucky?
VLADIMIR. C'est lui qui t'a attaqué hier.
ESTRAGON. Je te dis qu'ils étaient dix.
VLADIMIR. Mais non, avant, celui qui t'a donné des coups de pied.

Beckett, and other experimental dramatists of his generation, are
known for the way in which they pare down linguistic usage, suggesting perhaps an inadequacy in the way in which human beings
communciate with one another.
    Whereas rhetoric is about an effective means of communication,
usually geared towards action, the nature of the dialogue in
Beckett's play, and the conception of the action, seem to constitute

a denial of rhetoric. On closer inspection, however, it is only rhetoric as sustained persuasion that is called into question in *En attendant Godot*. The play is about the attempts of Vladimir and Estragon to fill the void of waiting, and they fill it with rhetoric; or, rather, Beckett does so for them. In particular, they have repeated recourse to the *figures* of *elocution* and the *places* of *invention*.

The *places* of *invention* usually supply enough material for a few exchanges. Vladimir probes Estragon for a *definition* of the word 'lié' (p. 15):

ESTRAGON (*la bouche pleine, distraitement*). On n'est pas lié?
VLADIMIR. Je n'entends rien.
ESTRAGON (*mâche, avale*). Je me demande si on est lié.
VLADIMIR. Lié?
ESTRAGON. Lié.
VLADIMIR. Comment lié?
ESTRAGON. Pieds et poings.
VLADIMIR. Mais à qui? Par qui?
ESTRAGON. A ton bonhomme.
VLADIMIR. A Godot? Lié à Godot? Quelle idée!

Estragon exploits the *place* of *comparison* to argue against Vladimir, who thinks he should put on his shoes (p. 47):

VLADIMIR. Mais tu ne peux pas aller pieds nus.
ESTRAGON. Jésus l'a fait.
VLADIMIR. Jésus! Qu'est-ce que tu vas chercher là! Tu ne vas pas tout de même te comparer à lui!
ESTRAGON. Toute ma vie je me suis comparé à lui.
VLADIMIR. Mais là-bas il faisait chaud! Il faisait bon!
ESTRAGON. Et on crucifiait vite.

In both these examples rhetoric is both used and subverted. In the first, *définition* provides the material for the exchange, but it is devoid of any argumentational framework, and just peters out. In the second, the *comparison* is used argumentationally by Estragon, but in his last line he develops it in a way quite irrelevant to his argument. The subversion of rhetoric contributes to the comic effect; yet at the same time the mention of crucifixion evokes pity.

When *invention* fails to fill the void, the characters try to fill it with the *figures* of *elocution*. Estragon uses triple *antithesis* and extreme *parataxis*, telegraphic style, to explain to Vladimir why they cannot both hang themselves on the tree: 'Gogo léger—branche pas casser—Gogo mort. Didi lourd—branche casser—Didi seul' (pp. 11-12). They amuse themselves and the audience with various kinds of word-play and with the mixing of registers. Estragon leaps, in a single exchange, from an elaborate *metaphor* in the *grand style* to a vulgar colloquialism in the *low style*: 'J'ai tiré ma roulure de vie au milieu des sables! Et tu veux que j'y voie des nuances! (*Regard circulaire.*) Regarde-moi cette saloperie!' (p. 53). Estragon uses the *low style* again, to underscore his annoyance that Vladimir will not believe that he has not been to the Vaucluse: 'Mais non, je n'ai jamais été dans le Vaucluse! J'ai coulé toute ma chaude-pisse d'existence ici, je te dis! Ici! Dans la Merdecluse!' (p. 53). Here the vulgarisms suggestive of irritability are all the more striking for being neologisms. The second is more remarkable still, constituting a *homoioteleuton*: the second half of the word 'Vaucluse' is repeated, but preceded, inappropriately, by the word 'Merde'. *Paronomasia*, playing with similar-sounding words, is a common device, as when Vladimir exclaims, using Estragon's familiar name: 'Gogo! C'est Godot!' (p. 65). Beckett, through his characters, delights in word-play, associating words through sound rather than substance, in a childlike way.

Repetitions

A particular range of *figures*, however, dominates the rhetoric of *En attendant Godot*, the figures of repetition. The characters enjoy *polyptoton* and its associated device *dérivation* (p. 63):

VLADIMIR. C'est toujours à la tombée de la nuit.
ESTRAGON. Mais la nuit ne tombe pas.
VLADIMIR. Elle tombera tout d'un coup, comme hier.

The idea of falling creates an opportunity for conversational expansion by dint of repetition in different forms. They are fond of *syllepsis*. Vladimir says: 'Pendant le petit pendant, et le bref après', reinforcing his comic *syllepsis* (the two senses of 'pendant') with an *alliteration* in /p/ (p. 54). Vladimir sums up their condition wittily, by juxtaposing the technical and proverbial senses of 'plateau': 'En effet, nous sommes sur un plateau. Aucun doute, nous sommes servis sur un plateau' (p. 66).

But the *figures* of repetition that Beckett deploys most often, in a seemingly unstoppable whirlwind of rhetorical display, are various combinations of *anaphora*, *isocolon*, *parison*, and *epitrochasmus*.

Sometimes these *figures* are used in the construction of single *répliques*. Estragon employs triple *anaphora* and *isocolon* when he says touchily to Vladimir: 'Ne me touche pas! Ne me demande rien! Ne me dis rien! Reste avec moi!' (p. 50). The linguistic patterning is reinforced by the way in which the central two of the four elements of this reply constitute a symmetrical pivot, the symmetry deriving from the *alliterative* /d/ and the further figure of repetition deployed here, the *epistrophe* with the repetition of 'rien' at the end of each command. The paradoxical nature of Estragon's request, wanting to be left alone and wanting to be with Vladimir, is brought out more forcefully by the descending *gradatio*, whereby the sequence ends with the shorter command 'Reste avec moi!', which negates the three preceding ones.

Most overwhelmingly, however, it is in the construction of exchanges between characters that Beckett combines the *figures* of repetition. For instance, Vladimir reminds Estragon of the request, a sort of prayer, that they had transmitted to Godot (pp. 12–13):

ESTRAGON. Et qu'a-t-il répondu?
VLADIMIR. Qu'il verrait.
ESTRAGON. Qu'il ne pouvait rien promettre.
VLADIMIR. Qu'il lui fallait réfléchir.
ESTRAGON. A tête reposée.
VLADIMIR. Consulter sa famille.
ESTRAGON. Ses amis.
VLADIMIR. Ses agents.
ESTRAGON. Ses correspondants.
VLADIMIR. Ses registres.
ESTRAGON. Son compte en banque.
VLADIMIR. Avant de se prononcer.

There are two distinct sequences of repetition here. The first expresses the temporizing nature of Godot's response, combining triple *anaphora* ('Qu'il') and *parison*. The second vividly evokes the reasons for the delay, and combines multiple *anaphora* ('Ses'), *epitrochasmus* ('famille', 'amis', 'agents', and so on), and *homoioteleuton*, the repetition of the same vowel sounds in the last syllables of 'famille'/'amis', and 'agents'/'correspondants'. As one further example, of very many, Vladimir and Estragon consider filling the time with physical exercise; while doing so, they fill it with rhetorical *figures* (pp. 67–8):

ESTRAGON. Qu'est-ce qu'on fait maintenant?
VLADIMIR. En attendant.
ESTRAGON. En attendant.
Silence.
VLADIMIR. Si on faisait nos exercices?
ESTRAGON. Nos mouvements.
VLADIMIR. D'assouplissement.
ESTRAGON. De relaxation.
VLADIMIR. De circumduction.
ESTRAGON. De relaxation.
VLADIMIR. Pour nous réchauffer.
ESTRAGON. Pour nous calmer.

First of all there is Estragon's immediate repetition of Vladimir's answer to his question (*reduplicatio*). Then there is the quadruple *anaphora* ('D'/De') indicating the different kinds of movements they might make. Finally there is the double *anaphora* and *isocolon*, expressing the purpose of the envisaged exercise ('Pour [. . .]'). Within this broad framework of repetition, there are other devices at work: *homoioteleuton* ('-ments'/'-ment'; '-tion'; '-er') and *geminatio*, when Estragon repeats 'relaxation' instead of fulfilling the expectation of the sequence and supplying a new word. The comic effect of this exchange derives also from the unexpectedly *grand style* of learned and Latinate vocabulary with which the simple question is answered.

How can we explain the importance in the play of *figures* of repetition as a basis for so many of the exchanges? Various responses are possible. The effect of the *figures* in the two examples above is to detract from the referential function of language and stress its poetic function, a shift from the utility to the pleasure of language. Vladimir and Estragon use language less to communicate purposefully than to pass time. They play with language. And the games they play are artfully controlled by Beckett for the amusement of the theatre audience. Repetition is important in the play on a much broader level than individual exchanges between characters. Whatever the differences between the first and second acts, it is the similarities that are most striking: with some variations, the second is a repetition of the first. Vladimir and Estragon meet and wait for Godot; Pozzo and Lucky pass by; a boy comes to say that Godot cannot come today, but will come tomorrow. The suggestion is that every day is more or less the same. Life is about waiting, our hopes go unfulfilled, but we must do our best to fill the time, because the wait cannot be avoided. Repetition is therefore a crucial thematic concern of the play, and it is a tribute to Beckett's artistry that he carries through that concern in even the smallest aspects of the play's construction: the individual exchange is a microcosm of the whole.

Beckett's Orators

For all that the play creates an impression of sameness, monotony, and repetition, Beckett cannot risk boring his audience. He avoids this danger by ringing the changes in the characters' rhetorical behaviour, and in particular by introducing two further characters with whom Vladimir and Estragon can engage. In rhetorical terms, Pozzo and Lucky are at diametrically opposed poles; they are also both different from Vladimir and Estragon. Whereas Vladimir and Estragon speak, for the most part, in short phrases and simple sentences, and whereas Lucky, but for one long speech in the first act, is silent, Pozzo makes great play of his abilities as a speaker. This characteristic goes hand in hand with his relative wealth and his authority over Lucky. Pozzo speaks more readily than the other characters; the silences diminish when he is on-stage. He also employs more complex sentences than the others, and positively invites them to admire his skills as a speaker.

Even so, in his depiction of Pozzo as a would-be orator, Beckett ridicules him mercilessly. It is the comedy of the authority figure undermined. Vladimir and Estragon want to know why Lucky will not put down Pozzo's bags. After avoiding the question for some time, Pozzo finally seizes on it as an opportunity for rhetorical display. Beckett dwells comically on the enormous disproportion between Pozzo's subject and his performance (p. 24):

POZZO. Je vais vous répondre. (*A Estragon.*) Mais restez tranquille, je vous en supplie, vous me rendez nerveux.
VLADIMIR. Viens ici.
ESTRAGON. Qu'est-ce qu'il y a?
VLADIMIR. Il va parler.
Immobiles, l'un contre l'autre, ils attendent.
POZZO. C'est parfait. Tout le monde y est? Tout le monde me regarde? (*Il regarde Lucky, tire sur sa corde. Lucky lève la tête.*) Regarde-moi, porc! (*Lucky le regarde.*) Parfait. (*Il met la pipe dans sa poche, sort un petit vaporisateur et se vapor-*

ise la gorge, remet le vaporisateur dans sa poche, se râcle la gorge, crache, ressort le vaporisateur, se revaporise la gorge, remet le vaporisateur dans sa poche.) Je suis prêt. Tout le monde m'écoute? *(Il regarde Lucky, tire sur sa corde.)* Avance! *(Lucky avance.)* Là! *(Lucky s'arrête.)* Tout le monde est prêt? *(Ils les regardent tous les trois, Lucky en dernier, tire sur la corde.)* Alors quoi? *(Lucky lève la tête.)* Je n'aime pas parler dans le vide. Bon. Voyons. *(Il réfléchit.)*
ESTRAGON. Je m'en vais.
POZZO. Qu'est-ce que vous m'avez demandé au juste?

Pozzo takes a long time preparing to answer the question about Lucky and his bags. His listeners constitute an audience, which he wants to be very attentive. He is nervous about speaking. Above all, he is so concerned about his *action*, his delivery, that he fussily prepares his throat with a vaporizer. Beckett intensifies the ridicule of his nervous orator by making him forget his subject after all his preparations (a lapse in *memory*, in rhetorical terms). Reminded of the question he has to answer, he launches into a reply (pp. 24–5):

POZZO. J'y suis. Il fallait me le dire plutôt. Pourquoi il ne se met pas à son aise. Essayons d'y voir clair. N'en a-t-il pas le droit? Si. C'est donc qu'il ne veut pas? Voilà qui est raisonné. Et pourquoi ne veut-il pas? *(Un temps.)* Messieurs, je vais vous le dire.
VLADIMIR. Attention!
POZZO. C'est pour m'impressionner, pour que je le garde.
ESTRAGON. Comment?
POZZO. Je me suis peut-être mal exprimé. Il cherche à m'apitoyer, pour que je renonce à me séparer de lui. Non, ce n'est pas tout à fait ça.

Rhetoric as both concept and practice is deeply embedded in these exchanges, and it is consistently held up to ridicule. After his lengthy preparations for speech, Pozzo's explanation is extraordinarily terse and simplistic, expressed in the form of an *enthymeme* in two *interrogations*: 'N'en a-t-il pas le droit? Si. C'est donc qu'il ne veut pas?' This response is all the more comic as it is followed by Pozzo's clumsily self-satisfied congratulation on the rhetorical skills he thinks he has demonstrated: 'Voilà qui est raisonné.' Having established that Lucky does not put the bags down because he does not want to, Pozzo warms to his audience, asking the question they had wanted to be answered all along, but asking it in the form of a *communicatio* (the kind of question that normally makes the interlocutor think) and leaving a pause to keep them in suspense. Finally, and with a flattering address to Vladimir and Estragon, he paves the way for his answer: 'Messieurs, je vais vous le dire.' Vladimir's *exclamation*

('Attention!') is presumably an *ironic* suggestion of anticipation. At last, Pozzo's explanation reveals something new about the relationship between Lucky and himself. Lucky wants to be sure to be kept in Pozzo's employ, so keeps hold of the bags in order to impress him favourably. This idea is interesting for the way it imputes rhetorical motivation to a character who has so far been mute. Lucky's *action* is, according to Pozzo, persuasive in intention; and, as he goes on to say, Lucky is making particular use of *pathos* ('Il cherche à m'apitoyer'). However, Estragon is puzzled by what Pozzo has said, and this leads Pozzo to begin a series of statements, all of which are examples of *correctio*, some explicit ('Je me suis peut-être mal exprimé'), others not, in which he restates his explanation in different words.

Pozzo is acutely aware of his audience. On a later occasion, after he has attempted, in a Beckettian parody of lyricism, to evoke the night sky, he obsessively grills Vladimir and Estragon for their comments on his rhetorical skill (p. 32):

POZZO. Comment m'avez-vous trouvé? (*Estragon et Vladimir le regardent sans comprendre.*) Bon? Moyen? Passable? Quelconque? Franchement mauvais?
VLADIMIR (*comprenant le premier*). Oh très bien, tout à fait bien.
POZZO (*à Estragon*). Et vous, monsieur?
ESTRAGON (*accent anglais*). Oh très bon, très très très bon.
POZZO (*avec élan*). Merci, messieurs! (*Un temps.*) J'ai tant besoin d'encouragement. (*Il réfléchit.*) J'ai un peu faibli sur la fin. Vous n'avez pas remarqué?
VLADIMIR. Oh, peut-être un tout petit peu.
ESTRAGON. J'ai cru que c'était exprès.
POZZO. C'est que ma mémoire est défectueuse.

Pozzo, who appears to be in authority, turns out to be full of insecurities and inadequacies. And this is conveyed by his attitude to this explicitly rhetorical performance. The good orator would observe the effect on his audience; he would not ask them, in schoolboy fashion, to grade his performance. Aware of his weakness, he himself points to his rhetorical defect, deficient *memory*.

The man carrying Pozzo's bags is silent. We are even told in the second act that he is incapable of speech (p. 83). But in Act I he makes the longest and most extraordinary speech in the whole play. It is an outrageous parody of serious public discourse. These are the opening lines (p. 37):

LUCKY (*débit monotone*). Etant donné l'existence telle qu'elle jaillit des récents travaux publics de Poinçon et Wattmann d'un Dieu personnel quaquaquaqua à barbe blanche quaqua hors du temps de l'étendue qui du haut de sa divine apathie sa divine athambie sa divine aphasie nous aime bien à quelques exceptions près on ne sait pourquoi mais ça viendra et souffre à l'instar de la divine Miranda avec ceux qui sont on ne sait pourquoi mais on a le temps dans le tourment dans les feux dont les feux les flammes pour que ça dure encore un peu [. . .].

This is presented as philosophical thought addressed to a public. Lucky is responding to the repeated command 'Pense'; he prepares himself by putting on his hat; and, before speaking, he turns to address the theatre audience. So there is a considerable degree of expectation before he actually speaks. His words contain sufficient suggestions of serious philosophical—indeed theological—discourse; but the context in which these suggestions occur, and Lucky's delivery, turn them into comic nonsense. Academic rhetoric is undermined, but by rhetorical means. Beckett parodies academic delivery by stating that Lucky's *action* should be monotonous. The stage direction is reinforced by the complete absence of punctuation. Suggestions of academic discourse are the recourse to *external proofs* (the public works of Poinçon and Wattmann), a relatively elevated vocabulary ('l'existence', 'jaillit', 'travaux publics', 'Dieu personnel', 'divine apathie'), and the hint of syntactic subordination ('Etant donné l'existence telle qu'elle jaillit', 'pour que'). But the context in which this would-be academic discourse is situated entirely undermines it. The *grand style* rubs shoulders with the *low style*. 'Un Dieu personnel' is juxtaposed with the *onomatopoeic* term for the quacking of a duck ('quaquaquaqua'). Elevated words are ridiculed by *paronomasia* ('apathie', 'athambie', 'aphasie'). *Paronomasia, geminatio*, and *hendiadys* combine to create nonsensical syntax ('dans les feux dont les feux les flammes'). The dominant *figure* that ensures the incomprehensibility of Lucky's speech is *anacoluthon*. Throughout, words are put together in syntactically impossible sequences. Lucky's monotonous nonsense is an extreme example of Beckett's verbal variety and dexterity and of his fundamental questioning of the efficacy of language as a mode of communication.

Vladimir's response to Pozzo's request for help can serve as a final example of Beckett's use of rhetoric to subvert rhetoric. In Act II, Pozzo is blind and falls to the ground. After much temporizing, Vladimir urges action (p. 71):

VLADIMIR. Ne perdons pas notre temps en de vains discours. (*Un temps. Avec véhémence.*) Faisons quelque chose, pendant que l'occasion se présente! Ce n'est pas tous les jours qu'on a besoin de nous. Non pas à vrai dire qu'on ait précisément besoin de nous. D'autres feraient aussi bien l'affaire, sinon mieux. L'appel que nous venons d'entendre, c'est plutôt à l'humanité tout entière qu'il s'adresse. Mais à cet endroit, en ce moment, l'humanité c'est nous, que ça nous plaise ou non. Profitons-en, avant qu'il soit trop tard. Représentons dignement pour une fois l'engeance où le malheur nous a fourrés. Qu'en dis-tu?
ESTRAGON. Je n'ai pas écouté.
VLADIMIR. Il est vrai qu'en pesant, les bras croisés, le pour et le contre, nous faisons également honneur à notre condition. Le tigre se précipite au secours de ses congénères sans la moindre réflexion. Ou bien il se sauve au plus profond des taillis. Mais la question n'est pas là. Que faisons-nous ici, voilà ce qu'il faut se demander. Nous avons la chance de le savoir. Oui, dans cette immense confusion, une seule chose est claire: nous attendons que Godot vienne.

The comedy derives from two major discrepancies. The first, in Vladimir's first *réplique*, is between his words and his actions. His words argue for help to be offered to Pozzo, but his speech stands in the way of his offer of help. The words in his second *réplique* contradict the words of his first. Having first urged helpful action, he now considers the desirability of honorable inaction. This discrepancy is compounded by his digression into a more general metaphysical question, far removed from Pozzo's earth-bound helplessness.

Prompted by the blind Pozzo's call for help, Vladimir draws on the *places* of *genus* and *species* to consider the distinction between himself and Estragon as individuals and as representatives of humanity. Having established the desirability of helping Pozzo, he then turns to other *places*. The *place* of *opposites* allows him to glimpse the prospect of inaction. *Comparison* lets him flesh out this prospect: a tiger would dash unthinkingly to help another tiger, but it is human to stop and think. However irrelevant it may be to the situation, rhetoric allows Vladimir to fill the time in an entertaining way.

In *Tartuffe* and *Britannicus* characters use rhetoric to engage in purposeful acts of persuasion; and Molière and Racine so deploy their characters' rhetoric as to secure the spectators' interest in their rhetorical behaviour. Characters try, more or less well, to speak in order to further their own self-interest; and the dramatist often shows their rhetoric failing, because that turns out to be dramatically more exciting for the audience. Beckett's world has no room for purposeful acts of persuasion. It is a world in which it is hard to envisage any actions or decisions of import. None the less, the characters use rhetoric, but inappropriately, in order to highlight the futility of their existence as judged by the criterion of purposeful action. Rhetoric keeps all the dramatic characters busy with each other, and offers diverse sources of entertainment for the audience. That is why it is crucial to the art of the dramatist, even one concerned with the pathetic inadequacy of human communication.

4

PROSE FICTION

Explicit links, like those between rhetoric and drama in the early modern period, have never existed between rhetoric and prose fiction. If we think of the minimalist definition of prose fiction as the telling of a story in prose, it may well seem difficult to see the relevance of rhetoric to the genre. Yet telling a story is a subject covered by the rhetorical theorists. *Narration* is conventionally seen as the second part of a *judicial* speech. The orator tells a story in order to secure his audience's belief in it, and tells it in such a way as to make it support whatever persuasive aim he has. When rhetoric is considered in this light, its links with some kinds of prose fiction will be immediately apparent, since some prose fiction—in particular some first-person narratives—enacts rhetorical situations that are very close to those faced by real orators.[1]

Rhetoric and the First-Person Narrative

A rhetorical novel *par excellence* is Camus's *La Chute* (1956).[2] The novel is composed of the words of Clamence as he addresses his

---

[1] One substantial book has attempted to use the terminology of traditional rhetoric to discuss the novel, looking very much at the interaction between narrator and reader, rather than at the representation of rhetoric as used by the characters: A. W. Halsall, *L'Art de convaincre: Le Récit pragmatique: rhétorique, idéologie, propagande* (Toronto: Paratexte, 1990). Halsall is also the author of a rhetorical study of Hugo's fiction: *Victor Hugo et l'art de convaincre: Le Récit hugolien: Rhétorique, argumentation, persuasion* (Montreal: Les Éditions Balzac, 1995). There is a study of eighteenth-century fiction concentrating exclusively on the rhetoric of the characters: J.-P. Sermain, 'Rhétorique et roman au XVIIIᵉ siècle: L'Exemple de Prévost et de Marivaux (1728–42)', *Studies on Voltaire and the Eighteenth Century*, 233 (1985). In this chapter I will argue that a rhetorical reading of prose fiction needs to take into account the complex interplay of rhetoric on the character axis and that on the narrator–reader axis.

[2] A. Camus, *La Chute* (Gallimard, 1956). For different approaches to this text see e.g. J. Lévi-Valensi, '*La Chute* ou la parole en procès', *Cahiers Albert Camus*, 3 (1970), 33–57; R. Jones, 'Modes of Discourse in *La Chute*', *Nottingham French Studies*, 15(2) (1976), 27–35; and B. T. Fitch, *The Narcissistic Text: A Reading of Camus's Fiction* (Toronto: University of Toronto Press, 1982). None of these approaches is specifically rhetorical, but all raise questions of language, irony, and narrative form.

interlocutor in a series of meetings in Amsterdam. Readers can guess the reactions of the interlocutor only from the way in which Clamence speaks to him. For a good deal of the time, it seems that Clamence is above all concerned to talk about himself, to tell stories about himself, but in a distinctly *judicial* mode. He is accusing himself of basic human failings. This kind of discourse is peculiarly appropriate, because the career that he had followed in Paris, prior to giving it up, was a legal one: he was a barrister. He seems strangely preoccupied with making his interlocutor reach an unfavourable verdict on him. Yet, towards the end of the novel Camus springs a surprise. Clamence turns the tables on his interlocutor, who is now urged to engage in *judicial* oratory at his own expense. The text engages the reader in an unremitting and intricate rhetorical situation. Clamence's *judicial* oratory is really *deliberative* oratory in disguise, and its purpose is to persuade the interlocutor to start accusing himself. The final twist in the last paragraph is the revelation that the interlocutor is, as Clamence was, a barrister in Paris.

La Chute is a text that foregrounds rhetoric explicitly, not only in the profession of the two main characters and in the nature of the situation in which they are involved; Clamence also talks openly about his rhetorical skill. Early in the text, he comments particularly on his *action* and his ability to make emotional appeals (*pathos*): 'Je suis sûr que vous auriez admiré l'exactitude de mon ton, la justesse de mon émotion, la persuasion et la chaleur, l'indignation maîtrisée de mes plaidoiries' (p. 22). At the end of the novel, he comments on the different rhetorical skills he deploys on his interlocutors in the bar in Amsterdam (p. 145):

[Ma profession actuelle] consiste [. . .] à pratiquer la confession publique aussi souvent que possible. Je m'accuse, en long et en large. Ce n'est pas difficile, j'ai maintenant de la mémoire. Mais attention, je ne m'accuse pas grossièrement, à grands coups sur la poitrine. Non, je navigue souplement, je multiplie les nuances, les digressions aussi, j'adapte enfin mon discours à l'auditeur, j'amène ce dernier à renchérir.

In rhetorical terms, this is his *peroration*, and in it he reveals his methods to his interlocutor. The techniques he employs as 'juge-pénitent' are less ostentatious and more subtle than those he deployed in the lawcourts. Above all, he knows how to suit his style to his audience.

Critics disagree over the interpretation of this text. Is Camus in pessimistic mood, speaking through Clamence, and inviting readers, like Clamence's interlocutor, to see the extent of the guilt they carry with them as human beings? Or is Camus ironizing Clamence, and inviting his readers to reject Clamence's unremittingly negative attitude to life? A rhetorical reading might favour the latter interpretation. It is as if Camus makes Clamence allude so frequently, and from so early on in the text, to his awareness of rhetorical strategies, that the reader is thereby forearmed against them and will observe them at work from an ironic distance.

Another work of prose fiction with a comparable rhetorical structure is Gide's *L'Immoraliste* (1902).[3] It is a first-person account by the young historian Michel, recounting his recovery from illness, his self-discovery, and his wife's illness and subsequent death. Almost the whole text is composed of Michel's words spoken to three friends who have made the journey from France to North Africa specially to listen to him, at his request. This context is established by some direct words of address to the friends and, more importantly, by the letter that one of them writes to his brother in France. Indeed, the fiction begins with this letter. Its author explains that the three friends have answered Michel's call for help, and requests that the well-placed recipient of the letter (Monsieur D. R., Président du Conseil) find Michel a suitable position. With the letter, the author sends his transcript of Michel's words.

Even within the fiction itself, the rhetorical situation is more complex than that enacted in *La Chute*. There are two levels in play: Michel speaks at length to his friends; and one of them writes to his brother to persuade him to find Michel a post, sending the text of Michel's speech, by way of *external proof*. But the complexity is even greater. What kind of speech does Michel make? It starts out in non-rhetorical terms, a simple, unbiased narration: 'Souffrez que je vous parle de moi; je vais vous raconter ma vie, simplement, sans modestie et sans orgueil, plus simplement que si je parlais à moi-même' (p. 17). But by the end, it is clear that we have heard no straightforward account, and that Michel himself is aware of the various degrees of distortion that might have entered his narrative: 'Ce n'est pas, croyez-moi, que je sois fatigué de mon crime, s'il vous plaît de

---

[3] A. Gide, *L'Immoraliste* (Gallimard, 1972). On the narrative framework of Gide's fictions, see D. Walker, *André Gide* (Basingstoke: Macmillan, 1990).

l'appeler ainsi,—mais je dois me prouver à moi-même que je n'ai pas outrepassé mon droit' (p. 180). It is a narrative that is both self-accusation ('crime') and self-defence ('je n'ai pas outrepassé mon droit').

This fundamental ambiguity is indicative of the delicate moral problems at the heart of the text. In regaining his own health, Michel has discovered the pleasures of the senses, and he has increasingly pursued an individualistic ethic to the point of extreme selfishness. His wife, who looked after him when he was ill and nursed him back to health, falls ill and is destroyed by the tiring journey he takes her on to North Africa in pursuit of his own interests. In responding to this behaviour, readers are in the position of Michel's friends, except that we cannot see him or hear his voice; we can only read his words. The writer of the letter intervenes towards the end of Michel's account, just after he has related his wife's death (pp. 179–80):

> Il nous semblait hélas! qu'à nous la raconter, Michel avait rendu son action plus légitime. De ne savoir où la désapprouver, dans la lente explication qu'il en donna, nous en faisait presque complices. Nous y étions comme engagés. Il avait achevé ce récit sans un tremblement dans la voix, sans qu'une inflexion ni qu'un geste témoignât qu'une émotion quelconque le troublât, soit qu'il mît un cynique orgueil à ne pas nous paraître ému, soit qu'il craignît, par une sorte de pudeur, de provoquer notre émotion par ses larmes, soit enfin qu'il ne fût pas ému.

This reported response makes plain the curious combination of objective appreciation, disapproval, and sympathy to which Michel's *action* in the narrative gives rise in his fictional audience, but also, perhaps, in readers of the story. That, in any event, is what Gide wanted. He uses explicitly rhetorical terminology in his preface. Aware that his text focuses centrally on a problem of moral judgement, he claims that he, as author, does not want his work to do any more than highlight the problem; he certainly does not want to persuade his readers that there is a right and a wrong approach to the ethical difficulties involved: 'je n'ai voulu faire en ce livre non plus acte d'accusation qu'apologie, et me suis gardé de juger' (p. 10). In choosing a form in which his narrator claims to tell a story objectively, whilst alternately (or simultaneously) accusing and defending himself, Gide has chosen a rhetorical structure ideally suited to the open-ended vision he wishes to promote.

Rhetoric and the Polyphonic Narrative

Even without detailed rhetorical analysis, it is clear that rhetorical structures underpin the basic form of these two predominantly first-person narratives. But it is perhaps too easy to claim the centrality of rhetoric in prose fiction by taking first-person narratives as examples, because this form, a primarily univocal text, is naturally close to the situation of the orator. For all the importance of first-person narrative in the history of prose fiction, however, the novel is perhaps most remarkable for its complexity of narrative voice: narrators who play a role in the action and see it only from their point of view (like Clamence and Michel); narrators who are hardly identifiable as individuals, who play no role in the action, and yet seem to know everything that all the characters are doing and feeling (like the narrator of Balzac's *Le Père Goriot*); characters within a narrator's story who themselves become, as it were, second-degree narrators (the narrator of Madame de Lafayette's *La Princesse de Clèves* tells a story in which many of the characters themselves become narrators of substantial stories).[4] The novel is the genre that most obviously and most intricately exploits polyphony, and it might be thought that this degree of polyphony has the effect of complicating the rhetorical structure to such an extent that the rhetorical framework ceases to be a useful one for the analysis of such stories. In cases of real oratory and in first-person narratives, it is a relatively straightforward task to identify the rhetorical voice and analyse its persuasive strategies. It is relatively easy to appreciate drama as a succession of rhetorical encounters between characters. But how can rhetoric illuminate novels of some narrative complexity?

To a certain extent, novels, like plays, show characters in conflictual situations, and aim to secure the interest of readers in the specifically rhetorical behaviour of characters. If there is a third-person narrator distinct from the characters, his narration works directly on readers, inviting them to see characters or scenes in certain ways, even if (as in most cases) it is the kind of narrator that does not explicitly acknowledge the act of narration or the existence of readers. The three novels considered in the remainder of this chapter will allow me to explore and illustrate contrasting sources

---

[4] Two standard works on narratology (among many) are G. Genette, *Figures*, vol. iii (Seuil, 1972), and S. Rimmon-Kenan, *Narrative Fiction: Contemporary Poetics* (Routledge, 1983).

of rhetorical interest in polyphonic prose fiction: Laclos's *Les Liaisons dangereuses* (1782), Zola's *Germinal* (1885), and Nathalie Sarraute's *Le Planétarium* (1959).

I. RHETORIC AND SEX IN LACLOS'S *LES LIAISONS DANGEREUSES*

With the exception of a few supposedly editorial notes explaining some references and omissions in this allegedly real correspondence, the text of *Les Liaisons dangereuses* is made up entirely of letters composed by the characters.[5] There are twelve different correspondents in all. To that extent it is obviously a polyphonic novel. But the apparent absence of an overarching narrator has the effect of making this novel, like other letter-novels, akin to drama, in that the characters are presented to the readers directly, without apparent narratorial mediation. It is particularly appropriate to invoke rhetoric in the case of this letter-novel, however, because the action revolves around the attempts by some characters either to manipulate others in order to obtain sexual favours, or to report their own sexual exploits in order to elicit praise for them. It is a novel about persuasion, and one of the main persuasive devices deployed is the writing of letters, which is also the form that the novel takes. The main focus of the readers' interest is the rhetorical strategies that the characters adopt, sometimes consciously, sometimes unconsciously, sometimes effectively, sometimes disastrously, to strike their targets, or to fend off their adversaries' blows.

Two explicit and contradictory views of epistolary communication are evoked in the novel. Danceny expresses the simplistic and naïve view: 'une lettre est le portrait de l'âme' (letter 150). This view supposes that when people write, they reveal themselves straightforwardly and transparently. This is the way in which Cécile de Volanges writes, and she is reprimanded for doing so by the Marquise de Merteuil, who expresses the alternative view of letter writing (letter 105):

[5] C. de Laclos, *Les Liaisons dangereuses*, ed. R. Pomeau (Flammarion, 1981). References will be to the letter number rather than the page number. The nature of the text seems to ensure that most critical studies raise issues relevant to a rhetorical reading, even though they may not be specifically rhetorical in approach. One of the older general studies of the work remains one of the best: J.-L. Seylaz, *'Les Liaisons dangereuses' et la création romanesque chez Laclos* (Geneva: Droz, 1958).

Vous écrivez toujours comme un enfant. Je vois bien d'où cela vient; c'est que vous dites tout ce que vous pensez, et rien de ce que vous ne pensez pas. Cela peut passer ainsi de vous à moi, qui devons n'avoir rien de caché l'une pour l'autre: mais avec tout le monde! avec votre amant surtout! vous auriez toujours l'air d'une petite sotte. Vous voyez bien que, quand vous écrivez à quelqu'un, c'est pour lui et non pas pour vous: vous devez donc moins chercher à lui dire ce que vous pensez, que ce qui lui plaît davantage.

For Merteuil, there are two distinct types of epistolary communication. Simple self-expression is legitimate only between intimate friends. All other correspondents, including lovers, need to be addressed with studied rhetorical skill. One achieves one's aim by saying not what one thinks, but what one thinks the recipient wants to hear. This is sound rhetorical advice, based on an awareness of the importance of *ethos* and *pathos*. Cécile ought to be alerted by it to Merteuil's own rhetorical manipulation, but instead she is taken in by it and becomes Merteuil's victim.

On a superficial reading, the main characters can be divided into two groups that equate with the two views of epistolary communication, the manipulative and the straightforward. The arch-manipulators are Merteuil and the Vicomte de Valmont, who seek to take their sexual pleasures when they please and with whom they please, inflicting revenge on those who stand in their way. The immediate victims of their rhetoric are the youthful Cécile and Danceny and the married Présidente de Tourvel. But they deceive others too: Mme de Volanges, Mme de Rosemonde, Père Anselme.

This neat division of characters into the rhetorical manipulators and the rhetorically manipulated fails, however, to take into account a crucial factor. The absence of a narrator means that readers are offered no objective guidance with which to assess the degree of manipulation which characters use. This structural factor focuses readers' attention entirely on the characters' rhetorical behaviour, and makes it all the more intriguing, because not easily fathomable. The two schemers are fully aware of the power of rhetoric, but when they write complicitously to each other, it can seem that they write frankly and without conscious persuasive intent. Indeed, it is such apparent frankness in Merteuil's letters 81 and 85, where she explains her method to Valmont and narrates an example of it in practice, that leads to her downfall when these letters are eventually circulated. And yet, even when they write to each other, there is rhetorical manipulation of a sort. They are trying to impress each other, and have recourse to *demonstrative* discourse; they boast of their exploits; they try to show that they are not dependent on each other's complicity. And it is this simmering conflict that sparks off the denouement, Valmont's death and Merteuil's disgrace.

The other characters, who often seem too innocent to write rhetorically, do, none the less, resort to rhetorical strategies. Tourvel adopts a *deliberative* discourse to deter Valmont's amorous affections (letter 50). Père Anselme also adopts a *deliberative* discourse to encourage Valmont in his apparent turn to religion (letter 123). Even Valmont's servant, Azolan, indulges in some grovelling *judicial* rhetoric to defend himself against his master's charge that he negligently failed to find out about Tourvel's flight from the château in which they were staying (letter 107). Mme de Volanges writes to Tourvel in *judicial* mode to accuse Valmont of vice (letter 32). Their experiences are a lesson to Cécile and Danceny in the art of rhetorical manipulation. So many characters are so skilled, or become so skilled, at expressing themselves in ways best calculated to affect their audience that the characters' authentic selves can only be penetrated, if at all, through a dense texture of rhetorical ploys. The pleasure of reading this novel lies in good measure in reading with acute sensitivity to the characters' rhetorical practices.

Valmont, Merteuil, Tourvel

The case of Valmont is particularly perplexing and fascinating from a rhetorical point of view. It appears that he will seduce Tourvel as a standard challenge, and that when he has dropped her, Merteuil will once again grant him sexual favours. But it seems increasingly that he is falling in love with Tourvel. He denies it, but the suspicion of it makes Merteuil jealous. Valmont writes letter 133 explicitly as an attempt to prove to Merteuil that he is not in love with Tourvel: 'vous me croyez amoureux, subjugué? [. . .] Ah! grâces au Ciel, je n'en suis pas encore réduit là, et je m'offre à vous le prouver. Oui, je vous le prouverai.' He tries at some length to demonstrate why this particular woman has retained his interest for longer than usual without, however, ensnaring him in any amorous ties. He finishes his letter by asserting confidently and hopefully the supreme value of his liaison with Merteuil, which he thinks is about to be resumed. Merteuil's reply (letter 134) is a systematic and withering

demolition of Valmont's self-defence. She is even prepared to
believe that he is deluded by his own specious argument, that he
really thinks he does not love Tourvel. But, by subjecting his letter
to a rhetorical reading, she asserts her own conviction that
Valmont's feelings for Tourvel are amorous: 'C'est de l'amour, ou
il n'en exista jamais: vous le niez bien de cent façons; mais vous le
prouvez de mille.' Her expression, with its use of balanced phrasing
(*parison*) and increasing *hyperbole* ('cent', 'mille'), makes her insight
seem decisive. She responds to his own arguments with a series of
aggressive *interrogations* and dismissive *exclamations*, and above all she
quotes him against himself. By way of *external proof* she quotes the
phrases he has used to describe Tourvel ('une femme étonnante, une
femme délicate et sensible', 'une femme rare enfin, et telle qu'on
n'en rencontrerait pas une seconde'), and presses them into the service of arguments opposite to those of Valmont himself. Such
phrases are signs of his love, or at least signs that after Tourvel he
would never find such love again. She sets a condition on the
resumption of their own affair, but does not for a second believe that
Valmont can fulfil it. She wants to be convinced that Tourvel represents nothing more for Valmont than 'une femme ordinaire, une
femme telle qu'elle est seulement'. Crucially, signalling her determination not to be taken in by the kind of rhetoric with which she
gladly dupes others, she indicates the kind of *proof* that she requires:
'mais, je l'avoue, je n'en croirais pas de vains discours. Je ne pour-
rais être persuadé que par l'ensemble de votre conduite.' Merteuil
knows that Valmont's words are empty. She will be convinced only
by tangible action.

Yet, writing and speaking rhetorically are habits in which
Valmont is so steeped that he will never be able to satisfy Merteuil's
condition. His constant recourse is to wily words, as the immediately
following episode shows. The event seems simple. Valmont's
response to it is not. He visits Tourvel, leaves her politely but
abruptly, and is later seen by her in their respective carriages; but
in his, there is Emilie, a woman of ill repute, who laughs scornfully
at Tourvel. The Présidente sends him a letter breaking with him
(letter 136). Readers are presented with three versions of this
episode. The first is Tourvel's to Madame de Rosemonde, full of
grief, pain, and hurt (letter 135). The second and third are the most
contrasting, and are both written by Valmont, to Tourvel and
Merteuil respectively (letters 137 and 138).

By the time we read his letter to Tourvel, we know only her perception of the event, and have no reason to disbelieve that she has
been grossly offended by Valmont and Emilie. When we read
Valmont's letter, it is very evidently the reply of a man keen to
defend himself and to re-establish relations with Tourvel. And given
the amount of pain we know he has inflicted, his task is an exacting
one. This letter follows closely the four parts of a speech recommended by rhetoricians. In a long and insinuating *exordium* ('On
vient seulement, Madame, [. . .] me livrer à mes remords') he skilfully exploits *ethos* and *pathos*, presenting an image of himself as distressed by her interpretation of events and appealing to her pity for
him as the misunderstood partner. The next section is the *narration*
('Cependant, qui le croirait? [. . .] me juger coupable'), in which he
gives an apparently innocent version of the story. The following
paragraphs constitute his *confirmation*, in which he glosses his *narration*, and admits guilt, albeit in a generalized way. But his admission
of a guilty encounter with Emilie is couched in terms of an argument based on the *place* of *comparison*, and is designed to persuade
her that the kind of love he feels for Tourvel is of a superior nature
to the kind he experienced with Emilie. Finally, his *peroration* makes
a climactic appeal to her emotions ('Si, tout à coup, [. . .] désespoir
éternel').

Given the extent to which appearances are against him, his skill
in the deployment of *ethos* in the *exordium* and of *parataxis* in the *narration* is extraordinary (letter 137):

[1] On vient seulement, Madame, de me rendre votre lettre; j'ai frémi
en la lisant, et elle me laisse à peine la force d'y répondre. [2] Quelle
affreuse idée avez-vous donc de moi! [3] Ah! sans doute, j'ai des torts; et
tels que je ne me les pardonnerai de ma vie, quand même vous les couvririez de votre indulgence. [4] Mais que ceux que vous me reprochez ont
toujours été loin de mon âme! [5] Qui, moi! vous humilier! vous avilir!
quand je vous respecte autant que je vous chéris; quand je n'ai connu
l'orgueil, que du moment où vous m'avez jugé digne de vous. [6] Les
apparences vous ont déçue; et je conviens qu'elles ont pu être contre moi:
mais n'aviez-vous donc pas dans votre cœur ce qu'il fallait pour les combattre? et ne s'est-il pas révolté à la seule idée qu'il pouvait avoir à se plaindre du mien? [7] Vous l'avez cru cependant! [8] Ainsi, non seulement vous
m'avez jugé capable de ce délire atroce, mais vous avez même craint de
vous y être exposée par vos bontés pour moi. [9] Ah! si vous vous trouvez
dégradée à ce point par votre amour, je suis donc moi-même bien vil à vos
yeux?

[10] Oppressé par le sentiment douloureux que cette idée me cause, je perds à la repousser, le temps que je devrais employer à la détruire. [11] J'avouerai tout; une autre considération me retient encore. [12] Faut-il donc retracer des faits que je voudrais anéantir, et fixer votre attention et la mienne sur un moment d'erreur que je voudrais racheter du reste de ma vie, dont je suis encore à concevoir la cause, et dont le souvenir doit faire à jamais mon humiliation et mon désespoir? [13] Ah! si, en m'accusant, je dois exciter votre colère, vous n'aurez pas au moins à chercher loin votre vengeance; il vous suffira de me livrer à mes remords.

[14] Cependant, qui le croirait? cet événement a pour première cause le charme tout-puissant que j'éprouve auprès de vous. [15] Ce fut lui qui me fit oublier trop longtemps une affaire importante, et qui ne pouvait se remettre. [16] Je vous quittai trop tard, et ne trouvai plus la personne que j'allais chercher. [17] J'espérais la rejoindre à l'Opéra, et ma démarche fut pareillement infructueuse. [18] Emilie que j'y trouvai, que j'ai connue dans un temps où j'étais bien loin de connaître ni vous ni l'amour, Emilie n'avait pas sa voiture, et me demanda de la remettre chez elle à quatre pas de là. [19] Je n'y vis aucune conséquence, et j'y consentis. [20] Mais ce fut alors que je vous rencontrai; et je sentis sur-le-champ que vous seriez portée à me juger coupable.

The *exordium*, in the first two paragraphs, constitutes an extremely dense exploitation of *ethos*. Valmont is setting off the image Tourvel has of him against the image he wishes her to have: the cruelly unfaithful lover versus the painfully misunderstood and despairing lover. In presenting these two images, he is attempting to make her feel guilty of misjudging him, and to arouse feelings of sympathy (*pathos*). His strategy is underpinned by a range of emotional and emphatic *figures*.

The opening sentence creates an impression of hasty composition. He has, he claims, taken up his pen immediately upon receipt of her letter of dismissal. This may, or may not, be true. Its effect, calculated or not, is to create the impression that the writing is spontaneous, unprepared, and honest. This is supported by the further claims in this sentence. Although he is communicating in writing, he still tries to make use of *action*. The emotional effect of her letter on him was horror, and this resulted in physical shuddering. The second physical effect, he says, continues at the point of writing: he is hardly able to produce words, a claim belied by the carefully constructed flow of words that follows.

The second sentence introduces the question of his image directly in an impassioned *exclamation* intended to indicate the force of the suffering her view of him has provoked. His self-presentation in the next three sentences (3–5) uses the device of *chleuasmos*, admitting some generalized weaknesses the better to convince her of his honesty and basic goodness. Two series of *antitheses* underscore the device. One sentence admits his wrongs, and suggests that he does not wish to diminish them, introducing them as he does with a *concessive exclamation* 'Ah!' and qualifying them in *hyperbolic* terms ('tels que je ne me les pardonnerai de ma vie') (3). The next sentence, by contrast, states that he is not guilty of the wrongs with which she charged him, the *exclamatory* form underlining the assertion (4). This basic *antithesis* is then repeated twice over with multiple *exclamations*, *isocolon*, and *parison* in the next sentence (5). The initial *exclamation* acts as a forceful and concise rebuttal of her charge ('Qui, moi!'). This is extended into two further *exclamations* expressed in *isocolonic* and *anaphoric* form and with *hendiadys*, both verbs having comparably similar meanings ('vous humilier! vous avilir!'). The densely concise, emphatic *figures* in this part of the *antithesis* make unambiguously plain his rejection of her view of him as someone who had sought to wound her. Just as the first part of the *antithesis* is expressed in double form with the two infinitives, so too is the second part, with two temporal clauses in the form of a *parison*. Not only does Valmont here try to defend his image as a respectable person; he subtly attempts to suggest a necessary connection between his respectability and his relationship with Tourvel. The underlying suggestion is that, in undermining him as the person he now is, she would be destroying her own creation.

There is a serious difficulty in Valmont's claims about his innocence and guilt, and it will become more evident as his letter progresses. In the first paragraph of the *exordium* he admits to wrongs, but denies that he is guilty of those of which Tourvel has accused him. This strategy potentially puts him in a good light, because it insinuatingly implies that the wrongs he would admit to are quite irrelevant to his relationship with Tourvel. In making his denial, what is he actually denying? Tourvel had raised two kinds of wrong (letter 136). She explicitly charges him with subjecting her to scorn and insult, presumably the laughter of Emilie. She fleetingly conjures up the question of his infidelity, only to let it drop: 'Je me tais sur [les torts] de l'amour; votre cœur n'entendrait pas le mien.' So although his denial of the wrongs with which she has taxed him seems, in expression, firm and unambiguous, it is in fact not at all clear at this stage what he is denying. He is certainly denying that he exposed her to scorn and insult. But does his denial extend to the charge of infidelity which she raised and dropped? It is evidently to his rhetorical advantage at this opening stage in his letter to maintain ambiguity here, while appearing simply to make a resolute denial. The interpretative difficulty resurfaces in the second paragraph of the *exordium*, where he claims that he will make a confession ('J'avouerai tout' (11)) and refers to 'un moment d'erreur' (12). It now appears that, after all, and contrary to the impression in the first paragraph, he is prepared to admit to a wrong in respect of the Emilie episode. But it is still unclear what it is. Only well into the *confirmation* does he return explicitly to the topic: 'vous vous taisez en vain sur [les torts] de l'amour: je ne garderai pas sur eux le même silence'. And even then, he writes only in the most *periphrastic* terms about his infidelity with Emilie: he does not explain how it came about, and he does not name her. From a rhetorical point of view, what is interesting about Valmont's treatment of his innocence and guilt is the way in which statements of truth, honesty, and confession are mediated through delaying tactics that ensure that at any point the proper measure of interpretative ambiguity is retained for the successful manipulation and persuasion of the letter's recipient.

After his initial passionate attempt to recast his self-image, Valmont's *exordium* adopts an accusatory tone, undermining Tourvel's confidence in her judgement (6–9). He prepares the way for his own version of events in the *narration* by claiming baldly that she has misunderstood what she saw, softening this with a *concession*: 'et je conviens [que les apparences] ont pu être contre moi'. Despite his admission that things looked against him, he asks two questions which turn the tables and seek to put Tourvel in the wrong for not searching beneath the appearance (*percontatio*) (6). In the first he uses *metaphor* to suggest her feebleness and the inadequacy of her love for him: her heart should have provided the weapons with which to combat the appearance. In the second, he again attempts to suggest the poverty of her love by *personifying* her heart and indicating the kind of response that it failed to make ('ne s'est-il pas révolté'). The suggestion of his incredulity at her lack of faith is maximized by the ensuing *exclamation* ('Vous l'avez cru cependant!' (7)). This dominant tone of incredulity continues as he explains two distinct points in her feelings on the matter (8). The first is her judgement, which he has overwhelmingly implied to be faulty, that he deliberately exposed

her to ridicule. The second is her self-accusation: had she not suc-
cumbed to her feelings for Valmont in the first place, she could not
have been hurt in this way. Valmont picks up this point to underscore more vigorously the view he had just been conveying about
the inadequacy of her love. And he clinches the point with another
exclamation and *percontatio* (9), using the language of moral turpitude
to describe both her ('dégradée') and himself ('vil') in an attempt to
provoke her to rebel against this view and find value in her love for
him. The effect of Valmont's rhetoric is, paradoxically, to make him
appear the victim of a capricious woman, whose feelings are so
insubstantial that they cannot be relied upon to give any prospect
of durability to their relationship.

The final stage of the *exordium* opens the way to an allegedly complete confession, while simultaneously developing ethical and emotional arguments that delay it (10–13). So far, Valmont has
demonstrated his hurt by his manner; now he states it explicitly and
hyperbolically ('Oppressé par le sentiment douloureux que cette idée
me cause' (10)). By commenting critically on his writing, he reinforces the impression that it is spontaneous. His comment is based
on an *antithesis* between rejecting Tourvel's version of events and
destroying it (10). It is a cunning strategy to say that he has been
wasting his time rejecting it when he should be destroying it,
because this potentially arouses some sympathy for him as an apparently wavering communicator; moreover, he plants the idea that her
version can easily be demonstrated to be false. His next statement,
unadorned, bolsters the impression that he can clarify the situation
simply: 'J'avouerai tout' (11). But it is followed by an explicit delaying tactic: 'une autre considération me retient encore' (11). These
two simple sentences contrast markedly with the long pleading one
that comes next (12). Whilst on the one hand he wants her to believe
that a simple confession will solve the problem, on the other he
wants to say that making it will in fact be difficult and painful for
him. Why does he say this? To delay getting to the point; to build
up in her more of a sense of expectation, but also to continue his
earlier strategy of transferring feelings of guilt to her for putting him
through a stressful confession; and above all, to convince her, with
all his tortured prevarication, that when he eventually writes his version of events, it will be truthful. *Antithesis* draws her attention to the
painful difference between what her accusation is forcing him to do
('retracer des faits') and what he would like to do ('[les] anéantir').

It is at this point that he refers *periphastically* to the topic of his confession ('un moment d'erreur'). The *periphrasis* is also an example of
litotes: he is trying to diminish the significance of his wrong. And the
pain that contemplating this moment of wrongdoing will cause him
is indicated by the three *parisonic* relative clauses with which it is now
fleshed out ('que [. . .], dont [. . .], et dont [. . .]'). Whatever it is he
is about to confess, he states *hyperbolically* that he would like to atone
for it ('un moment d'erreur que je voudrais racheter du reste de ma
vie'). He subtly prepares for any inadequacies in the explanation he
is about to give, and also tries to arouse some sympathy for himself
by implying that he might momentarily have been unhinged and
cannot adequately understand the cause of his error himself. The
third clause is the most emotional, combining *hyperbole* and *isocolon*
to paint a picture of himself as a wreck ('dont le souvenir doit faire
à jamais mon humiliation et mon désespoir'). There is, of course, a
gross discrepancy between his earlier claim that he is guilty of none
of the wrongs she mentioned and the desperate picture he now
paints. But it is a discrepancy that is lost in the flow of reading. Or,
if it is noticed, it is accounted a sign of his strong emotion. Either
way, Valmont gains by it. This long sentence acquires even more
emotional impact by being framed as an *interrogation*. It engages
Tourvel directly. Valmont extracts much more emotion at this point
than rhetoricians would normally recommend for the *exordium*. He
capitalizes on this in the last sentence (13), beginning with an *exclamatory* 'Ah!' and evoking the possibility of three different passions that
might result from his confession: her anger and vengeance, his
remorse. He is careful to present himself as her ready victim: 'il vous
suffira de me livrer à mes remords'.

After a long and emotional *exordium*, in which he has sought to
reverse their respective roles as victim and tyrant, the *narration*, with
its predominantly simple sentence structure and relative absence of
figures, contrives to confirm his claim that a straightforward explanation of what happened will show her the reality beneath the
appearances. The opening sentence (14) is the least straightforward
and, from a rhetorical point of view, the cleverest and most con-
trived part of his explanation. Valmont chooses to explore the *cause*
of the Emilie episode, and turns the tables unexpectedly by claiming that Tourvel is herself the main cause: he loves her so much that
he delayed leaving her, missed his appointment, and accidentally
met Emilie, who asked for a lift in his carriage. The short *interroga-*

tion inserted into his explanation ('qui le croirait?') is intended to disarm obvious objections. The *parataxis* with which most of the account is delivered creates the impression of an unexceptionable sequence of events, requiring no subordinating clauses by way of justification: 'Ce fut lui qui [. . .], et qui [. . .]' (15); 'Je vous quittai [. . .], et ne trouvai plus [. . .] (16); 'J'espérai [. . .], et ma démarche' (17); 'Emilie [. . .] n'avait pas [. . .], et me demanda [. . .]' (18); 'Je n'y vis [. . .], et j'y consentis' (19). The exception within this smooth flow of simple sentences is the one which mentions Emilie by name (18). Although the basic structure of this sentence is the same as the others, it includes an interesting sequence of relative clauses that serve to gloss the infamous Emilie in the most favourable light possible: 'Emilie que j'y trouvai, que j'ai connue dans un temps où j'étais bien loin de connaître ni vous ni l'amour'. The first relative clause ('que j'y trouvai') reinforces explicitly the impression that the whole sequence of sentences is trying to create: namely, that his meeting with Emilie was accidental. The second situates his relationship with Emilie in the past, and manages to suggest an *antithesis*, underscored by the *polyptoton* ('connu', 'connaître'), between then and now, Emilie and Tourvel, flirtation and real love. The flattery of his recipient is furthered by the juxtaposition of Tourvel and love as joint objects of the verb 'connaître', conspiring to suggest that the two terms are synonymous. The sequence of events has so far been presented as unproblematic, but even Valmont concedes that he saw a problem when his carriage met Tourvel's: 'je sentis sur-le-champ que vous seriez portée à me juger coupable'.

This explicitly *judicial* terminology heralds the end of the *narration* and the start of the *confirmation*. It is not that he has finished narrating the key episodes. It is rather that they require such delicate presentation that they are woven into an argumentation which seeks constantly to diminish their potentially damaging significance. So he explains away Emilie's scornful laughter as laughter directed at himself. And while using a resolutely *periphrastic* terminology that gives little away, he explains his night spent with Emilie as a contrast between cheap love and the purely divine love that Tourvel offers him. In his *peroration* he elaborates a series of passionate *antitheses* between the punishment that he is prepared for her to inflict on him and the love and consolations that he still hopes for, nevertheless. His letter closes with a desperate plea for her sympathy: 'Ah! Madame, me livrerez-vous aujourd'hui à un désespoir éternel?'

What is the relationship between rhetoric and truth in this letter? One of the main pleasures of the text is that it is impossible to answer this kind of question with any certainty. For her part, Tourvel is persuaded by all Valmont says to revise her version of events and to adopt his. She gives a clear account of the effect of Valmont's letter on her to Madame de Rosemonde (letter 139):

Valmont est innocent; on n'est point coupable avec autant d'amour. Ces torts graves, offensants, que je lui reprochais avec tant d'amertume, il ne les avait pas et si, sur un seul point, j'ai eu besoin d'indulgence, n'avais-je donc pas mes injustices à réparer?

Je ne vous ferais point le détail des faits ou des raisons qui le justifient; peut-être même l'esprit les apprécierait mal: c'est au cœur seul qu'il appartient de les sentir.

Tourvel believes Valmont's version of events; she takes his expressions of love and pain at face value; and she forgives him his fleeting and unplanned infidelity with Emilie. For Tourvel, Valmont's rhetoric tells the truth, because he has adapted his strategy to an audience he knows well.

Valmont also comments on his rhetoric in a letter to Merteuil (letter 138), in which he gives a different version of the Emilie episode. He calls his letter to Tourvel 'une grande épître de sentiments': 'j'ai donné de longues raisons, et je me suis reposé sur l'amour, du soin de les faire trouver bonnes'. For Valmont, at least in his account to Merteuil, his rhetoric does not tell the truth: he persuades Tourvel to believe a false version of events by writing passionately and relying on the deep love he knows she feels for him. He tells Merteuil what he claims to be the real version of events: he had been with Tourvel and left her abruptly to demonstrate his indifference to her; he had arranged to meet Emilie, and they had spent a blissful night together; when their carriage met Tourvel's, Emilie had laughed insultingly at her.

A third character comments, implicitly, on Valmont's rhetoric, and that is Merteuil. She does not believe the version of events he has given her; or rather, she points out the real difficulty of fathoming the relationship between Valmont's words and the truth (letter 141):

Parlez-moi vrai; vous faites-vous illusion à vous-même, ou cherchez-vous à me tromper? la différence entre vos discours et vos actions, ne me laisse de choix entre ces deux sentiments: lequel est le véritable? Que voulez-vous donc que je vous dise, quand moi-même je ne sais que penser?

Valmont claims that, in truth, he arranged the Emilie episode to show his detachment from Tourvel; but why does he then write Tourvel a letter based on a false version of events and false sentiments? Perhaps what is factually true gives a false account of his feelings; and conversely, what is factually false gives a true account of them. The reader has to decide. There is no narrator to offer guidance. Laclos has employed rhetorical polyphony to represent the subtleties of elusive emotions in Valmont and to suggest the links between human psychology and the art of rhetoric.

Laclos's Rhetoric

Laclos has woven a fascinatingly complex and, at times, impenetrable web of truths and falsehoods to sustain the reader's interest throughout the novel. Is there anything of which he, as author, wants to persuade the reader through his manipulation of this fictional polyphony? There are two occasions in the text when we hear would-be authoritative voices commenting on the letters, the voice of the publisher in the 'Avertissement de l'éditeur' and the voice of the editor of the supposedly real letters in the 'Préface du rédacteur'. Both precede the text of the letters and are juxtaposed, and both are almost certainly the voice of Laclos. Both suggest ways in which the text might work on the reader, but they suggest different ways.

The 'publisher' is scathing about the work. He minimizes its likely rhetorical impact on the reader. He thinks the letters are not real, but only a novel, and a far-fetched one at that. Although the setting is contemporary France, he thinks the characters' preoccupations so far removed from the real concerns of French people that the impact on the reader is likely to be minimal. The 'editor' asserts the reality of the correspondence, and describes his editorial work. He claims that the correspondence in its edited form is both pleasing and useful. Its pleasure, he says, lies in the variety of correspondents. He presents its usefulness in clearly rhetorical terms: 'On y trouvera aussi la preuve et l'exemple de deux vérités importantes.' The whole correspondence is seen here as an example of *external proof* which will convince the reader that women cannot consort with immoral men without becoming their victims (the Tourvel story), and that mothers should not entrust their daughters to the care of anyone else (Cécile's story).

Now, the contradictory views of the 'publisher' and 'editor' about the rhetorical impact of the letters need to be understood rhetorically. Both views defend the work in different ways against possible attacks: it should not be taken seriously, because it is too fantastic; if taken seriously, it is positively useful. But the conflicting voices that precede the correspondence also prepare the reader for the kind of rhetorical reading that the letters themselves call for. The reader has always to be attentive to the rhetorical situation of the writer, but the polyphonic effect is such that the reader's constant attempts to establish a firm vantage-point from which to view the rhetorical effect of either the individual letters or the work as a whole will nearly always be frustrated. The text's resistance to simplistic interpretation ensures its perennial fascination.

2. RHETORIC AND POLITICS IN ZOLA'S *GERMINAL*

The rhetorical structure of *Les Liaisons dangereuses* is close to the kind found in drama. The reader experiences the communication between characters almost without any noticeable narratorial mediation. Third-person narration is more common in prose fiction, however, and is the mainstay of the realist novel, canonically represented by Stendhal, Balzac, Flaubert, and Zola. In the third-person form, the rhetorical situation is more complex for the reader, who has not only to attend to the communication between characters but also to be aware of the constant and explicit mediation of the narrator. In novels of this kind, the predominance of the third-person narrator might seem to militate against the presence of rhetoric. But rhetoric is in fact richly present in the realist novel. At the very least, the narrator is trying to persuade readers that the story he is telling is lifelike, though he does not use conventionally rhetorical arguments to do so. He may also maintain the reader's interest by deploying the specifically rhetorical behaviour of his characters in ways likely to engage and compel: not only their verbal rhetoric, but their gestural rhetoric too, on which the narrator exercises his powers of description. And sometimes the narrator may tell a story which explicitly raises intellectual, social, or political issues, on which sides may be taken. Here rhetoric comes into its own. This is what happens in Zola's *Germinal*.[6]

Zola's novel depicts a conflict between mine-owners and mine-workers in northern France in the 1860s. There is no doubt that real-life miners, whether they had read it or not, thought of *Germinal* as a story promoting the interests of the oppressed working classes and denouncing their exploitation by the bourgeoisie. Delegations of miners attended Zola's funeral in 1902, and shouted 'Germinal! Germinal!' The novel certainly evokes sympathy for the mining community: its cramped living conditions, poor diet, perilous working practices, its dreary round of thankless, relentless, and exhausting labour. The picture is intensified into poverty, starvation, and desperation when the miners strike. It would be possible to read the novel as a succession of *hypotyposes* deployed by the narrator to arouse the reader's emotions for the suffering miners and their families. Such a reading would be reinforced by the contrasting *hypotyposes* in which the more comfortable lives of the mine-owners and managers are described, prompting, perhaps, the reader's horror and disgust at the all too evident social inequality. The conclusion to the story seems to intensify the reader's sympathy with its apparent bleakness: the strike is crushed, the large mining company's position is consolidated, the miners have gained nothing. But at the very end, the narrator offers the reader a new vision and a new emotion, hope, expressed in the form of a surrealistic *hypotyposis*. The narrator surveys the plain (VII, 6, pp. 502–3):

Aux rayons enflammés de l'astre, par cette matinée de jeunesse, c'était de cette rumeur que la campagne était grosse. Des hommes poussaient, une armée noire, vengeresse, qui germait lentement dans les sillons, grandissant pour les récoltes du siècle futur, et dont la germination allait faire bientôt éclater la terre.

The closing sentences finally allow the reader to interpret the novel's mysterious title as a *syllepsis*. The literal meaning of 'Germinal' is the month in the revolutionary calendar running from late March to

---

[6] E. Zola, *Germinal*, ed. A. Dezalay (Le Livre de Poche, 1983). Some of the techniques used by realist novelists to persuade readers of the illusion of reality have been identified by P. Hamon in 'Un Discours contraint', in R. Barthes, L. Bersani, P. Hamon, M. Riffaterre, and I. Watt (eds.), *Littérature et réalité* (Seuil, 1982), 119–80. G. Declercq has examined a section of Pt. IV, ch. 7, of *Germinal*, and has concluded that a rhetorical approach reveals some of the ambiguities of Zola's narrative technique (*L'Art d'argumenter: Structures rhétoriques et littéraires* (Éditions Universitaires, 1992), 217–23). My own analyses will confirm this view and explore it more fully.

late April. The narrator tells us that this final scene is set in April. But the *metaphorical* senses of the word are foregrounded with the imagery of germination, expressed by means of a *dérivation* ('germait', 'germination'), and revolutionary change ('faire bientôt éclater la terre'). The narrator's story and descriptions might be read as a kind of *judicial* discourse, defending labour and attacking capital.

A rhetorical reading at this level, however, neglects the polyphony of voices that the narrator produces. It is important to note that the narrator avoids any explicit political comment, whereas his charac-ters engage in it frequently. At key moments of crisis, the narrator displays characters engaging in explicitly rhetorical confrontations. Readers certainly weigh up the various stances adopted by the char-acters; but the reader has also to weigh up the narrator's stance, indicated not in explicitly rhetorical form, but by the way he chooses to present the characters' rhetoric. What emerges is no clear politi-cal line, but rather a suggestion of ideological ferment. More signif-icantly, perhaps, the narrator's presentation suggests that political argument is often coloured by the complex motivation of those engaging in it.

Politics at the Bon-Joyeux

Part IV, chapter 4, sensitizes readers to the importance of rhetori-cal skill in those who would claim to offer the striking miners polit-ical leadership. The chapter narrates a meeting at an inn, the Bon-Joyeux, of strikers who have come to listen to Pluchart, a visi-tor and representative of the Workers' International. The narrator parades a diversity of political positions, whilst showing that it is the tricks of rhetoric that determine which one the collectivity eventu-ally appears to espouse.

At one extreme, Souvarine proposes anarchy. The narrator's presentation of Souvarine's speech makes it clear why it has little persuasive impact on his audience and simultaneously implies that it should have little persuasive impact on the reader (IV, 4, pp. 233–4):

'[. . .] Il faut qu'une série d'effroyables attentats épouvantent les puissants et réveillent le peuple.'

En parlant, Souvarine devenait terrible. Une extase le soulevait sur sa chaise, une flamme mystique sortait de ses yeux pâles, et ses mains déli-cates étreignaient le bord de la table, à la briser. [. . .]

'Non! non! murmura Étienne, avec un grand geste qui écartait ces abominables visions, nous n'en sommes pas encore là, chez nous. [. . .]'

Extreme argument delivered with unusual *action* and followed by the immediate objections of Étienne and the explicitly negative evaluation (by Étienne or the narrator?) of Souvarine's stance ('ces abominables visions') ensures that the reader judges Souvarine's rhetoric and his views as unattractive.

At the other extreme is Rasseneur, who has long had the miners' ear. He wants to improve their lot by moderate means; he is pragmatic and uninterested in abstract politics. The narrator comments explicitly on Rasseneur's rhetorical strategy, particularly his use of *action* (IV, 4, p. 237):

Il semblait très ému, il toussa avant de lancer à pleine voix:
'Camarades . . .'
Ce qui faisait son influence sur les ouvriers des fosses, c'était la facilité de sa parole, la bonhomie avec laquelle il pouvait leur parler pendant des heures, sans jamais se lasser. Il ne risquait aucun geste, restait lourde et souriant, les noyait, les étourdissait, jusqu'à ce que tous criassent: 'Oui, oui, c'est bien vrai, tu as raison!' Pourtant, ce jour-là, dès les premiers mots, il avait senti une opposition sourde.

Without opposition in the past, or with only Souvarine's mad opposition, Rasseneur's calming rhetoric, fluent and uneventful, deliberately avoiding the use of gesture, perfectly suited his message of moderation and the needs of his audience as they perceived them. But, sensitive to his new rhetorical situation, Rasseneur is aware that this approach is not working. Rasseneur's old rhetoric gives way to Pluchart's new, which the assembled crowd is waiting to hear.

The crowd greets Rasseneur's familiar rhetoric with noisy insults, but falls silent to hear Pluchart's new voice. Once again, the narrator comments explicitly on the character's *action* (IV, 4, p. 238):

Sa voix sortait, pénible et rauque; mais il s'y était habitué, toujours en course, promenant sa laryngite avec son programme. Peu à peu, il l'enflait et en tirait des effets pathétiques. Les bras ouverts, accompagnant les périodes d'un balancement d'épaules, il avait une éloquence qui tenait du prône, une façon religieuse de laisser tomber la fin des phrases, dont le ronflement monotone finissait par convaincre.

Not only is Pluchart's voice new; it is more varied in its effects than Rasseneur's. The narrator's witty *zeugma* in the phrase 'promenant sa laryngite avec son programme' is not necessarily at the expense of Pluchart, but certainly invites the reader to assess his rhetoric from the same distance as the narrator. Pluchart is able to change the volume of his voice, he uses it to heighten effects of *pathos*, and, unlike Rasseneur, he deploys gestural rhetoric. The narrator even identifies that aspect of Pluchart's rhetoric that most persuades audiences to believe his arguments. It is the repeated low monotone with which he delivers the ends of his sentences.

If *Germinal* is a novel about politics, it is also about all those personal and rhetorical traits that come into play when human beings interact with each other. This political meeting ends with hastily and chaotically assembled support for Pluchart and the International, when the gendarmes arrive to disperse the illegal gathering. But as much as a battle of ideologies, the narrator has offered the reader a picture of those interpersonal rivalries through which ideologies are expressed, and which, in the end, determine their success or failure.

Mass Politics in the Forest

The meeting at the Bon-Joyeux is important for the subsequent political gathering, which is, in a sense, the rhetorical highpoint of the novel (IV, 7). There is a danger that the strike might collapse. Étienne summons a meeting of miners with a view to strengthening support for the strike. The place for the meeting is, significantly, the forest of Vandame. Étienne explains: the gendarmes expelled them from the Bon-Joyeux; nobody will drive them from the forest (p. 270). The forest is also important for some descriptive details that the narrator gives to guide the reader's response to the scene. The meeting takes place in the evening, and throughout his account the narrator makes recurrent reference to the moon, not only a temporal marker, not only an aspect of Zola's poeticization of realistic narrative, but also a technique deployed by the narrator for passing indirect comment on the characters' rhetorical behaviour.

At the beginning of the meeting there is a dispute between Rasseneur and Étienne. Rasseneur is still smarting from his defeat at the Bon-Joyeux, and 'il s'était juré d'avoir sa revanche' (p. 270). Already the narrator is isolating those feelings of personal pride that drive the contributions of the participants; and it is unwillingness to see the dispute with Rasseneur drag on that prompts Étienne suddenly to change the rhetorical situation. He jumps on to a tree trunk to address the 3,000 assembled miners. What follows is predominantly the narrator's account of Étienne's speech. He is later described by the narrator as an 'orateur' (p. 274). A worker, formally uneducated, Étienne delivers a speech which the narrator presents to the reader in explicitly rhetorical terms, and which lends itself to traditional rhetorical analysis. It is fascinating for the reader to observe the interaction between Étienne and the crowd: the crowd's reactions are carefully noted by the narrator. A second source of interest arises from the interaction between Étienne's speech and the narrator's own response to it.

He begins by satisfying briefly the conventional requirements of an *exordium*, using *action* ('une voix éclatante' (p. 270)) to secure the attention of his listeners, and winning them over with suggestions of solidarity and righteousness (ibid.): 'Ici, nous sommes libres, nous sommes chez nous, personne ne viendra nous faire taire, pas plus qu'on ne fait taire les oiseaux et les bêtes!' The three short phrases, each restating the same idea, and the *comparison* (they are as free as the birds and the beasts) all suggest the simplicity and directness of his appeal to a mass audience. The narrator indicates the crowd's immediate approval after this concise *exordium*: 'Un tonnerre lui répondit, des cris, des exclamations' (ibid.). The narrator also introduces the moon imagery. Although Étienne is raised above the crowd, everyone is in darkness, because the moon is too low to strike anything other than the highest branches on the trees.

Étienne proceeds with the *narration*. The narrator relies predominantly on narratorial comment and free indirect speech in presenting this part of Étienne's address. The orator's *action* is first described ('Il leva un bras dans un geste lent, il commença' (p. 271)), then his tone of voice, which changes from the *exordium* ('sa voix ne grondait plus, il avait pris le ton froid d'un simple mandataire du peuple qui rend ses comptes' (ibid.)). The narrator's next comment forces the reader to stand back and make a critical assessment of Étienne's rhetoric. The reader is told that Étienne now delivers the speech that he had prepared to give at the Bon-Joyeux, but had been prevented from doing so by the arrival of the gendarmes: 'il débutait par un historique rapide de la grève, en affectant l'éloquence scientifique: des faits, rien que des faits' (ibid.). It is of course entirely appropriate, in rhetorical terms, that the *narration* should appear to be a dispassionate, objective account of events. But the narrator's account of the speech makes it clear that Étienne inevitably puts the miners in a more favourable light than the management. The narrator also manages to suggest a certain *naïveté* in Étienne's belief in Pluchart and the International in the way he sums up Étienne's excuses for their inadequate assistance: '[il] excusait en quelques phrases l'Internationale, Pluchart et les autres, de ne pouvoir faire davantage pour eux, au milieu des soucis de leur conquête du monde' (p. 270). In this phrase we hear the narrator's own rhetoric, his use of *irony*, working on the reader and superimposed on the rhetoric of Étienne. Étienne's *narration* lays bare the worsening nature of the strike for the miners, and ends with two questions which focus the strikers on the decision that they need to take now; this is the crux of his speech. Should the strike continue, and how can they make it succeed?

It is the aim of Étienne's *deliberative* speech to persuade them to continue to strike. After a pause, he begins the *confirmation*. Again the narrator comments on Étienne's *action*: he speaks 'd'une voix changée' (p. 270); and he is described with exaggerated *antonomasias*, which once again make the reader stand back and assess Étienne's rhetoric critically: 'Ce n'était plus le secrétaire de l'association qui parlait, c'était le chef de bande, l'apôtre apportant la vérité' (p. 271). The confusion of ideologies already paraded before the reader suggests that the narrator is being ironically sceptical in his reference to Étienne's speech as the repository of truth. The narrator's recourse to free indirect speech conjures up something of the flavour of Étienne's style (IV, 7, pp. 271–2):

[1] Est-ce qu'il se trouvait des lâches pour manquer à leur parole? [2] Quoi! depuis un mois, on aurait souffert inutilement, on retournerait aux fosses, la tête basse, et l'éternelle misère recommencerait! [3] Ne valait-il pas mieux mourir tout de suite, en essayant de détruire cette tyrannie du capital qui affamait le travailleur? [4] Toujours se soumettre devant la faim jusqu'au moment où la faim, de nouveau, jetait les plus calmes à la révolte, n'était-ce pas un jeu stupide qui ne pouvait durer davantage? [5] Et il montrait les mineurs exploités, supportant à eux seuls les désastres des crises, réduits à ne plus manger, dès que les nécessités de la concurrence abaissaient le prix de revient. [6] Non! le tarif de boisage n'était pas acceptable, il n'y avait là qu'une économie déguisée, on voulait voler à chaque homme une heure de son travail par jour. [7] C'était trop cette fois, le temps venait où les misérables, poussés à bout, feraient justice.

[8] Il resta les bras en l'air.

[9] La foule, à ce mot de justice, secouée d'un long frisson, éclata en

applaudissements, qui roulaient avec un bruit de feuilles sèches. [10] Des voix criaient:

'Justice! . . . Il est temps, justice!'

The narrator amply conveys the powerful directness of Étienne's communication with his audience through the use of *interrogation*, the simplest and most compelling form of rhetorical question (1, 3, 4), short *exclamatory* phrases ('Quoi!' (2), 'Non!' (6)), and an *exclamatory* sentence (2). It is significant that these emotional *figures* predominate at the very beginning of the *confirmation*, when his tone of delivery changes after the more measured *narration*. In fact this passage is striking for its use of *pathos* so early in the speech. Étienne intimidates and threatens, suggesting that only cowards would abandon the strike (1). With a brief *hypotyposis*, evoking a return to work, he aims to make them feel afraid at the thought of accepting once again intolerably low wages and the consequences of poverty (2). He stokes them up, wanting them to feel a destructive hatred for the exploitative proprietors (3). He tries to make them feel the pointlessness of repeatedly going back to work only to have to strike again later (4). He probes their weak spots, the degrees of hunger with which they are so familiar, whether at work or on strike, supporting this point with the *figure* of *geminatio* ('se soumettre devant la faim jusqu'au moment où la faim [. . .]' (4)). He develops a *hypotyposis* ('il montrait' (5)), in which he dwells on the suffering and hunger of the miners, and bases it on an argument from the *place* of *opposites*: the narrator's phrase 'les mineurs [. . .] supportant à eux seuls' suggests a contrast between the miners' life-style and that of the managers. From this graphic evidence of a wretched future, Étienne draws the conclusion that the reduction in wages is not acceptable (6), and intimates the consequence of this view, that the miners will have to take action to demand justice. The narrator's account implies that Étienne is being rousing rather than specific in this early stage in the *confirmation*. This more inspirational, less rationalistic verbal rhetoric is accompanied by equally rousing gestural rhetoric: 'Il resta les bras en l'air' (8). One interpretation of this *action*, thrown into prominence by the single paragraph in which it is expressed is that Étienne appeared to the mass of strikers as a Christ-like saviour figure. The narrator certainly indicates the rapturous reception of the first part of Étienne's *confirmation* (9–10).

At this point the narrator's account becomes momentarily more distant from Étienne's words, and he passes judgement in explicitly rhetorical terms on Étienne's performance. His tone rises: 'Étienne s'échauffait' (p. 272). His *elocution* is rough-hewn: 'Il n'avait pas l'abondance facile et coulante de Rasseneur. Les mots lui manquaient souvent' (ibid.). The narrator is even attentive to links between *elocution* and unconscious *action*: 'il devait torturer sa phrase, il en sortait par un effort qu'il appuyait d'un coup d'épaule' (p. 272). The narrator isolates those aspects of Étienne's rhetoric that have most impact on his audience, his use of imagery and *action*: 'il rencontrait des images d'une énergie familière, qui empoignaient son auditoire; tandis que ses gestes d'ouvrier au chantier, ses coudes rentrés, puis détendus et lançant les poings en avant, sa mâchoire brusquement avancée, comme pour mordre, avaient eux aussi une action extraordinaire sur les camarades' (ibid.). Although the narrator maintains the reader's critical distance from Étienne's speech by avoiding significant amounts of direct speech, he gives an example of the orator's direct and simple imagery, taken from what is in effect the beginning of the second part of the *confirmation* (ibid.):

Le salariat est une forme nouvelle de l'esclavage, reprit-il d'une voix plus vibrante. La mine doit être au mineur, comme la mer est au pêcheur, comme la terre est au paysan . . . Entendez-vous! la mine vous appartient, à vous tous qui, depuis un siècle, l'avez payée de tant de sang et de misère!

The *metaphor* of wage as enslavement, the argument from *comparison* (mine/miner, sea/fisherman, earth/peasant), and the financial *metaphor* justifying their alleged right to ownership of the mine ('payée de tant de sang et de misère') all draw on simple concepts within the personal experience of Étienne's audience, and are powerfully woven together by an emotional delivery ('une voix plus vibrante') and by the climactically *exclamatory* tone, engineered by the pause, the imperative, and then the longer *exclamatory* statement.

For the rest of the speech, the narrator prefers to interweave concise paraphrase with his own comments, both explicit and implicit: 'Carrément, il aborda des questions obscures de droit, le défilé des lois spéciales sur les mines, où il se perdait' (pp. 272–3). The criticism of Étienne for addressing issues that are beyond not only his listeners' competence, but also his own, is ironically balanced by the narrator's physical description of the scene and of the audience's response to it. From these obscure legal topics Étienne concludes that the miners should reclaim the mine, and he accompanies this with a gesture, extending his arm over the land around him. The narratorial irony lies in the reintroduction, at this point, of the moon. It is the narrator's description of the combined effect of the moon and Étienne's gestures that accounts for the audience's rapturous reaction, not Étienne's words themselves: 'A ce moment, la lune, qui montait de l'horizon, glissant des hautes branches, l'éclaira. Lorsque la foule, encore dans l'ombre, l'aperçut ainsi, blanc de lumière, distribuant la fortune de ses mains ouvertes, elle applaudit de nouveau, d'un battement prolongé' (p. 273). Here is yet another image of Étienne as a saviour figure, engineered ironically, and without Étienne's knowledge, by the chance angle of the moonlight.

The last part of his *confirmation* merges into a *peroration*. He broadens the scope of his speech substantially, no longer addressing the problem of the strike, but issues of a very general social and political nature. The narrator again avoids direct speech, and his favourite device in recounting Étienne's views is *gradatio*. In fact, the narrator uses this *figure* so insistently here that it almost becomes *conglobatio*, a heavy-handed piling up of different elements. It can be substantival (ibid.):

Puis, quand le peuple se serait emparé du gouvernement, les réformes commenceraient: retour à la commune primitive, substitution d'une famille égalitaire et libre à la famille morale et oppressive, égalité absolue, civile, politique et économique, garantie de l'indépendance individuelle grâce à la possession et au produit intégral des outils du travail, enfin instruction professionnelle et gratuite, payée par la collectivité.

It can be a list of verbs, as in the immediately following sentence (pp. 273–4):

Cela entraînait une refonte totale de la vieille société pourrie; il attaquait le mariage, le droit de tester, il réglementait la fortune de chacun, il jetait bas le monument inique des siècles morts, d'un grand geste de son bras, toujours le même, le geste du faucheur qui rase la moisson mûre, et il reconstruisait ensuite de l'autre main, il bâtissait la future humanité, l'édifice de vérité et de justice grandissant dans l'aurore du vingtième siècle.

The narrator's relentlessly and obsessively enumerative style to evoke Étienne's vision of a socialist future leads the reader to question the narrator's appreciation of that vision. Étienne seems to be moving ever further away from the pressing needs of his immediate audience, and he seems to be sketching out abstractions without any

realistic sense of how they can be realized. It is the narrator's preferred *figure*, *gradatio*, that persuades the reader to adopt a critical
stance towards Étienne's rhetoric here. But this stance is confirmed
by the narrator's explicit comment: 'la raison chancelait, il ne restait
que l'idée fixe du sectaire' (p. 274). Having prompted this critical distance from Étienne's words, the narrator, with further irony, quotes
the final words of the speech directly, before describing the audience
response and the new position of the moon (ibid.):

> 'Notre tour est venu, lança-t-il dans un dernier éclat. C'est à nous d'avoir
> le pouvoir et la richesse!'
> Une acclamation roula jusqu'à lui, du fond de la forêt. La lune main-
> tenant blanchissait toute la clairière, découpait en arêtes vives la houle des
> têtes, jusqu'aux lointains confus des taillis, entre les grands troncs grisâtres.
> [. . .] Ils ne sentaient plus le froid, ces ardentes paroles les avaient chauffés
> aux entrailles. Une exaltation religieuse les soulevait de terrre, la fièvre
> d'espoir des premiers chrétiens de l'Église, attendant le règne prochain de
> la justice.

On the one hand, the narrator's evocation of the moon suggests
some connivance between nature and ideology, as well as intimat-
ing the favourable reception of Étienne's ideas. On the other hand,
the narrator's use of *hyperbole* in his choice of *metaphor* ('exaltation
religieuse', 'premiers chrétiens de l'Église', 'le règne prochain de la
justice') invites a certain scepticism about the feasibility of Étienne's
vision and a smile at the naïve enthusiasm with which it is greeted.
There is a clear contradiction between hope, on the one hand, and
the possibility of its realization on the other. The narrator describes
the reception in some detail before noting Étienne's reaction to it.
It is a reaction that suggests mixed motivation in Étienne: 'Étienne
goûtait l'ivresse de sa popularité. C'était son pouvoir qu'il tenait,
comme matérialisé dans ces trois mille poitrines dont il faisait d'un
mot battre les cœurs' (p. 275). His pleasure is as much the personal
satisfaction of adulation as the success at broadcasting his ideas. Étienne will speak again before the meeting is over, and the narrator
will suggest further complications in his motivation.

The narrator now contrasts Étienne's unpolished but effective
rhetorical skills with those of other speakers. Rasseneur has been
provoked by Étienne's message to address the crowd in different and
more moderate terms. But the narrator indicates how the strikers'
rhetorical tastes have changed in these desperate times: 'Son élocu-
tion facile, sa parole coulante et bonne enfant, qui avait si longtemps

charmé, était traitée à cette heure de tisane tiède, faite pour endormir les lâches' (ibid.). Rasseneur is not heard, and is driven away to shouts of 'A bas le traître!' (pp. 275–6). A differently contrasting speaker is the old man Bonnemort, whose well-intentioned, rambling digressions are conjured up in free indirect discourse until the narrator reports Étienne's sudden interruption.

To the crowd listening to Bonnemort's recollections, bored but polite, it must seem that Étienne is seizing the moment to inject new passion into Bonnemort's contribution. The narrator uses direct speech to record Étienne's opening words: 'Camarades, vous avez entendu, voilà un de nos anciens, voilà ce qu'il a souffert et ce que nos enfants souffriront, si nous n'en finissons pas avec les voleurs et les bourreaux' (p. 277). The old man before him and all that he has said are efficiently turned into *external proof* of the miners' suffering. Appealing to the concerns of his audience, he breezily argues that, without decisive action, the future will be full of suffering Bonnemorts. And he fuels hatred of the mine-owners with a dual *antonomasia* ('les voleurs et les bourreaux'). The narrator is careful to indicate Étienne's revitalizing *action* too: 'Il fut terrible, jamais il n'avait parlé si violemment. D'un bras, il maintenait le vieux Bonnemort, il l'étalait comme un drapeau de misère et de deuil, criant vengeance' (ibid.). And as if spurred on by this use of graphic *external proof*, he proceeds to use further examples from the crowd. The Maheu family are used as a kind of *hypotyposis*, passionately evoked in all their suffering. In retrospect, this speech is the real *peroration* of his earlier address, heavily exploiting *pathos* as he reaches his climax with the *personification* of capital as a monster to be slain (p. 278). When he then asks the questions to which all his *deliberative* oratory has been leading (will they continue the strike? and how?), the crowd gives him answers that show he has their full support: yes, death to the strike-breakers.

But this final speech, which appears to the crowd as the height of Étienne's involvement and support, is read differently by the reader of the novel. The narrator indicates a motivation underlying Étienne's speech, one that is quite different from political or social concern. Étienne speaks as a jealous rival of Chaval for the love of Catherine Maheu: 'Il venait de reconnaître Chaval parmi les amis au premier rang. L'idée que Catherine devait être là l'avait soulevé d'une nouvelle flamme, d'un besoin de se faire acclamer devant elle' (p. 277). Running through the novel is the story of Étienne's love for

Catherine. It is significant that when he appears to be his most politically active, spurring on 3,000 miners to continue the strike, he is
also, and perhaps above all, trying to impress the woman he loves
by his skills as a public speaker. The narrator adds further ironies.
At the end of his speech, Étienne realizes that Catherine is not there
to hear it after all. The climax of the meeting is an enraged clash
between Chaval and Étienne, on the surface a clash of ideologies,
but not far beneath it a struggle between two men for one woman.
Chaval, who had been claiming the right to carry on working at his
pit, Jean-Bart, changes tack, and tries to impress by expressing the
intention to persuade other workers at Jean-Bart to strike. The
chapter ends with apparent unanimity for a strike: 'L'ouragan de ces
trois mille voix emplit le ciel et s'éteignit dans la clarté pure de la
lune' (p. 280). The narrator again indicates the presence of the
moonlight, ironic or sympathetic, at the reader's choice.

The next chapter (V, 1) shows the consequences at Jean-Bart the
following day. Chaval clashes with Catherine, who wants to work,
and then with Deneulin, the mine-owner, who eventually persuades him not to strike. So, having begun the chapter by urging
his fellow-workers to put down their tools, he closes it by pleading
with them to pick them up again. What persuades Chaval to perform such a potentially shaming volte-face? Not Deneulin's eco-
nomic arguments. Deneulin has the skill to read his interlocutor's
character, and plays up to his vanity by promising promotion.
Chaval, meanwhile, thinks of getting one up on Étienne: 's'il s'en-
têtait dans la grève, il n'y serait jamais que le lieutenant d'Étienne,
tandis qu'une autre ambition s'ouvrait, celle de passer parmi les
chefs' (p. 288). Once again, the individual's personal motivation,
hidden from public view, determines the public statement of political opinion.

There are so many conflicting voices in *Germinal*—characters
clashing, now politically, now personally; the narrator presenting
their views, now ironically, now sympathetically—that it is impossible to see the novel as attempting to persuade the reader of any
particular political creed. Rather, Zola shows rhetoric at work in
complex ways in the realist novel: how ordinary characters use verbal and gestural rhetoric in their daily lives, how the narrator uses
it to influence the reader's responses to the characters. Above all,
there is a subtle exploration of the shifting relationship between
rhetoric, the expression of ideas, and human psychology. What

seems to be a rhetoric of political ideology turns out to be a rhetoric of rivalry in love.

3. DOMESTIC RHETORIC IN NATHALIE SARRAUTE'S
LE PLANÉTARIUM

When we turn to Nathalie Sarraute's *Le Planétarium*, we might expect to engage in a different kind of rhetorical reading from that elicited by most other novels.[7] Written in the same decade as Beckett's *En attendant Godot*, it exhibits a similar spirit of iconoclasm and experimentalism. It is generally seen as an example of the *nouveau roman*, which was consciously practised to undermine the narrative techniques which the realist novel of the nineteenth century had developed so successfully. The *nouveau roman* alerted readers to the alleged easy comprehensibility and artificiality of character, plot, and narrator in the realist novel by offering characters, plots, and narrators that challenged or frustrated the expectations of readers accustomed to the traditional realist narrative.

Readers of *Le Planétarium* are dimly aware of the presence of fictional characters for some time before they can give them names and a social context; and some characters are never named. As they turn the pages, readers become conscious of a series of recurrent preoccupations that can be pieced together to form a story; but it might seem a banal story for a novel of 250 pages (a young Parisian couple want to take over their aunt's flat, which is larger than theirs, and the man in the couple, Alain Guimier, is keen to impress the writer Germaine Lemaire). Although, strictly speaking, *Le Planétarium* is a third-person narrative, the narrator offers the readers little purchase on the characters and the story. The narrator is highly elusive. It must be presumed that he or she determines the order in which the scenes are arranged, the point of view from

---

[7] N. Sarraute, *Le Planétarium* (Gallimard, 1959). Her theoretical work *L'Ère du soupçon* (Gallimard, 1956) is crucial reading. The best introductory study of Sarraute is V. Minogue, *Nathalie Sarraute and the War of Words* (Edinburgh: Edinburgh University Press, 1981), which deals (among other things) with questions of narrative perspective. On the metaphorical language of *Le Planétarium*, see J. A. Fleming, 'The Imagery of Tropism in the Novels of Nathalie Sarraute', in W. M. Frohock (ed.), *Image and Theme: Studies in Modern French Fiction* (Cambridge, Mass.: Harvard University Press, 1969), 74–98. On the *nouveau roman* in general see A. Jefferson, *The Nouveau Roman and the Poetics of Fiction* (Cambridge: Cambridge University Press, 1980).

which they are seen, and the mode of discourse (direct speech or, much more commonly, free indirect discourse) in which they are presented to the reader. But the narrator seems, otherwise, to be hard to pin down.

In terms of its rhetorical structure, therefore, the novel is clearly very different from *Les Liaisons dangereuses* and *Germinal*. Whatever the differences between these two earlier novels, both set up a series of rhetorical encounters, which are contextualized so sharply that readers can clearly identify the orator figure and his or her inter-locutor(s). It could be Valmont writing seductively to Tourvel, or Étienne addressing the assembled strikers, or the narrator of *Germinal* persuading readers to take a distance from Étienne's rhetoric. The rhetorical situation could usually be clearly delineated, and the reader's pleasure lies in part in the observation of the rhetorical strategies at work. There is nothing simplistic about this. Both these novels depict numerous orators, and the reader's task is to weigh up the significance of all the voices in the polyphony. None the less, Laclos and Zola always help the reader to focus on the rhetorical situation depicted within the fictional world and (in the case of Zola) the rhetorical situation involving the narrator and readers.

This clearly identifiable rhetorical situation on which readers have traditionally been invited to focus seems to have dissolved in *Le Planétarium*. The preponderance of free indirect discourse has the unsettling effect of making the reader uncertain as to whose voice can be heard (character's or narrator's or even which character's) and whether a character is speaking or thinking. This structure might seem to remove the rhetorical situation from the centre of the reader's interests. However, the characters' preoccupations that fill the pages of the novel seem compellingly to invite a rhetorical approach. It is true that they are not engaged in seduction and cover-up, even less in social and political struggles. Their concerns seem banal: the choice of a door handle, the preference for an old-fashioned *bergère* over leather armchairs, a distaste for carrots. Despite the displacement of the traditional rhetorical situation, Nathalie Sarraute writes in such a way as to extract enormous con-flictual potential from the plainest episodes of daily life; and her recourse to free indirect discourse suggests that our daily conflicts and rivalries occupy us relentlessly, whether we are speaking aloud or not. Many of the recurrent images in the text liken human beings to animals, birds, and insects. What such images aim to convey is the pattern of attack and defence, the struggle for survival, which are very much the preoccupations of an orator.

The climax of the novel is Alain's and Gisèle's move into the flat of Aunt Berthe, who finally agrees to move into a smaller flat. This is the result of a long sequence of confrontations. Alain's father, Pierre, puts to his sister, Berthe, the proposition that she move into a smaller flat so that Alain and Gisèle can move into hers; he is rebuffed (pp. 176–83). Alain tries to bully his aunt into moving, claiming that she has no right to occupy a large flat alone (pp. 184–8). Named and nameless acquaintances debate Alain's methods (pp. 189–98). The negative assessment is that he has gone beyond acceptable methods of persuasion: 'chez moi, dans ma famille, c'est impensable, tout ça . . . Je ne parle même pas d'employer des procédés pareils, évidemment il ne peut en être question, mais d'essayer, même par la persuasion . . .' (p. 196). The positive assessment is sceptical of hearsay: 'Vous êtes méchants. Moi vous aurez beau dire tout ce que vous voudrez contre les Guimier, je ne le croirai pas tant que je ne l'aurai pas vu de mes yeux' (ibid.). This particular section of the novel (the sections are not numbered in the way that chapters conventionally are) engages readers in a kind of *judicial* rhetoric. Alain's character is weighed up, but no clear verdict is reached.

In the next two sections the *judicial* discourse focusing on Alain continues, but is intermingled with more *deliberative* discourse focused on the aunt's move. A further meeting between Pierre and Berthe ensues in which Berthe is reassured about Alain's good character, and decides that a move is well worth consideration after all; she also confirms that her wealth will eventually secure Alain's future. This meeting is presented first from Berthe's point of view (pp. 199–214), then from Pierre's (pp. 215–28). As far as the reader can tell from the surface appearance of this encounter, Pierre defends Alain's character, but positively deters Berthe from giving way to Alain over the flat. It appears to be Berthe's own decision to consider the move. At the end of the second version, however, Pierre's strategy in dealing with his sister is called into question, and there is a very slight suggestion that he may have calculated his approach carefully to bring Berthe round to taking, apparently by herself, the decision that all along he really wanted her to take (p. 227):

L'avenir d'Alain est assuré . . . Eh bien, tant mieux, parbleu . . . Il n'y a plus à s'inquiéter. Son rôle, à lui, de père, est depuis longtemps achevé. Il faut enfin savoir prendre ses distances, se détacher. Il est grand temps . . . Tout cela ne le concerne plus. Son devoir est accompli. Il ne reste plus rien à faire. La tâche est terminée. Aucun effort ne pourrait plus rien modifier. Et c'est très bien ainsi, c'est parfait. Il sent un bien-être dans tous ses membres tandis qu'il s'étire . . . une exquise sensation de légèreté, un goût d'autrefois qu'il avait oublié, de liberté, d'insouciance . . . Libre enfin, délesté. Qu'ils fassent tout ce qu'ils voudront . . . Elle l'observe, on dirait qu'elle a compris, elle paraît contente, apaisée.

This passage is ambiguous. It is also crucial, retrospectively, for assessing the nature of the confrontational strategies deployed in the encounter between Pierre and Berthe. This is free indirect discourse giving readers a glimpse into Pierre's thoughts now that the encounter is, to all intents and purposes, finished. The insistent suggestion of a task successfully completed ('rôle [. . .] achevé', 'devoir [. . .] accompli', 'tâche [. . .] terminée') might invite readers to see Pierre's aim all along as that of persuading Berthe to consider moving out of her flat. In this light his expressed preference for her not to move, not to give into Alain, not to continue to spoil him as she has always done, would be a deception. The phrases 'Elle l'observe, on dirait qu'elle a compris' might support this view: Pierre wanted to hide his rhetorical ploy and his contentment with its success, but she looks now as if she has penetrated it. Yet this passage can also be read without any suggestion of deviousness. Though the outcome is not the one he had recommended, he is content with it because it means that he need no longer intervene on behalf of his spoilt son. The passage would then speak of his huge personal relief to be freed of the burden of his inadequately resourced son ('bien-être', 'exquise sensation de légèreté', 'liberté', 'insouciance'). These two interpretations may seem contradictory: Pierre the underhand orator, Pierre the sincere orator. So two possible versions of Pierre—underhand or sincere—are seen retrospectively to cohabit in both of the two different accounts of this meeting with Berthe.

It is illuminating to compare the narrator's two presentations of a vital moment in the encounter, when Pierre explicitly discourages Berthe from helping Alain. This is the version that is presented second, from Pierre's point of view (pp. 221–2):

[1] Mais bien sûr, mais tu céderas. [2] Ils peuvent dormir tranquilles. [3] C'est déjà fait . . . [4] La douleur, la fureur chez lui ont atteint leur point

culminant. [5] Tu n'a jamais rien fait d'autre que de céder à tous ses caprices idiots . . . [6] Tu l'as rendu comme il est . . . [7] Il n'y a plus rien à faire maintenant . . . [8] Il n'y a qu'à continuer. [9] Seulement moi je vais te dire . . . [10] Je vais te dire moi ce qu'il lui faut, à Alain, en ce moment. [11] Et ce n'est pas ton appartement. [12] Est-ce que tu te rends compte de sa situation? [13] Est-ce que tu vois où il en est? [14] Il ferait mieux de se dépêcher de finir sa thèse et de demander un poste quelque part . . . [15] S'il y arrivait, ce serait déjà beau. [16] S'il pouvait être nommé dans n'importe quel trou, ce serait mieux que de courir les salons, de meubler les appartements, de vivre aux crochets—parfaitement—de ses beaux-parents . . . [17] la douleur qu'il ressent est celle qu'on éprouve quand on vous cautérise une plaie, quand on vous coupe un membre gangrené, il le faut, jusqu'au bout, il faut couper carrément, il faut arracher de soi cette tumeur, cette chair malade qui est en train de le contaminer, il ne faut pas se laisser pourrir tout entier . . . [18] il crie presque et elle se recule effrayée . . . [19] Voilà ce qu'il lui faut à notre Alain, si tu veux le savoir: songer à son avenir . . . [20] Les beaux-parents ne leur laisseront à peu près rien, ce n'est que de la frime, tout ça, ce luxe, de la poudre aux yeux . . . [21] et il n'est pas reluisant, son avenir, si tu veux tout savoir . . . [22] je te dis toute ma pensée . . . [23] ce mariage l'a abruti et ce milieu snob, idiot, cette Germaine Lemaire, moi je l'ai vue, une vieille fausse gloire qui s'entoure de jeunes imbéciles comme lui pour se faire encenser . . . [24] Ah, il s'agit bien d'appartements luxueux . . . [25] Il a devant lui—je sais ce que je dis—un tout petit avenir et il devra s'en contenter . . . [26] la douleur maintenant, encore vive, est en train de régresser . . . [27] Un petit avenir bien modeste, une petite sécurité, une retraite, un traitement. [28] Encore heureux s'il arrive à décrocher un poste quelconque, il n'est pas agrégé, sa thèse, je ne sais pas ce qu'elle vaudra . . . [29] s'il parvient à obtenir un poste de suppléant, de lecteur, ce sera encore beau . . . [30] La douleur se fait plus sourde, il semble qu'elle s'apaise peu à peu . . . [31] Il s'agit bien de s'installer à Paris, dans cinq pièces, dans les beaux quartiers, de donner des réceptions . . . des fêtes . . . comme ils disent . . . des fiestas, comme il dit . . .

Whatever intention lies behind Pierre's words, their effect is to persuade Berthe to contemplate leaving her flat to make way for Alain and to promise him a secure financial future. It is fascinating for the reader to observe Pierre's persuasive manner in action, particularly in a text in which one might not have expected to see traditional rhetoric at work. Yet Sarraute shows how the basis of traditional rhetoric (deliberation, judgement, praise, and blame) is deeply embedded in the human psyche.

At four points in this speech, though without any typographical indication of a change in the use of language, the words cease to be those addressed by Pierre to his sister. At these four points (4, 17–18, 26, 30) the words represent either the narrator's intervention, commenting on Pierre's *action*, or Pierre's thoughts about his own feelings as he speaks. What all four comments have in common is a reference to Pierre's pained emotion: the word 'douleur' is used four times. And there is a logical pattern to Pierre's pain. It is at its height at the beginning, and gradually diminishes as his speech develops. This is significant, because the beginning of this speech marks a new direction in the confrontation. Until this moment, the dialogue had been constituted primarily of Berthe's attack on Alain's character and Pierre's defence of it. But now the tables are suddenly turned. As soon as Berthe is reassured about Alain's character, she affirms her affection for him, and suggests that she might easily have given into his request, had he been gentler. Pierre seizes on this point to begin a speech which is partly in *judicial* mode, attacking his sister's weakness for her nephew, and partly in *deliberative* mode, appearing to persuade her not to move out of her flat. It is therefore appropriate for his speech to seem most pained at the moment of the initial attack, and for him gradually to calm down as he moves into *deliberative* mode.

Pierre's *elocution* is characterized by elements of the *low style*. His sentences are short and predominantly simple, and he uses a colloquial style ('n'importe quel trou' (16), 'que de la frime, tout ça' (20)) and an equally colloquial sentence structure: there are several examples of *hyperbaton* (e.g. 'et il n'est pas reluisant, son avenir' (21), 'sa thèse, je ne sais pas ce qu'elle vaudra' (28)). This *low style* is at its most acutely pointed and aggressive in the *paratactic* opening sentences when Pierre is accusing Berthe of weakness (1–3, 5–8). With a mixture of *irony* ('Ils peuvent dormir tranquilles' (2)), feigned or real despair ('C'est déjà fait' (3)), and direct accusation ('Tu l'as rendu comme il est' (6)), his words seem to seek to shame her for her weakness, though without any hope of her redemption. Pierre seems to be suggesting that she will never be able to act otherwise towards her nephew than by spoiling him. This impression is reinforced by his recourse to *hyperbole* ('Tu n'a jamais rien fait d'autre', 'céder à tous ses caprices' (5)). The climax of this accusatory section makes explicit the point about her inability to reform herself: 'Il n'y qu'à continuer' (8). But what appears to have been *judicial* discourse up to this point turns out to have been a preparation for the *deliberative* discourse that follows. Together they form an *antithesis*: what appears to be the only way forward, continuing to spoil Alain, is contrasted with what Pierre claims Alain needs, and that is not the kind of easy and immediate assistance that Berthe is ready to offer.

Pierre introduces his new topic, what Alain really needs, with a complex, but still colloquial, pattern of repetitions. First, repetition of the same words in close proximity (*geminatio*) in *chiastic* arrangement: 'moi je vais te dire . . . Je vais te dire moi' (9–10). This same sentence is completed by a repetition of the same referent as both pronoun and noun, a kind of *metabole*: 'ce qu'il lui faut, à Alain' (10). Readers assume that these devices are designed to ensure an arresting start to the presentation of Pierre's main point. This arresting rhetoric is enhanced next by the plain negative ('ce n'est pas ton appartement' (11)), and then by a double *communicatio*, the kind of question designed to force the interlocutor to think: 'Est-ce que tu te rends compte de sa situation? Est-ce que tu vois où il en est?' (12–13). These questions lead Pierre to exploit the *place* known as *circumstances*, and, in an *antithesis*, he contrasts Alain's potential circumstances (if he were to complete his thesis and secure a job) (14–15) with his actual circumstances. His expressed preference for Alain finding 'n'importe quel trou' (16), with all the lowly connotations that the pejorative term implies, constitutes a devastating critique of the pretentious literary life-style he currently cultivates but cannot afford. This life-style is conjured up emphatically in a triple *parison* in the form of an ascending *gradatio*: 'de courir les salons, de meubler les appartements, de vivre aux crochets—parfaitement—de ses beaux-parents' (16). The *parenthesis* is presumably *ironical*. His emotional delivery at this point is characterized as almost shouting, and either he, or the narrator, notes its effect on Berthe: she is frightened and shrinks back (18).

Pierre insistently reiterates his main theme ('Voilà ce qu'il lui faut à notre Alain' (19)), but this time sums up his message concisely and positively ('songer à son avenir' (19)). His choice of words here and the way he goes on to develop this message are significant for the ambiguity inherent in the rhetorical situation. Thinking of Alain's future could mean denying him the flat he wants and forcing him to make his own way in life. This appears to chime in with Pierre's views so far. But thinking of Alain's future could imply making financial provision for him in the future. This sense is implicit in his next point when he turns to the *effects* of Alain's currently empty life-style: he and his wife will end up with almost nothing because his parents-in-law have almost nothing to give them. The flimsiness of the parents-in-law and their life-style are satirically expressed in two *isocolonic* phrases *chiastically* arranged: 'ce n'est que de la frime, tout ça, ce luxe, de la poudre aux yeux' (20). It is by tying this picture of Alain's bleak future to his parents-in-law and their minimal financial support that Pierre's language creates an implicit contrast between them and Berthe, who is in a position to help much more. Pierre may, or may not, be intending Berthe to step in and bail Alain out; he certainly does not invite her to do so explicitly. But his persuasion can be read that way, and is certainly read that way by Berthe.

Pierre continues to explore the current and future *circumstances* of Alain in ways that simultaneously mock him and paint him as a victim. It is as if there was nothing wrong with Alain's character until it was corrupted by the circles into which his marriage introduced him ('ce mariage l'a abruti et ce milieu snob' (23)). Pierre certainly describes him as a young imbecile blithely following in the camp of Germaine Lemaire. But it is implied that he is in a crowd of others whose circumstances have put them in that position. Whether the effect is intentional or not, Pierre's presentation of Alain, though satirical, still leaves scope for pity; that is the effect his speech has on Berthe. Pierre continues to play off *antithetically* the very modest future that he can foresee for Alain (25, 27–8, 29) with his son's current pretensions (24, 31). *Epitrochasmus* is the device he uses to make these contrasts stand out: on the one hand, 'Un petit avenir bien modeste, une petite sécurité, une retraite, un traitement' (the modesty emphasized by the adjectival *geminatio*) (27), on the other, the double sequence 's'installer à Paris, dans cinq pièces, dans les beaux quartiers, de donner des réceptions . . . des fêtes . . . comme ils disent . . . des fiestas, comme il dit' (the speaker making his sceptical stance plain with the qualifying phrases 'comme ils disent' and 'comme il dit') (31). The most belittling, yet also pathetic, image of his son is in the evocation of the kind of jobs he might hope to obtain: 's'il parvient à obtenir un poste de suppléant, de lecteur, ce sera encore beau' (29): these are the lowest positions in the teaching hierarchy.

Readers know the effect on Berthe of Pierre's rhetoric, not from what they read in this passage, but from their memory of the previous account of this same episode from her point of view. But the precise intention behind Pierre's words is difficult to pin down. The reader can only be intrigued by his combination of criticism of Berthe for wanting to help Alain, his mockery of his son, and his fleetingly pathetic evocations of his son's future. He seems to speak with colloquial vigour and determination, but his words have a life of their own through the patterning created by the *figures* of *chiasmus*, *isocolon*, *antithesis*, and *gradatio*, and offer an uncertain purchase on his real feelings. It is as if to assert the primacy of words and their ultimate independence of human control that Sarraute writes an extraordinary digression, quite at odds with the surrounding language (17):

la douleur qu'il ressent est celle qu'on éprouve quand on vous cautérise une plaie, quand on vous coupe un membre gangrené, il le faut, jusqu'au bout, il faut couper carrément, il faut arracher de soi cette tumeur, cette chair malade qui est en train de le contaminer, il ne faut pas se laisser pourrir tout entier . . .

This is the second of the interventions that comment on Pierre's delivery and feelings, but it is quite different from the others and quite different from his own spoken words. In a speech which in part mocks Alain's literary pretensions, is it possible to interpret this short burst of purple prose as free indirect discourse? The narrator might then be mocking Pierre, imputing the *grand style* to the thoughts of a man whose speech is in the *low style*. It might be preferable to read this sentence as the eloquent intervention of the narrator reading the character's mind. The sense of this *conglobatio* of medical and surgical imagery is clear: Pierre wants to be free from the burden of worry that his son imposes on him. But the question as to whom the expression of this thought should be attributed is teasingly unclear.

One response to this puzzle is to take the view that *Le Planétarium* is a text about language as much as about people. The very structures adopted for the 'telling' of the story make readers think constantly about the source and purpose of the language that they read on the page, the relationship between a character's language and his or her feelings, and the way in which language affects those who hear it. The sense that these matters are important in the text is reinforced when we remember how differently the same moment of the encounter between Pierre and Berthe is presented to the reader in the immediately preceding section of the novel, from Berthe's point of view (pp. 209–10):

[1] 'Mais bien sûr, à qui le dis-tu? Mais tu céderas sûrement. Ils peuvent dormir tranquilles. C'est déjà fait. [2] Elle sent qu'il fait un effort pour contenir la rage méprisante qui affleure dans sa voix, mais il n'y parvient pas, elle s'échappe en un fin sifflement . . . [3] Tu n'as jamais rien fait d'autre que de céder à tous ses caprices . . . tu l'as rendu comme il est, un enfant gâté, pourri. Il n'y rien à faire maintenant. Seulement moi je vais te dire . . .'

[4] C'est donc là en lui toujours, après tant d'années, aussi virulent qu'autrefois, quand cela lui faisait si peur qu'elle n'osait pas emmener le petit dans une pâtisserie, lui acheter un jouet . . . le pauvre petit savait bien qu'il était inutile de demander à son père—bien trop égoïste, trop mesquin—c'était à elle que le pauvre amour s'adressait, à sa Tatie . . . Mais cela, justement, il ne pouvait pas le supporter, cette tendresse de l'enfant pour elle, leur joie quand ils sortaient ensemble, ce bonheur qu'elle éprouvait à le gâter un peu, pauvre petit bonhomme toujours un peu triste, qui n'a pas connu la tendresse d'une mère . . . Le voilà parti maintenant, elle connaît l'antienne, elle sait, c'est de sa faute à elle, bien sûr, voilà ce qu'elle en a fait: un faible, un bon à rien . . . [5] 'Ce n'est pas ton appartement qu'il lui faut à Alain, en ce moment . . . L'idée même est absurde, je l'ai toujours pensé . . . Mais ils m'ont tellement assommé avec ça, supplié . . . j'étais ravi que tu aies refusé . . . Je vais te dire, moi, ce qu'il lui faut . . . Est-ce que tu te rends compte de sa situation? Il ferait bien mieux, crois-moi, de se dépêcher de finir sa thèse et de se faire nommer n'importe où, dans n'importe quel trou . . . Il aurait un traitement assuré, au moins, et une retraite, plus tard, ce n'est pas à négliger, ce serait mieux que de vivre de bricoles, d'expédients, de demander à ses beaux-parents . . . Un avenir modeste, ah, bien sûr . . .' [6] Il est content maintenant, il les a arrachés l'un à l'autre, ils sont séparés, il les tient serrés chacun dans une main, il les tourne l'un vers l'autre et la force à regarder: voilà avec qui elle allait s'acoquiner, avec qui elle allait préparer l'avenir, marcher la main dans la main, ah il est joli, son compagnon, son enfant chéri . . . un petit snob, un paresseux . . . [7] 'Ce mariage . . . Germaine Lemaire . . . il ne s'agit pas de vivre à Paris dans cinq pièces, dans les beaux quartiers . . . qu'ils se regardent donc . . . passer son temps à faire des installations . . . [8] il les cogne l'un à l'autre . . . [9] donner des réceptions . . . des fiestas, comme ils disent . . . [10] il lui fait mal . . . il rit, ravi, là, encore un bon coup: et sois tranquille, ce ne sera pas pour nous . . .'

The two versions of this episode are roughly comparable, but, in places, crucially different. Pierre's speech is recognizable as the same in both passages: the order is the same and there is a substantial overlap in phraseology. But sometimes one version gives a more, and the other a less, elaborate account of his words. For instance, in the account in Pierre's perspective, his preliminary accusation against Berthe is expressed as: 'Tu l'as rendu comme il est . . .' (6); but in Berthe's perspective Pierre is recorded as saying 'tu l'as rendu comme il est, un enfant gâté, pourri' (3). Conversely, in Pierre's perspective, he speaks a neat combination of *antithesis, parison*, and *gradatio*, when deriding Alain's current arrangements: 'S'il pouvait être nommé dans n'importe quel trou, ce serait mieux que de courir les salons, de meubler les appartements, de vivre aux crochets—parfaitement—de ses beaux-parents . . .' (16); but in Berthe's perspective this whole development is fractured and intermingled with other elements: 'Il ferait bien mieux, crois-moi, de se dépêcher de finir sa thèse et de se faire nommer n'importe où, dans n'importe quel trou . . . Il aurait un traitement assuré, au moins, et une retraite, plus tard, ce n'est pas à négliger, ce serait mieux que de vivre de bricoles, d'expédients, de demander à ses beaux-parents . . .' (5). Most significantly, the phrase that in Pierre's perspective suggests that he might possibly be asking her to support Alain financially in the future ('songer à son avenir' (19)) is missing in Berthe's perspective. The effect of these variations, by the time readers have read both accounts, is to unsettle any belief that language might be able to record the world accurately. What Pierre says is different when filtered through his own mind from the version as filtered through Berthe's. The narrator sets both accounts in direct speech, with all its apparent authoritativeness, the better to reinforce the reader's puzzlement.

The two accounts differ more significantly still in their narratorial interventions, and the differences are of the utmost importance for a rhetorical reading, and suggest the text's compelling interest in the intricate processes of persuasion. The account in Pierre's perspective indicates the changing degree of passion and vigour with which he speaks. There is something of this in the account in Berthe's perspective. The reader observes her attentiveness to his most pained *action* at the start of this speech: 'Elle sent qu'il fait un effort pour contenir la rage méprisante qui affleure dans sa voix' (2). And towards the end of this passage, what is presented in his perspective as the gradual recovery of calm, in Berthe's perspective looks like a smiling satisfaction with his own rhetoric as he makes more and more points that tell against Berthe: 'il lui fait mal . . . il rit, ravi, là, encore un coup' (10). This comment, and other more explicit ones (4, 6), show the unexpected way in which Pierre's rhetoric operates on his sister. Whatever his intentions, his words seem to be criticizing her for indulging her nephew. The effect is to open up old wounds in their brother–sister relationship. She sees him as the unloving father, envious of the close bond she has been able to establish between herself and Alain; rightly or wrongly, she sees the purpose of his rhetoric as being to drive aunt and nephew definitively apart. It is this interpretation of his speech that prompts Berthe to do the opposite of what her brother seems to be urging, and to make further gestures of indulgence towards Alain, moving out of her flat and securing his financial future.

Despite the iconoclastic aims of the *nouveaux romanciers*, traditional rhetoric is present in ever more complex ways in their work. Subtextually Nathalie Sarraute is waging a campaign against the realist novel and its allegedly simplistic account of the relationship between words and reality. In *Le Planétarium* she does this with the help of her narrator, who does not unambiguously reveal himself or herself to the reader, but whose deliberately unsettling presence can be felt all along: in the reluctance to name and contextualize characters, in the relentlessly indeterminate use of free indirect discourse, and in the apparently authoritative use of direct speech, the truthful status of which is thrown open to question when the same speech is recorded twice and differently. With unconventional rhetorical means, Sarraute argues the case for the subjectivity of reality and for the pre-eminence of language in fiction. It is a case she makes explicitly in her collection of theoretical essays, *L'Ère du soupçon*. Her attention to language, and especially her awareness of the importance of *elocution*, in her campaign to write a new kind of novelistic dialogue is here abundantly apparent (p. 121):

[Le lecteur] sait qu'ici chaque mot compte. Les dictons, les citations, les métaphores, les expressions toutes faites ou pompeuses ou pédantes, les platitudes, les vulgarités, les maniérismes, les coq-à-l'âne qui parsèment habilement ces dialogues ne sont pas, comme dans les romans ordinaires, des signes distinctifs que l'auteur épingle sur les caractères des personnages pour les rendre mieux reconnaissables, plus familiers et plus 'vivants': ils sont ici, on le sent, ce qu'ils sont dans la réalité: la résultante de mouvements montés des profondeurs, nombreux, emmêlés, que celui qui les perçoit au-dehors embrasse en un éclair et qu'il n'a ni le temps ni le moyen de séparer et de nommer.

Sarraute here associates the use of language in her writing with her interest in the subconscious forces at work in the human mind. She implies a major difference between her use of language and that of more traditional novelists. But, whilst it is true that the reader of *Le Planétarium* faces real obstacles in identifying any conscious persuasive or linguistic intention behind her characters' words, it is also the case that there are uncertainties in the persuasive intention behind the words of Valmont and Étienne in Laclos's and Zola's allegedly more traditional novels.

The rhetorical structures of the three novels examined in this chapter could hardly be more varied. In *Les Liaisons dangereuses* it is the character axis that predominates; in *Germinal* the reader has to be equally attentive to the character axis and the narrator–reader axis; and in *Le Planétarium* the reader is interested in the rhetoric on the character axis whilst being constantly frustrated as to the degree of interference operating on the narrator–reader axis. There are obviously also glaring differences in subject-matter: sex, politics, domestic trivia. Yet all these novels are built around probing explorations of human behaviour and human psychology. Rhetoric, an art of persuasive interaction, affords the critic numerous insights into the psychological complexities of fictional characters, as well as into the communicative practices of their creators.

5

POETRY

Some modern readers might be reluctant to see poetry in a rhetorical perspective, believing it to be the domain of originality and imagination. Such a reluctance might derive from the attitude to the poet propagated by the romantics in the first half of the nineteenth century. For them, the poet was a special kind of individual, using language in ways not entirely explicable in rationalistic terms. Earlier generations of poets, it is true, had anticipated the romantic view. In the ancient world poets sometimes claimed to have the power of prophecy, and in Renaissance France some poets, like Ronsard, claimed to be divinely inspired ('les vers viennent de Dieu, / Non de l'humaine puissance').[1] Yet, despite the special status to which poets in the early modern period occasionally laid claim, no poet would have seen rhetoric as alien to poetry. In two respects poets needed technical knowledge that went beyond that offered by rhetoricians: they needed to know the conventions of versification and those attaching to the different genres of poetry, like epic, ode, or madrigal. The works of poetics written to teach these skills sometimes referred to poetry as the art of second rhetoric. Poetry was seen to require its own skills not instead of, but in addition to, the skills of traditional rhetoric.

For all that Ronsard evokes divine inspiration, his prose writings on poetry clearly advertise the technical skill required, and make plain the links between poetry and rhetoric. His *Abbrégé de l'art poëtique françois* of 1565 contains sections on *invention, disposition,* and *elocution.* When he writes the 1587 preface to his epic poem *La Franciade,* he discusses *elocution* in explicitly rhetorical terms (*Œuvres,* xvi. 334):

---

[1] P. de Ronsard, *Œuvres complètes,* ed. P. Laumonier, I. Silver, and R. Lebègue (20 vols., Hachette, then Droz, then Didier, 1914–75). The lines quoted are from the 'Ode à Michel de l'Hospital', 475–6 (*Œuvres,* iii. 145). On poetic theory in the sixteenth century see G. Castor, *La Poétique de la Pléiade: Etude sur la pensée et la terminologie du XVIe siècle,* trans. Y. Bellenger (Champion, 1998) (first pub. as *Pléiade Poetics* (Cambridge: Cambridge University Press, 1964)).

Tu dois davantage, Lecteur, illustrer ton œuvre de paroles recherchees & choisies, & d'arguments renforcez, tantost par fables, tantost par quelques vieilles histoires, pourveu qu'elles soient briefvement escrites & de peu de discours, l'enrichissant d'Epithetes significatifs & non oisifs, c'est a dire qui servent à la substance des vers & par excellentes, & toutefois rares sentences.

The interesting point here is that Ronsard envisages rhetorical devices in the way rhetoricians themselves traditionally conceived them. The carefully chosen words, arguments, stories, fables, and epithets are not to be employed simply for decorative purposes (though they certainly enrich the text); they are there to fulfil some other useful communicative function within their context.

A century later the rhetorical perspective remains crucial in Boileau's poem about the composition of poetry, *L'Art poétique* (1674). At the very beginning he refers to the poet's need for divine inspiration, without which he might as well remain silent:[2]

> C'est en vain qu'au Parnasse un téméraire auteur
> Pense de l'art des vers atteindre la hauteur.
> S'il ne sent point du Ciel l'influence secrète,
> Si son astre en naissant ne l'a formé poète,
> Dans son génie étroit il est toujours captif.

After this preliminary caution, the rest of Boileau's poem gives practical advice to be followed. The poet is expected to work hard on the technical side of composition. Above all, he is to think constantly of the effect of his writing on the reader or audience. Readers want variety: 'Voulez-vous du public mériter les amours?/Sans cesse en écrivant variez vos discours' (canto I, 69–70). Readers want harmonious verse: 'N'offrez rien au lecteur que ce qui peut lui plaire./Ayez pour la cadence une oreille sévère' (I, 103–4). Spectators of tragedies want passionate conflict, not drily argued debate (III, 21–4):

> Vos froids raisonnements ne feront qu'attiédir
> Un spectateur toujours paresseux d'applaudir,
> Et qui, des vains efforts de votre rhétorique
> Justement fatigué, s'endort ou vous critique.

---

[2] N. Boileau-Despréaux, *Œuvres*, ed. J. Vercruysse (2 vols., Garnier–Flammarion, 1969), ii. 87–115 (Chant I, 1–5). On Boileau's conception of the role of the poet see D. C. Potts, ' "Une carrière épineuse": Neoplatonism and the Poet's Vocation in Boileau's *Art poétique*', *French Studies*, 47 (1993), 20–32.

Spectators want a concise exposition: 'Je me ris d'un acteur qui, lent à s'exprimer,/De ce qu'il veut d'abord, ne sait pas m'informer' (III, 29–30). In recommending that poets think carefully about what they want to write before choosing the words in which to express themselves, Boileau is following the traditional rhetorical order according to which *invention* comes first and *elocution* later (I, 150–2):

> Avant donc que d'écrire, apprenez à penser.
> Selon que notre idée est plus ou moins obscure,
> L'expression la suit, ou moins nette, ou plus pure.

Though a work of poetics and not of rhetoric, Boileau's poem embodies a rhetorical conception of poetry as ideas and words carefully chosen to have the desired impact on readers and audiences.

Towards the end of the eighteenth century, André Chénier's poem 'L'Invention', calling for a new attitude to poetry in France, anticipates some of the views of the romantic poets a few decades later, but without entirely breaking with tradition. It accords with some of his other poems, like 'La République des lettres' and 'Le Poète divin, tout esprit, tout pensée', in claiming a mysterious and divine power in the best poets. But it suggests that the subject-matter of poetry needs to change. Instead of pursuing well-worn themes, poets should write about subjects that are new to the age. This might, for instance, include the poetic expression of Newtonian physics:[3]

> Et qu'enfin Calliope, élève d'Uranie,
> Montant sa lyre d'or sur un plus noble ton,
> En langage des Dieux fasse parler Newton!

The title of the poem is ambiguous, and the ambiguity helps to put Chénier's poem on the threshold of romanticism. He could be referring to rhetorical *invention*, advising poets to turn to new sources for their material. But he could also be gesturing to the modern, non-rhetorical sense of 'invention' as inventiveness. The poet as someone inventive, creative, imaginative, working with material from the modern world, is an idea that the romantics will take further. Chénier's understanding of *invention* may look forwards, but his approach to *elocution* does not. For him, though the material might be new, the poetic genres to be practised and the language to be

---

[3] A. Chénier, *Poems*, ed. F. Scarfe (Oxford: Blackwell, 1961); 'L'Invention', ll. 296–8 (p. 68).

deployed continue to be those of the ancients, or imitations of them. This combination of new *invention* and traditional *elocution* is expressed in the most memorable line of the poem: 'Sur des pensers nouveaux faisons des vers antiques' ('L'Invention', 184). The (limited) novelty of Chénier's vision does nothing to detract from the continuing rhetorical perspective in which poetry was viewed.

It is Hugo who attempts most vigorously and most eloquently to shatter the bonds that for centuries linked rhetoric and poetry. In his poem 'Réponse à un acte d'accusation', published in his collection *Les Contemplations* in 1856 (book I, poem 7), written in 1854, though, for polemical reasons, dated 1834, Hugo adopts a *judicial* discourse to defend himself retrospectively against the attacks of those republicans who thought that, as a writer, Hugo was not making an adequate contribution to the promotion of democratic principles.[4] Hugo implicitly makes the point that poetry does not have to be art for art's sake, and explicitly argues that the poetic style he adopted participated in the revolutionary spirit of contemporary politics. Thus poetic revolution becomes a *metaphor* for political change, and, in circular fashion, this is expressed by *metaphors* relating to the *ancien régime* and the Revolution. His greatest contribution, he claims, is to have demolished linguistic hierarchies, just as the Revolutionaries toppled social ones. First he evokes the rigid separation of terms (p. 43):

> La poésie était la monarchie; un mot
> Etait un duc et pair, ou n'était qu'un grimaud;
> Les syllabes pas plus que Paris et que Londre
> Ne se mêlaient; ainsi marchent sans se confondre
> Piétons et cavaliers traversant le Pont-Neuf;
> La langue était l'état avant quatre-vingt-neuf.

Then he narrates the linguistic revolution and accords himself a central role (ibid.):

> Alors, brigand, je vins; je m'écriai: Pourquoi
> Ceux-ci toujours devant, ceux-là toujours derrière?
> Et sur l'Académie, aïeule et douairière,
> Cachant sous ses jupons les tropes effarés,
> Et sur les bataillons d'alexandrins carrés,
> Je fis souffler un vent révolutionnaire.
> Je mis un bonnet rouge au vieux dictionnaire.

[4] V. Hugo, *Les Contemplations*, ed. P. Albouy (Gallimard, 1973).

Hugo's use of political imagery to describe the state of poetic language before and since his own compositions is sustained. It is particularly interesting to see how he uses rhetoric in his argumentational framework. Rhetoric is unambiguously linked to a former age, and is presented as an active participant in the linguistic rigidity which Hugo claims to have swept away. Hence the *tropes* are linked to the aged and conservative Académie Française. Rhetorical *figures* are like timid aristocrats before the guillotine (p. 44):

> Discours affreux!—Syllepse, hypallage, litote,
> Frémirent; je montai sur la borne d'Aristote,
> Et déclarai les mots égaux, libres, majeurs.

Periphrasis is singled out for special destruction: 'J'ai de la périphrase écrasé les spirales' (p. 46). The *ethos* and *pathos* of *invention* suffer too: 'Sur leur axe,/On vit trembler l'athos, l'ithos et le pathos' (p. 45). It is all-out war on rhetoric: 'Guerre à la rhétorique et paix à la syntaxe!' (p. 45). Hugo's poem is rousing, but profoundly inconsistent. For the devastating attack on rhetoric is conducted by means of an extraordinary array of rhetorical devices. The lines 'Syllepse, hypallage, litote,/Frémirent' combine *personification, epitrochasmus,* and *alliteration* in /l/. The line 'On vit trembler l'athos, l'ithos et le pathos' combines *personification, homoioteleuton* (with the repetition of the /ɔs/ ending), and a witty *zeugma* ('l'athos', Mount Athos, having a quite different sense from 'l'ithos' and 'le pathos', and phonetically burlesquing the Greek rhetorical terms). Hugo's attack on rhetoric is, therefore, deeply rhetorical. Rhetoric is obliging and lends itself to the case for its own destruction; yet it thereby asserts its indestructibility.

For Hugo, poetic language is not a rhetorical construct. It is a mysterious creation. The poem immediately following the 'Réponse', called simply 'Suite', dwells on the mystery of poetic language: 'Les mots sont les passants mystérieux de l'âme' (p. 49). Hugo concludes the poem with a clear indication of the divine inspiration from which the poet benefits: 'Car le mot, c'est le Verbe, et le Verbe, c'est Dieu' (p. 51). His theoretical (if not practical) rejection of rhetoric is accompanied by this assertion of the spirituality inherent in the poetic medium.

In order to defend himself in the 'Réponse', Hugo vastly overstates his case. It is true that he makes some contribution towards extending the range of vocabulary in French poetry and that he goes further than some of his predecessors in breaking the tight relationship between sentence structure and alexandrine. This latter achievement is the sense of his battle-cry 'Guerre à la rhétorique et paix à la syntaxe!' The obvious manifestations of syntax's allegedly greater freedom is the more liberal use of *enjambement*. It is this same point that lies behind Verlaine's violent attack on rhetoric in his poem 'Art poétique', first published in 1874: 'Prends l'éloquence et tords-lui son cou!'[5] The sense in which the words 'rhétorique' and 'éloquence' are being used here by both Hugo and Verlaine is quite different from rhetoric as the art of persuasion. It is a much diminished sense. If the attack on rhetoric is focused primarily on the alleged constraints it imposes on the length of a poet's sentences, rhetoric as a whole emerges relatively unscathed.

Baudelaire was more generous and more perceptive in his understanding of the potential of rhetoric (and prosody). In the *Salon de 1859* he writes:[6]

Il est évident que les rhétoriques et les prosodies ne sont pas des tyrannies inventées arbitrairement, mais une collection de règles réclamées par l'organisation même de l'être spirituel. Et jamais les prosodies et les rhétoriques n'ont empêché l'originalité de se produire distinctement. Le contraire, à savoir qu'elles ont aidé l'éclosion de l'originalité, serait infiniment plus vrai.

This could almost be a response to Hugo. Baudelaire uses a similar pattern of imagery (tyranny and spirituality) to make a point that contradicts Hugo's. Without denying the spiritual role of the artist, he shatters the link Hugo made between rhetoric and rigidity, claiming that rhetoric is an open-ended art that can be used with different degrees of expressivity depending on the user. Whilst rejecting Hugo's poetic theory, Baudelaire's comment serves as a good defence of Hugo's, and his own, practice. Moreover, Baudelaire's intuition of a link between rhetoric and our spiritual being tallies with the observation that emerged from the analysis of the works of Laclos, Zola, and Sarraute in Chapter 4, that the operations of rhetoric are closely related to the workings of the human psyche.

Theorists of poetry in the twentieth century do not discuss traditional rhetoric very much. Paul Valéry is an exception. It is true that, in a romantic perspective, he evokes the linguistic abuses to

---

[5] P. Verlaine, *Œuvres poétiques*, ed. J. Robichez (Garnier, 1969), 261–2, at 261.
[6] C. Baudelaire, *Curiosités esthétiques, L'Art romantique, et autres œuvres critiques*, ed. H. Lemaitre (Garnier, 1962), 328.

which he believes the *figures* can give rise; but he then vigorously and
eloquently defends their role in poetry:[7]

Or ces figures, si négligées par la critique moderne, jouent un rôle de première importance, non seulement dans la poésie déclarée et organisée, mais
encore dans cette poésie perpétuellement agissante qui tourmente le vocabulaire fixé, dilate ou restreint le sens des mots, opère sur eux par symétries
ou par conversions, altère à chaque instant les valeurs de cette monnaie
fiduciaire; et tantôt par les bouches du peuple, tantôt par les besoins
imprévus de l'expression technique, tantôt sous la plume hésitante de
l'écrivain, engendre cette variation de la langue qui le rend insensiblement
tout autre.

Valéry is very much of his age in restricting the field of rhetoric to
the *figures* of *elocution*. But at least he offers a lyrical defence of their
transforming powers and their ability to make readers see anew.

The preceding pages do no more than allude to some of the key
moments in the history of the theoretical links between rhetoric and
poetry. Their purpose is mainly to suggest that, whatever shifts there
may have been over the centuries in the attitude of poets to rhetoric,
rhetoric is consistently, from the sixteenth to the twentieth centuries,
an issue with which poets grappled in one way or another. The rest
of this chapter considers the fruitfulness of a rhetorical reading of
the work of two poets, both of whom clearly belong to a rhetorical
tradition: d'Aubigné's *Les Tragiques* (1616) and two of Baudelaire's
love poems from *Les Fleurs du Mal* (1861); and turns finally to assess
the suitability of rhetoric for approaching a twentieth-century poem,
Aimé Césaire's *Cahier d'un retour au pays natal* (1939), written in part
as an attempt to break away from the earlier traditions of French
verse.

1. PROTESTANT RHETORIC IN D'AUBIGNÉ'S *LES TRAGIQUES*

Nobody familiar with d'Aubigné's long poem *Les Tragiques* will be
surprised to find it in a work on rhetoric.[8] Indeed a standard criti-

---

[7] P. Valéry, *Œuvres*, ed. J. Hytier, Bibliothèque de la Pléiade, (2 vols., Gallimard,
1957–60), i. 1289–90 (from an article entitled 'Questions de poésie', first pub. in 1935).

[8] A. d'Aubigné, *Les Tragiques*, ed. J.-R. Fanlo (2 vols., Champion, 1995). The text of
the poem is in vol. i. I quote exactly from this edition, which preserves d'Aubigné's original and often unusual spelling. M. Quainton, *D'Aubigné: 'Les Tragiques'* (Grant and Cutler,
1990), offers an excellent introduction to the poem, very sensitive to its use of rhetoric
and wisely critical of those who treat d'Aubigné's rhetorical practice dismissively (e.g.

cal response to the poem has been to deplore d'Aubigné's abuse of rhetoric. Yet the sort of rhetoric to be found in *Les Tragiques* is entirely consistent with the kind of poem that it is. Much of it was written between 1577 and 1579, inspired by the violent persecution of Protestants by Roman Catholics in the French religious wars. D'Aubigné continued to work on it, and finally published it in 1616. It is an unambiguously partisan poem in which the narrative voice is firmly on the side of the Protestants. The poem's rhetoric is designed to make this abundantly plain.

It is difficult to fit the poem into any existing genre. It is often called an epic, though it lacks the clear narrative line of most epic poetry. It is perhaps best seen as an example of *demonstrative* writing, the poetry of praise and blame. This is clearly the approach envisaged by d'Aubigné in some remarks in his verse preface (Préface, 367–72):

> Je n'excuse pas mes escrits
> Pour ceux-là qui y sont repris:
> Mon plaisir est de leur desplaire:
> Amis, Je trouve en la raison,
> Pour vous et pour eux fruict contraire,
> La medecine et le poison.

The poem is intended to displease Roman Catholics, even to destroy them in words. Its privileged readers, the author's friends, are Protestants, who are intended to be fortified by what they read. There is some speculation that d'Aubigné chose to publish the poem finally in 1616 in order to urge Protestants not to accept any compromise with Roman Catholic political authority. If this is so, the poem also had a *deliberative* function on publication.

Although d'Aubigné claims that he has put little thought into the *disposition* of the poem ('Il y a peu d'artifice en la disposition' ('Aux lecteurs', p. 13), his claim is somewhat belied by his demonstration of the work's structure and the relationship between structure and *elocution*. Book I ('Misères') depicts contemporary France torn asunder by the religious wars; it is characterized by 'un style bas et tragicque n'excedant que fort peu les loix de la narration' ('Aux lecteurs', p. 11). Book II ('Princes') attacks the Valois kings and their

J. Bailbé, *Agrippa d'Aubigné, poète des 'Tragiques'* (Caen: Publications de la Faculté des Lettres et Sciences Humaines, 1968), who comments that 'les beautés éclatantes sont ternies par de graves défauts, qui tiennent au fait que d'Aubigné n'a pas su se dégager de ses souvenirs d'érudit et des procédés artificiels de la rhétorique' (p. 396)).

role in the persecution of Protestants, adopting 'un style moyen, mais satyrique en quelque façon' (p. 11). Book III ('La Chambre dorée') employs the same style as book II and attacks corrupt figures in the legal establishment. Book IV ('Les Feux') marks a further notch up in the stylistic hierarchy ('un style tragicque moyen', p. 11), portraying a succession of Protestant martyrs. Book V ('Les Fers') depicts once again the suffering of the Protestants during the religious wars, this time clearly in the context of a cosmic confrontation between God and Satan; again there is an increase in the stylistic register ('du style tragicque eslevé, plus poeticque et plus hardy que les autres [livres]', p. 11). Finally books VI ('Vengeances') and VII ('Jugement') employ the highest stylistic register, which even d'Aubigné presents with a hint of apology: these two books 'd'un style eslevé tragicque, pourront estre blasmez pour la passion partizane: Mais ce genre d'escrire a pour but d'esmouvoir, et l'autheur le tient quitte s'il peut cela sur les esprits des-jà passionnez ou pour le moins aequanimes' (p. 13). The two books depict in turn the persecutors of the true Church over the centuries and the Last Judgement, when both good and bad will rise from the dead and receive their just rewards. D'Aubigné's account of the structure of the poem and its gradually developing *elocution* suggests that he is deliberately building up to an emotional crescendo when Roman Catholics will be filled with horrific fear and Protestants with teeming hope.

Whilst the poem clearly exhibits more structural design than d'Aubigné explicitly admits, there is a certain amount of repetitiveness between and within the seven long books. A strictly logical account of the poem's structure might highlight redundancies, but there is another way of accounting for the structure that leaves nothing spare. The whole poem is a vast and elaborately woven *antithesis* between Protestants and Catholics, God and Satan, Good and Evil. Every detail serves insistently to evoke the reader's sympathy for what d'Aubigné sees as the right side of the *antithesis*. This structure is evident in d'Aubigné's alternation between a rhetoric of praise and one of blame. The following examples will show how d'Aubigné's blatant and insistent use of rhetorical *figures* leaves the reader no room for manoeuvre in assessing degrees of praise and blame. A detailed rhetorical approach can sometimes reveal a writer's ambiguities and uncertainties, but, when applied to *Les Tragiques,* it serves to confirm d'Aubigné's vision of a world of absolute religious certainty. A rhetoric of undiluted blame is reserved for Catherine de Médicis and the Cardinal de Lorraine, both leaders in the Roman Catholic cause, whilst a rhetoric of praise evokes the heavenly delights that await the favoured few.

Catherine de Médicis

Catherine de Médicis, widow of Henri II and mother of succeeding kings François II, Charles IX, and Henri III, is seen by d'Aubigné as one of the Protestants' prime contemporary enemies. He makes a sustained, vitriolic attack on her character in 'Misères', of which the following lines are a part (I, 815–38):

> Neron laissoit en paix quelque petite part,
> Quelque coing d'Italie esgaré à l'escart
> Eschappoit ses fureurs; quelqu'un fuioit de Sylle
> Le glaive et le courroux en la guerre civille:
> Quelqu'un de Phalaris evitoit le Taureau;   5
> La rage de Cinna; de Caesar le couteau:
> Et (ce qu'on feint encor' estrange entre les fables)
> Quelqu'un de Diomede eschappoit les estables:
> Le lion, le sanglier qu'Hercule mit à mort,
> Plus loing que leur buisson ne faisoient point de tort: 10
> L'Hydre assiegoit Lerna, du Taureau la furie
> Couroit Candie, Anthee affligeoit la Lybie.
>   Mais toy qui au matin de tes cheveux espars
> Fais voile à ton faux chef branslant de toutes parts,
> Et desploiant en l'air ta perruque grisonne,   15
> Les païs tous esmeus de pestes empoisonne:
> Tes crins esparpillez, par charmes herissez,
> Envoient leurs esprits où ils sont addressez:
> Par neuf fois tu secouë, et hors de chaque poincte
> Neuf Demons conjurez descochent par contraincte.   20
>   Quel antre caverneux, quel sablon, quel desert,
> Quel bois, au fond du quel le voiageur se perd,
> Est exempt de malheurs? Quel allié de France
> De ton breuvage amer n'a humé l'abondance?

This passage is part of an *ethopoeia*, an attack on Catherine's character. D'Aubigné wants to paint the Queen Mother as a tyrant who has plumbed new depths of tyranny. The *place* that is the basis of the above passage is *comparison*. In order to suggest her inescapable tyranny, d'Aubigné compares her to some legendary tyrants, and then implies that she is worse. He builds up a degree of expectation by listing first the famous tyrants (1–12), then Catherine's relationship to them (13–24).

A characteristic feature of d'Aubigné's style is his enthusiastic overstatement. This can be seen in the *conglobatio* of tyrants. He begins with tyrants from ancient history: Nero, whose cruel pleasure at watching Rome burn he has evoked just before the start of this passage; Sulla's, Cinna's, and Caesar's cruelty during the Roman civil wars; and the picturesque cruelty of Phalaris, tyrant of Agrigentum, who had a bronze bull made, in which he burnt his enemies. In his presentation of these tyrants d'Aubigné is already shaping the argument that will eventually establish the point of contrast between them and Catherine. It is the claim that whatever cruelties they perpetrated, they were never universal. The point is spelt out most clearly in the case of d'Aubigné's first example, Nero. The idea that there were parts of Italy that avoided his ravages is reinforced by a combination of *anaphora*, *hendiadys*, and *alliteration* first in /p/, then in /k/: 'quelque petite part/Quelque coing d'Italie' (1–2). Thereafter this argumentational point is made more deftly ('quelqu'un fuioit' (3), 'Quelqu'un [. . .] evitoit' (5)), and other *figures* highlight the bloodthirstiness of the various tyrants: *zeugma* for Sulla ('quelqu'un fuioit de Sylle/Le glaive et le courroux' (3–4)); *chiasmus* and *alliteration* in /s/ for Caesar and Cinna ('La rage de Cinna; de Caesar le couteau' (6)); and Phalaris's bull stands *metonymically* for his cruelty ('Quelqu'un de Phalaris evitoit le Taureau' (5)).

Although the *conglobatio* of tyrants continues, there is a significant change in direction, or rather an intensification of the kind of tyranny evoked. What follows is a list of beasts and a giant, so frightening and dangerous that in all cases it took Hercules with his legendary courage to conquer them. This change in direction towards the mythical is signalled by the *parenthesis* indicating the strangeness of these examples (7). D'Aubigné then adumbrates five of Hercules' twelve labours, and concludes with one of his other glorious deeds: the man-eating horses of Diomedes, the Nemean lion with its invulnerable hide, the gigantic boar of Mount Erymanthus, the many-headed hydra of Lerna, the fire-breathing Cretan bull, and the Libyan giant, Antaeus, whom Hercules had to hold in the air and squeeze to death. Whilst d'Aubigné could rely upon a degree of classical learning that would have helped his original readers to decipher these references easily, his presentation of them is such that all readers are equipped with the information needed to appreciate the image of Catherine that he is preparing. Like the historical tyrants, the ones killed by Hercules exercised a local rather than a universal tyranny: the stables of Diomedes, Lerna, Heraklion ('Candie') in Crete, Libya. In the case of the lion and the boar, d'Aubigné makes the point less precisely and more picturesquely: 'Plus loing que leur buisson ne faisoient point de tort' (10). Although Hercules was able to overcome these threats, they represent an increase in horror over and above the historical tyrants by virtue of their being animals and giants. The sense of overwhelming danger is conveyed by the triple *parison* of short phrases with which d'Aubigné's long list (eleven tyrants in all) comes to an end: 'L'Hydre assiegoit Lerna, du Taureau la furie/Couroit Candie, Anthee affligeoit la Lybie' (11–12).

Having established his points of comparison, d'Aubigné returns to the subject of his portrait, and describes her in a way that makes her seem more inescapably horrific than any of history's and mythology's famous tyrants. To mark the shift from vehicle (the other tyrants) to tenor (Catherine), he adopts the dramatic *figure* of *apostrophe*, addressing Catherine directly. Initially the poet evokes her by describing her hair in such a way as to demonize her and make her more frightening than the tyrants he has just listed and described much more briefly (13–20). Her wild hair suggests madness and the influence of black magic, which is reinforced by the explicit reference to spells ('Tes crins esparpillez, par charmes herissez' (17), and by the repeated number nine ('Par neuf fois tu secouë' (19), 'Neuf Demons conjurez' (20)). This monstrous head of hair, *metaphorically* spreading pestilence around the land (16), dehumanizes Catherine, and equates her more with the mythological than with the historical tyrants. The poet's voice implies spluttering outrage at her behaviour by recourse to *anacoluthon*, whereby the syntax of this section of the passage (13–20) cannot be construed in any logical way. The enthusiastic opening 'Mais toy qui' anticipates a main verb with a second-person singular subject, but the next main verb has a plural third-person subject ('Tes crins esparpillez' (17)). As well as suggesting uncontrollable outrage, the effect of this is to make Catherine's hair stand, by means of *synecdoche*, for all her personal evil.

The last part of the passage continues the *apostrophe* to Catherine (21–4), and, now that her monstrosity has been conveyed, turns to the point in the comparison that makes her much worse than any of the tyrants listed earlier. Whereas their tyranny was localized, hers knows no bounds. The repeated *interrogations*, supported by the multiple *anaphora* with 'quel', make the point that her evil reaches everywhere: it even reaches the country's friends (23–4). An *epitrochasmus* of four unlikely locations ('antre', 'sablon', 'desert', 'bois') suggests the universality of Catherine's evil, and clinches the main argumentational point of this passage: that she is, to date, the worst tyrant ever.

Cardinal de Lorraine

In d'Aubigné's version of contemporary history, Catherine has a partner in crime. The Cardinal de Lorraine came to wield great political power and is portrayed in another *ethopoeia*, immediately following the one devoted to Catherine, as the next greatest persecutor of the Protestants. He died in 1574 on a stormy day. D'Aubigné builds this climatically dramatic death into his portrait (I, 993–1020):

> Tel fut l'autre moien de noz rudes miseres,
> L'Achitophel bandant les fils contre les peres:
> Tel fut cette autre peste, et l'autre malheureux,
> Perpetuelle horreur à nos tristes neveux:
> Ce Cardinal sanglant, couleur à point suivie   5
> Des desirs, des effects, et pareill' à sa vie:
> Il fut rouge de sang de ceux qui au cercueil
> Furent hors d'aage mis, tüez par son conseil:
> Et puis le cramoisy encores nous avise
> Qu'il a dedans son sang trempe sa paillardise,   10
> Quand en mesme subject se fit le monstrueux
> Adultere, paillard, bougre, et incestueux.
> Il est exterminé, sa mort espouvantable
> Fut des esprits noircis une guerr' admirable:
> Le haut ciel s'obscurcit, cent mille tremblements   15
> Confondirent la terre, et les trois elements:
> De celuy qui troubloit, quand il estoit en vie,
> La France et l'Univers, l'ame rouge ravie
> En mille tourbillons, mille vents, mille nœuds,
> Mille foudres ferrez, mille esclairs, mille feux: 20
> Le pompeux appareil de cette ame si saincte
> Fit des mocqueurs de Dieu trembler l'ame contrainte:
> Or n'estant despouillé de toutes passions,

De ses conseils secrets et de ses actions
Ne pouvant oublier la compagne fidelle,   25
Vomissant son Demon il eut memoire d'elle,
Et finit d'un à Dieu entre les deux amants
La moitié du conseil, et non de noz tourments.

Lines 1–4 introduce the subject and establish his key characteristics, before these are developed in sustained *metaphorical* language in lines 5–12. The remainder of the passage is a *narration* of the death of the cardinal.

He is introduced not by name, but by means of *antonomasia* ('L'Achitophel' (2)) and *periphrasis* ('l'autre moien de noz rudes miseres' (1), 'cette autre peste, et l'autre malheureux,/Perpetuelle horreur' (3–4)). The effect of not naming the cardinal is to ensure that his most repellent qualities are fixed in the reader's mind before he is identified. These qualities then dominate the portrait. Like the Old Testament figure Achitophel, who supported Absalom in his rebellion against his father David, the cardinal provokes discord and dissent. But whereas the biblical Achitophel provoked one son to rebel against one father, his Counter-Reformation counterpart is worse. The plural forms 'les fils contre les peres' (2) indicate the general societal discord with which the cardinal is taxed. The other feature that is fixed firmly in this introductory section by means of *geminatio* (the triple repetition of 'autre') is the relationship of complicity between the cardinal and Catherine: they share the same destructive and persecutory aims. Moreover, the introduction anticipates the depressing note adopted by the end of this passage. Although the cardinal is dead, he remains a baleful influence, the adjective 'Perpetuelle' (4) *hyperbolically* conveying the perceived longevity of this influence.

D'Aubigné's practice of the *ethopoeia* relies upon closely focused visual imagery. In the earlier passage about Catherine, the focus is on her hair. In the description of the cardinal, it is on the purple of his ecclesiastical garb (5–12). The cardinal is introduced with an arresting epithet: 'Ce Cardinal sanglant' (5). 'Sanglant' is clearly both literal and *metonymic*, but it is such a striking word to use that the *metonymic* connotations stand out. Not only is the cardinal dressed in purple; he is dripping with blood. D'Aubigné then explains, as if to drive the point home, that this colour has special connotations when applied to the life of this man (5–6). These connotations are then developed: first, the expected sense of bloodthirstiness (7–8), then, perhaps unexpectedly, the sense of gross sexual immorality (9–12). The colour he wears stands *metonymically* for the blood he has ordered to be shed. The killing is evoked insistently by means of *hendiadys*: 'ceux qui au cercueil / Furent hors d'aage mis, tüez par son conseil' (7–8). Then there is the murky evocation of the adulterous and incestuous sexual relationship he is alleged to have enjoyed with his sister-in-law (Anne d'Este). The colour now has a different *metonymic* sense, the blood relation ('il a dedans son sang trempe sa paillardise' (10)). The *epitrochasmus* of adjectives ('Adultere, paillard, bougre, et incestueux' (12)), following on from and explaining the *antonomasia* 'le monstrueux' (11), forms a devastatingly forceful conclusion to this character portrait, dominated by its insistent colour imagery: repetition of words with the same range of meanings ('sanglant', 'rouge', 'cramoisy'), *geminatio* ('sang'), and *dérivation* ('sang', 'sanglant').

The description changes abruptly to *narration* with the concise indication that the monster is no more: 'Il est exterminé' (13). The account of his death is constructed neither simply to inform readers nor to hold them in suspense. It is a *narration* engineered to contribute to the character assassination. The first part (13–22) dwells on the *circumstances* of the cardinal's death, and the circumstances that d'Aubigné exploits are the weather conditions, which were notoriously tempestuous. The story is told in such a way as to imply a necessary link between the climate and the death of the evil persecutor. The weather is the physical manifestation of the war of the black spirits, which is itself the *metaphor* employed to explain the cardinal's death (13–14). The polysyllabic rhyming adjectives applied to both tenor (death) and vehicle (war) foreground the portentous nature of the event ('espouvantable', 'admirable'). *Parataxis* serves to suggest the rapid simultaneity of the darkening of the sky and the quaking of the earth, the latter reinforced by numerical *hyperbole*: 'Le haut ciel s'obscurcit, cent mille tremblements/Confondirent la terre' (15–16). As if to capitalize on the climatic confusion, d'Aubigné makes not only the earth quake, but, in a kind of *zeugma*, the other elements too (water, fire, and air). The next stage in the narrative is based on a *comparison* between the living and the dying cardinal. Alive, the cardinal created chaos in France and the universe, but the words used to describe this ('troubloit [. . .]/La France et l'Univers' (17–18)) are stylistically modest compared to the words describing the physical chaos engendered by his death as his soul leaves his body. A verbal whirlwind of *anaphora, hyperbole,* and *conglobatio* suggests the climatic disturbances accompanying the movements of the cardinal's evil soul: 'En mille tourbillons, mille vents, mille nœuds,/Mille foudres ferrez, mille esclairs, mille feux' (19–20). The effect is heightened by the *alliteration* in /f/ and, across a sequence of lines (17–22), by the syntactic disturbance occasioned by an *anacoluthon*: 'l'ame rouge' (18) 'De celuy qui troubloit' (17) seems to be the subject of an impending verb, but when the next main verb arrives it has a different subject ('Le pompeux appareil' (21)). Hidden away amidst d'Aubigné's energetically tortuous sentences is the cause of the chaos, the cardinal's red soul. Since colour is a physical phenomenon, 'rouge' is an extraordinary adjective to apply to the immaterial soul; but it is here instantly enriched by all the *metonymic* associations which d'Aubigné has attributed to it a few lines earlier. He concludes his description of the unnatural storm with an indication of its terrifying effect on those Catholics who attended the cardinal's death. He dismisses them pejoratively in a *periphrasis,* 'moqueurs de Dieu' (22), and with supremely bitter *irony* describes the cardinal as 'cette ame si saincte' (21).

The last stage in the narrative is the account of the cardinal's final act: he takes his leave of Catherine. D'Aubigné builds up to this in a series of participial clauses, the effect of which is to suggest evil passions and scheming at work right up to the moment of death (23–6). The *periphrasis* evoking Catherine ('De ses conseils secrets et de ses actions/[. . .] la compagne fidelle' (24–5)) seals in the reader's mind the complicity between queen and cardinal, though their complicity in crime is suggested even more memorably by the two juxtaposed hemistiches: 'Vomissant son Demon, il eut memoire d'elle' (26). It is as if he thinks most acutely of Catherine at the point at which his evil soul leaves his body, a concept expressed by d'Aubigné in a deliberately revolting *metaphor* ('vomissant'). As he narrates the leave-taking, d'Aubigné is most explicit about yet another illicit sexual relationship, between Catherine and the cardinal, calling them 'les deux amants' (27). The final line of the narrative includes a *zeugma*: momentary optimism at the death of the cardinal ('La moitié du conseil' (28)), but the crushing return of pessimism with the awareness that the persecutions will live on in Catherine ('et non de noz tourments' (28)).

It is hard to imagine a more insistent rhetoric of blame than that deployed by d'Aubigné in his treatment of the Roman Catholics.

Unfavourable comparisons and *metonymic* associations of the most accusing kind paint Catherine and the Cardinal de Lorraine in the darkest hue, and the style adopted for the narrative voice is characterized by such denunciatory vigour that the predominant *figures* of repetition, enumeration, and syntactic confusion come thick and fast.

Heaven

D'Aubigné needs a different narrative voice for the rhetoric of praise, with which he treats the heavenly delights awaiting the elect at the end of his poem. The devices he uses, however, are equally suggestive of vigour and commitment, and give Protestant readers hope for a blissful salvation. D'Aubigné structures the latter part of 'Jugement' around an *antithesis* between heaven and hell. After conjuring up all the torments of hell, he turns abruptly to heaven with a brief but significant transition (VII, 1045–62):

> Mais de ce dur estat le poinct plus ennuyeux
> C'est sçavoir aux enfers ce que l'on faict aux cieux,
> Où le camp triomphant gouste l'aiz' indicible,
> Connoissable aux meschants, mais non pas accessible:
> Où l'accord tres-parfaict des douces unissons   5
> A l'univers entier accorde ses chansons:
> Où tant d'esprits ravis esclattent de louanges,
> La voix des saincts unis avec celle des Anges,
> Les orbes des neuf cieux, des trompettes le bruict
> Tiennent tous leur partie à l'hymne qui s'ensuit.   10
>   Sainct, sainct, sainct le seigneur, ô grand Dieu des armees
> De ces beaux cieux nouveaux les voutes enflammees,
> Et la nouvelle terre, et la neufve cité,
> Jerusalem la saincte annoncent ta bonté:
> Tout est plein de ton nom, Sion la bien-heureuse   15
> N'a pierre dans ses murs, qui ne soit precieuse,
> Ni cytoyen que Sainct, et n'aura pour jamais
> Que victoire, qu'honneur, que plaisir et que paix.

The transitional passage (1–4) introduces the picture of heaven as something that is beyond description ('indicible') and therefore a rhetorical challenge; yet it simultaneously constitutes the climax of the picture of hell with the claim that knowledge of heaven's ineffable comforts is the lowest nadir of hell's torments. These four lines are a cameo of the large-scale *antithesis* between heaven and hell, the point at which the two meet most tellingly.

Syntactically the opening four lines flow into the following ones with the series of three *anaphoric* relative clauses in which the poet tries to do what the word 'indicible' implies is not possible, to conjure up heaven in words ('aux cieux/Où [. . /Où [. . .]/Où [. . .]'). He sets about the task here by combining two principal devices, musical *metaphor* and *prosopopoeia*. D'Aubigné uses a wealth of musical terminology to evoke a celestial sound: 'l'accord' (5), 'douces unissons' (5), 'accorde ses chansons' (6), 'trompettes' (9), 'hymne' (10). These terms are supported by others denoting sound ('esclattent de louanges' (7), 'voix' (8), 'bruict' (9)), by an *epitrochasmus* of musical elements suggesting a choral symphony (5–10), and by a language of balance that is in perfect accord with the divine harmonies it is intended to evoke (*parison* in the two hemistiches of line 8 ('La voix des saincts unis avec celle des Anges') and *chiasmus* in line 9 ('Les orbes des neuf cieux, des trompettes le bruict')).

The musical description builds up to the *prosopopoeia*, the words uttered by the choir of heavenly voices (11–18). Appropriately for a *demonstrative* passage in praise of heaven, the words in the *prosopopoeia* are also words of praise. As well as praising God and his heaven, these words have also to convey the blissful state of those who sing them. D'Aubigné achieves this by various means. The hymn of praise begins with two emphatic and balanced *apostrophes* (11), the first of which is rendered all the more arresting by its combination of *reduplicatio* and *alliteration* in /s/: 'Sainct, sainct, sainct le seigneur'. It continues with a *personification* of the three main geographical elements of the heavenly sphere ('voutes', 'terre', 'cité'), which also join in the hymn of praise. And a sense of overwhelming plenitude is conveyed by the *polysyndeton* linking these three items: 'les voutes enflammees,/Et la nouvelle terre, et la neufve cité' (12–13). *Hyperbole* characterizes the appearance of the new city: every stone is precious, every person a saint; and its future is described with resounding quadruple *anaphora* and *epitrochamsus*: 'Que victoire, qu'honneur, que plaisir et que paix' (18). The climactic effect is underscored by the symmetrical rhythm (3/3/3/3) and, in the second hemistich, by the *alliterative* /p/ in initial position.

D'Aubigné's evolving image of heaven is built up by the exploitation of a series of different dominant rhetorical devices. For example, a later passage is a sustained *antithesis* between earthly and heavenly pleasures, based on the *place* of *comparison*. The best things on earth are as nothing compared to heaven (VII, 1093–1106):

> Les honneurs de ce monde estoient hontes au prix
> Des grades eslevez au celeste pourprix:
> Les thresors de là haut sont bien d'autre matiere,
> Que l'or qui n'estoit rien qu'une terre estrangere:
> Les jeux, les passe-temps et les esbats d'ici,   5
> N'estoient qu'amers chagrins, que colere, et soucy,
> Et que gehennes au prix de la joye eternelle,
> Qui sans trouble, sans fin, sans change renouvelle:
> Là sans tache on verra les amitiez fleurir,
> Les amours d'icy bas n'estoyent rien que hair   10
> Au prix des hauts amours dont la saincte armonie
> Rend une ame de tous en un vouloir unie:
> Tous noz parfaicts amours reduicts en un amour
> Comme noz plus beaux jours reduicts en un beau jour.

D'Aubigné makes his point insistently with a repeated pattern of *chiastic antitheses*. In the first four lines earth is contrasted with heaven, then heaven with earth. In lines 5–8 earth is again contrasted with heaven, and then in the following lines heaven with earth, though, in the last few lines, the *chiasmus* gives way to a series of concisely repeated *antitheses* driving home an image of the unity of divine love, a stark contrast with the earthly divisions that have dominated the poem so far. D'Aubigné's method is to identify an earthly good and to evoke a corresponding heavenly one, but each time to supply a term which, in the divine perspective, reduces the earthly good to nothing. So 'honneurs' (1), 'or' (4), 'jeux', 'passe-temps', 'esbats' (5), 'amours' (10), and 'parfaicts amours' (13), on the earthly side, are weighed, on the heavenly side, against 'grades eslevez' (2), 'thresors' (3), 'joye eternelle' (7), 'amitiez' (9), 'hauts amours' (11), 'un amour' (13). The result is that celestial beings see the earthly goods as 'hontes' (1), 'une terre estrangere' (4), 'amers chagrins', 'colere', 'soucy' (6), 'gehennes' (7), 'hair' (10). The torrent of *antitheses* swells with devices of *epitrochasmus* (5, 6) and *anaphora* (8). And, as if these insistent patterns were not enough to impose on the reader an image of the supreme heavenly pleasure as an intensely harmonious love, d'Aubigné ends this short development with recourse to a quite different device, a climatic and *hyperbolic simile* (14).

The description of heaven is the end of d'Aubigné's poem, but what new and compelling rhetorical strategy can he find for his closing lines? He exploits *aposiopesis*, and self-consciously draws himself as poet into his description (VII, 1209–18):

> Chetif je ne puis plus approcher de mon œil
> L'œil du ciel, je ne puis supporter le soleil,
> Encor tout esblouy en raisons je me fonde
> Pour de mon ame voir la grand' ame du monde,
> Sçavoir ce qu'on ne sçait, et qu'on ne peut sçavoir,   5
> Ce que n'a ouy l'oreille, et que l'œil n'a peû voir:
> Mes sens n'ont plus de sens, l'esprit de moy s'envolle,
> Le cœur ravy se taist, ma bouche est sans parole:
> Tout meurt, l'ame s'enfuit, et reprenant son lieu
> Extaticque se pasme au giron de son Dieu.   10

He alludes to the ineffability of heaven with which his description had begun, even though in the meantime he has, with the help of rhetoric, found many different verbal formulations with which to describe it. He uses a new *metaphor* to convey heaven's resistance to further description. Heaven is presented *metaphorically* as the sun and, in a secondary *metaphor*, as 'L'œil du ciel' (2). This secondary *metaphor* allows d'Aubigné to use a *syllepsis* ('mon œil' (1), 'l'œil' (2)), which helps to convey the idea that describing heaven is like looking at the sun. This same idea is repeated as a series of impossibilities that he has been trying to overcome in vain: knowing what cannot be known, hearing what cannot be heard, and seeing what cannot be seen. These are expressed in part through *polyptoton* and *dérivation*: 'Sçavoir', 'sçait' (5); 'ouy', 'l'oreille', and, comparably, 'l'œil', 'voir' (6). In the last four lines of the whole poem, d'Aubigné exploits *aposiopesis*: his reduction to silence, as an indication that the poem is over, as a further sign of the inexpressibility of celestial happiness, and, most boldly of all, as an intimation of the divine ecstasy that the elect will enjoy. The last word, 'Dieu', represents the end to which the whole poem has tended, as well as the motivating force that prompted its beginning. Rhetoric has, after all, given d'Aubigné the means with which to say what in theory cannot be said. It is the overwhelming recourse to rhetorical devices in this poem that conveys the exceptional degree of passion in the poetic voice. Those critics who blame rhetoric for leading d'Aubigné into lapses of taste bring to the poem a modern sensibility that perhaps fails to appreciate the indissoluble link between d'Aubigné's religious commitment and its rhetorical expression.

2. AMATORY RHETORIC: BAUDELAIRE'S 'LE POISON' AND 'A UNE MADONE'

From a Protestant propagandist epic of the Renaissance to love lyrics of the nineteenth century the distance might seem great. Yet in the first edition of *Les Fleurs du Mal*, published in 1857, Baudelaire provided an explicit link between his own poetry and that of d'Aubigné in the form of an epigraph quoting six lines of *Les Tragiques* (II, 1083–8):[9]

> On dit qu'il faut couler les execrables choses
> Dans le puits de l'oubli et au sepulchre encloses,
> Et que par les escrits le mal resuscité
> Infectera les mœurs de la postérité.
> Mais le vice n'a point pour mère la science
> Et la vertu n'est pas fille de l'ignorance.

D'Aubigné's verses justify his attack on alleged Roman Catholic abuses, corruption, and persecution. As an introduction to *Les Fleurs du Mal*, they alert the reader to the vicious nature of some of the poems and, perhaps, conspire to present the collection as a whole as a moral crusade against vice. If this was the persuasive intention behind the epigraph, it could be interpreted as an instance of *external proof*, the poet claiming to speak with the same moral urgency as his well-known predecessor. But, if the epigraph was a rhetorical ploy, it failed. After the publication of the first edition, Baudelaire was tried for offences against public morality. Whereas in the same year (1857) Flaubert was acquitted of the same charge, Baudelaire faced the censure of six of his poems, which had to be removed from further editions.

The epigraph from *Les Tragiques* can prompt reflections about other links between the two works. Both insist to a remarkable degree on the *figure* of *antithesis*. The *antithesis* between Protestants and Catholics, good and evil, subtends the whole of *Les Tragiques*. Baudelaire highlights this same *figure* in the very title of his work (flowers on the one hand, evil on the other), in the title of the first and largest section within the work ('Spleen et Idéal'), and in the

---

[9] C. Baudelaire, *Les Fleurs du Mal*, ed. A. Adam (Garnier, 1961), 2. Specifically on Baudelaire and traditional rhetoric see N. Wing, 'The Stylistic Function of Rhetoric in Baudelaire's "Au Lecteur" ', *Kentucky Romance Quarterly*, 19 (1972), 447–60, and J.-P. Saint-Gérand, ' "Une singulière noirceur d'expression": Baudelaire et la rhétorique', *L'Information grammaticale*, 39 (1988), 30–7.

recurrent struggle evoked throughout between the awfulness of life
and the various means employed to overcome it. But whilst, for
d'Aubigné, the *antithesis* is always a stark one, an unbridgeable gap
between good and evil, Baudelaire's voice distinguishes itself as new
by refusing any sharp and unambiguous contrast between the two
sides of his *antitheses*.

This *antithetical* ambiguity is evident in some of Baudelaire's love
poems. *Demonstrative* rhetoric is common in the love lyric. Poets often
praise the loved one; rather less often, they might attack the loved
one, especially if their love is unrequited. Baudelaire, however, combines praise and blame in teasingly ambivalent ways. The titles of his
love poems 'Le Poison' (no. 49) and 'A une Madone' (no. 57) might
suggest that the former would be primarily a poem of blame and the
latter one of praise, but a rhetorical reading suggests otherwise.

Poisons

Both poems come from the section 'Spleen et Idéal'. Within this section critics have traditionally, but not unproblematically, identified
three different cycles of love poems, each addressed to a different
woman. 'Le Poison' and 'A une Madone' are particularly significant
in being, respectively, the first and last poems in the third cycle,
whose addressee is conventionally identified as Marie Daubrun.
Poems in praise of a loved one often focus on one or more physical
features. 'Le Poison' concentrates on the loved one's eyes and saliva:

> Le vin sait revêtir le plus sordide bouge
>   D'un luxe miraculeux,
> Et fait surgir plus d'un portique fabuleux
>   Dans l'or de sa vapeur rouge,
> Comme un soleil couchant dans un ciel nébuleux.   5
>
> L'opium agrandit ce qui n'a pas de bornes,
>   Allonge l'illimité,
> Approfondit le temps, creuse la volupté,
>   Et de plaisirs noirs et mornes
> Remplit l'âme au delà de sa capacité.   10
>
> Tout cela ne vaut pas le poison qui découle
>   De tes yeux, de tes yeux verts,
> Lacs où mon âme tremble et se voit à l'envers . . .
>   Mes songes viennent en foule
> Pour se désaltérer à ces gouffres amers.   15

Tout cela ne vaut pas le terrible prodige
   De ta salive qui mord,
Qui plonge dans l'oubli mon âme sans remord,
   Et, charriant le vertige,
La roule défaillante aux rives de la mort!   20

The title of the poem signals its ambiguities. Poison is most obviously interpreted literally as a harmful, even fatal, substance or
potion, associated with the crimes of suicide and murder. Yet in the
nineteenth century the word 'poison' often referred *metaphorically* to
drugs and alcohol. This poem plays on the standard *metaphorical*
associations of poison (in stanzas 1 and 2 on wine and opium), and
develops new associations for the word (in stanzas 3 and 4 on eyes
and saliva), whilst never quite forgetting the unpleasant and deadly
consequences of literal poison.

The stanza divisions mark out very sharply the poem's intellectual structure. It is based on the *place* of *comparison*. Greater
things, the loved one's eyes and saliva, are compared with
allegedly lesser things, wine and opium, so that the former seem
all the more impressive. The particular point of comparison is
their transformative and intensificatory powers. To develop this
point, the poet exploits within each stanza, though to different
degrees, the *places* of *cause* and *effect*. The poem's structure also
stands out, thanks to the use of verbal parallelism and repetition.
The first and second stanzas begin with the noun that indicates
the subject of the stanza, respectively 'Le vin' and 'L'opium'. It
is only with the third and fourth stanzas that the reader realizes,
first, that it is a love poem and second, what its argumentational
structure is. The *anaphoric* repetition of 'Tout cela ne vaut pas' at
the beginning of these stanzas followed by the *metaphorical* identi-
fication of their subjects (eyes and saliva) adjusts the reader's
understanding of the significance of wine and opium in the first
half of the poem: they have not been described for their intrinsic
interest, but as a point of comparison with the attributes of the
loved one. Moreover, it is only in the second half of the poem
that the reader realizes that the verses enact a communicative situation. The poet's words do not merely provide a description for
the benefit of the reader; they are addressed to the loved one ('tes
yeux' (12)). So the rhetoric is addressed primarily to the loved
one, persuading her of the power she has to affect him. The
reader stands back, watches and appreciates this intratextual com-

munication from a distance. This is quite different from the rhetoric of d'Aubigné, meant directly for the reader.

The first stanza dwells on the transformative powers of wine, while repeatedly evoking the unreality of the transformations it appears to effect. Two examples are given (1–2, 3–4), the second supported by a *simile* (5). The first example works by means of *antithesis*. The wine-drinker may be in a hovel, emphasized by a superlative adjective ('le plus sordide bouge' (1)), but alcohol can transform his surroundings into undreamt-of luxury. The phrase used to describe the transformed state of the hovel ('un luxe miraculeux' (2)) is foregrounded by a *chiastic* pattern of repeated phonemes: /lyk/ /kyl/. The effect is to draw particular attention to the rhyme word 'miraculeux', which, in its ordinary sense, can be read as a term of extravagant praise of the newly created luxury, but, in its more etymological sense, calls into question the reality of the vision, induced merely by alcohol. The word 'miraculeux' is also important, because the two words that subsequently rhyme with it, very richly, fulfil the same function of undermining the delights that wine seems to offer ('fabuleux' (3), 'nébuleux' (5)). The second example, like the first, is architectural. But instead of repeating the *antithesis* of former state and transformed state, it adopts a dual pattern based on *cause* and *effect*. The *cause* is the heady wine ('l'or de sa vapeur rouge' (4)); the *effect* is the appearance of porticoes ('fait surgir plus d'un portique fabuleux' (3)). Just as the previous transformed state of miraculous luxury is foregrounded phonetically, so too is this one, with another *alliterative chiasmus*: /fppf/ ('fait', 'plus', 'portique', 'fabuleux'). This example is developed into a *simile* whereby the portico is equated to a sunset, and the wine vapours to a hazy sky. The *simile* maintains, and even reinforces, the ambiguous implications of the stanza. Sunsets are beautiful and are really there, but they are fleeting, and if the sky is misty, our appreciation of them may be limited; alternatively, the misty sky might make them seem more mysteriously beautiful than they really are.

The second stanza moves in apparently enumerative fashion to a second kind of *metaphorical* poison, opium. The focus here is on the drug's ability to intensify experience. The subject, opium, is followed by five verbal phrases, each conveying different kinds of experience that the drug can influence, but the poet uses terms that suggest simultaneously excitement and scepticism. The first two phrases celebrate opium's spatial powers in the form of two paradoxical *antitheses*: 'agrandit ce qui n'a pas de bornes' (6), 'Allonge l'illimité' (7). The second of these phrases is made all the more striking by its combination, in so short a space, of triple *alliteration* in /l/ and triple *assonance* in /i/. On the one hand, opium seems to be able to work the impossible; on the other hand, it is the impossibility and unreality of its effects that these phrases foreground. The next two *effects* of the drug are conveyed in a line characterized by *isocolon* ('Approfondit le temps, creuse la volupté' (8)): no scepticism is implied here about the drug-taker's capacity to sense time more fully or to feel pleasure more intensely. Both verbs seem to concentrate straightforwardly on the potency of the drug. Yet, in a sense, all the claims made so far in this stanza are qualified by its fifth, more fully developed claim, which once again foregrounds the ambiguity of these intense experiences. By means of *metaphor* the soul is rendered concrete, transformed into a vessel which drug-induced pleasures fill to overflowing. But these pleasures are described by yet another paradoxical *antithesis* as 'plaisirs noirs et mornes', the two adjectives foregrounded by their *chiastic* repetition of the phonemes /n/, /R/, /R/, /n/.

By celebrating the extraordinary powers of wine and opium, whilst also suggesting their real limits, the poet seems to have paved the way for an account of the loved one which could invoke her equally extraordinary powers whilst attaching no limit to them. But Baudelaire's strategy is not so simple. The *metaphorical* language employed to evoke the loved one's eyes and saliva certainly suggests their overwhelming power over the poet; and there is nothing to imply that their power is at all limited. But the noxious effects of poison, largely overlooked in the evocation of wine and opium, resurface in the presentation of the loved one's physical attractions, whose powers are asserted emphatically and explicitly in the repeated phrases 'Tout cela ne vaut pas' (11, 16).

The first and only mention of poison in the poem is a *metaphorical* reference to the loved one's eyes. Their unusual power is conveyed by the *reduplicatio* ('De tes yeux, de tes yeux verts' (12)) and by the strangeness of the *metaphor*. Poison works its effect by being taken into the body, like wine and opium. This stanza tries to create the impression that the eyes are so captivating that it is as if they are imbibed by the poet. The impression is built up gradually. The reader is first sensitized to the possibility of the eyes giving off the equivalent of an intoxicating liquid by the relative clause qualifying poison 'qui découle/De tes yeux' (11–12) and by the juxtaposition of this with the insistence on the green of the eyes, an emphasis which is the result of the *reduplicatio* and the stressed position of the adjective 'verts' at the end of the line. Mention of the colour is the justification for a new *metaphor* introduced in apposition to the eyes: 'Lacs où mon âme tremble et se voit à l'envers . . .' (13). In its context this *metaphor* seems appropriate, because both eyes and lakes can be green, and because it is possible to stare into someone's eyes as into a lake and see one's reflection. This image therefore suggests an intensity of visual contact between poet and loved one, conveyed all the more forcefully by the *synecdoche* whereby the poet is represented by his soul. A reflection in water is rarely still. Baudelaire capitalizes on this with his choice of the verb 'trembler', but in addition to evoking the shimmering reflection in the water, the word has connotations of fear and anxiety. These are entirely appropriate here in the light of Baudelaire's continuation of the image. His dreams are *personified* and presented as returning obsessively ('en foule' (14)), as if thirsty, to the loved one's eyes, which quench the thirst. But the final *metaphor* for the eyes stresses not so much their transforming power as their mysterious and dangerous side. 'Gouffres' suggests impenetrability and unknowability, whilst 'amers' implies a positively unpleasant taste (15), the taste indeed of poison. By combining *metaphor*, *synecdoche*, and *personification* in rapid succession, Baudelaire makes a pair of eyes as compellingly mysterious for the reader as he contrives to suggest they are for the poet.

The final stanza is presented climactically in the sense that mention of the loved one's saliva is preceded by a *metaphorical* introduction making this attribute seem more overwhelming in its effect even than the eyes of the previous stanza ('le terrible prodige/De ta salive' (16–17)). Resolutely ambiguous, the *metaphor* presents the woman as both wondrous and monstrous: the word 'prodige' carries both connotations; and similarly, the adjective 'terrible' can be intepreted as awe-inspiring or frightening. The *metaphor* is foregrounded by *assonance*, the repeated /i/ in stressed position in 'terrible' and 'prodige', echoed immediately afterwards in the tenor 'salive'. The physical act implied in this stanza is penetrative kissing, whence the exchange of saliva. The vigour of the kissing that the lovers have enjoyed is suggested by the application of the description 'biting' to the saliva, a *synecdoche* for the woman herself, or for her lips. The overwhelming effect of her kisses is conveyed by a *gradatio* of three verbal phrases: 'plonge dans l'oubli' (18), 'charriant le vertige' (19), and 'La [mon âme] roule défaillante' (20). These phrases describe a journey from forgetfulness, through loss of self-control, to death, 'mort' being the last word in the poem. The poet's soul again stands by way of *synecdoche* for the poet himself, who is presented as the victim of a violent tidal wave that washes him lifeless on to the shore. Death is the ultimate effect of any poison, and it is therefore fitting that the fourth and final kind of poison mentioned in the poem should be shown to have this effect. But perhaps here the emphasis is less on the literal connotations of the word 'death' than on its associations with sexual ecstasy. In its conclusion, it is a poem celebrating the transfiguring effects of sexuality.

Madonna

Ecstasy, both religious and sexual, is the subject of 'A une Madone'. The title implies a poem in praise of a woman, using religious imagery, in much the same way as Molière's Tartuffe expresses his desire for Elmire. The subtitle 'Ex-voto dans le goût espagnol' reinforces this impression: monuments to cherish the memory of the deceased are characteristic of Spanish religious art. But the expectation of a *demonstrative* poem in praise of the loved one is defeated by an increasingly ambiguous, and ultimately violent, expression of the poet's feelings for her, as he seems racked by jealousy.

> Je veux bâtir pour toi, Madone, ma maîtresse,
> Un autel souterrain au fond de ma détresse,
> Et creuser dans le coin le plus noir de mon cœur,
> Loin du désir mondain et du regard moqueur,
> Une niche, d'azur et d'or tout émaillée,   5
> Où tu te dresseras, Statue émerveillée.
> Avec mes Vers polis, treillis d'un pur métal
> Savamment constellé de rimes de cristal,
> Je ferai pour ta tête une énorme Couronne;
> Et dans ma Jalousie, ô mortelle Madone,   10
> Je saurai te tailler un Manteau, de façon
> Barbare, roide et lourd, et doublé de soupçon,
> Qui, comme une guérite, enfermera tes charmes;
> Non de Perles brodé, mais de toutes mes Larmes!
> Ta Robe, ce sera mon Désir, frémissant,   15
> Onduleux, mon Désir qui monte et qui descend,
> Aux pointes se balance, aux vallons se repose,

Et revêt d'un baiser tout ton corps blanc et rose.
Je te ferai de mon Respect de beaux Souliers
De satin, par tes pieds divins humiliés,   20
Qui, les emprisonnant dans une molle étreinte,
Comme un moule fidèle en garderont l'empreinte.
Si je ne puis, malgré tout mon art diligent,
Pour Marchepied tailler une Lune d'argent,
Je mettrai le Serpent qui me mord les entrailles   25
Sous tes talons, afin que tu foules et railles,
Reine victorieuse et féconde en rachats,
Ce monstre tout gonflé de haine et de crachats.
Tu verras mes Pensers, rangés comme les Cierges
Devant l'autel fleuri de la Reine des Vierges,   30
Etoilant de reflets le plafond peint en bleu,
Te regarder toujours avec des yeux de feu;
Et comme tout en moi te chérit et t'admire,
Tout se fera Benjoin, Encens, Oliban, Myrrhe,
Et sans cesse vers toi, sommet blanc et neigeux,   35
En Vapeurs montera mon Esprit orageux.
Enfin, pour compléter ton rôle de Marie,
Et pour mêler l'amour avec la barbarie,
Volupté noire! des sept Péchés capitaux,
Bourreau plein de remords, je ferai sept Couteaux   40
Bien affilés, et, comme un jongleur insensible,
Prenant le plus profond de ton amour pour cible,
Je les planterai tous dans ton Cœur pantelant,
Dans ton Cœur sanglotant, dans ton Cœur ruisselant.

The use of *metaphor* is both crucial and complex in this poem. The monument to the lover evoked from the very beginning is not a real one, but a *metaphorical* one. The monument is the vehicle, and the tenor is the poet's verses. This would be straightforward: the poet's monument to his lover is not a statue but a poem. But two factors complicate the imagery. The first is the wide range of equivalences that Baudelaire establishes between the creation of a statue and the composition of a poem. The second is the suggestion, as the poem continues, that the *metaphorical* monument is really a *synecdoche* for the living lover, and the verses a *synecdoche* for the loving, suffering poet. The result is that the poem that is notionally about a memorial to a deceased lover reads increasingly like an expression of feelings about a loved one who is very much alive and whose frenzied murder becomes the poem's climax. Moreover, the poem is addressed

directly to the loved one, to whom it must seem a poem of violent
threat.

Lines 1–6 tentatively introduce the addressee and the reader to
the poem's *metaphorical* substructure and its latent ambivalence. The
opening words ('Je veux bâtir pour toi'), which might be interpreted
literally at first, need to be reinterpreted *metaphorically* in the light of
the claim that the altar will be built invisibly deep within the poet's
heart. The ambiguous nature of the monument is promptly made
plain. Its first associations are with the poet's dark distress (2–3),
though it will not lack celebratory associations: it will be 'd'azur et
d'or tout émaillée' (5), and the statue that will be its central feature
is described as 'émerveillée' (6).

It is only after this introduction, which readers must imagine to
unsettle the addressee as much as it unsettles them, that the tenor is
spelt out. The monument will be a poetic one. The overall *disposition* of the poem now follows an enumerative pattern: it is built upon
an extended *epitrochasmus*. Four features of the *metaphorical* female
statue are evoked: crown (7–9), cloak (10–14), dress (15–18), and slip-
pers (19–22); after which, four of the statue's accessories are evoked:
the serpent beneath its feet (23–8), the candles that surround it
(29–32), the fragrances that perfume it (33–6), and the seven swords
that are associated with some images of the Virgin Mary, but which
here become the instrument of the poet's imagined sacrifice of his
Madonna (37–44).

In presenting each item in the list, Baudelaire maintains a balance between the literal (the poet composing) and the *metaphorical*
(the statue), but the feelings that motivate the poet change unpre-
dictably from physical desire and admiration to jealous rage and
hatred. A variety of rhetorical *figures* is drawn in to support the elaborate *metaphorical* play and the variously positive or negative
responses of the poet to his Madonna. *Hypallage* combines the
metaphorical and the literal when the statue's cloak is described as
'doublé de soupçon' (12). *Zeugma* does likewise when evoking the
cloak's embroidery: 'Non de Perles brodé, mais de toutes mes
Larmes!' (14). The poet's physical longing for his lover is conveyed
by the *metaphorization* of the dress as desire, and the *metaphor* is
extended over four lines that suggest intimate physical contact
(15–18), the woman's contour suggested by the *antithetical isocolon*
('Aux pointes se balance, aux vallons se repose' (17)). The serpent is
an *allegory* of the poet's jealousy which both causes him to suffer ('qui

me mord les entrailles' (25)) and makes him react violently ('Ce monstre tout gonflé de haine et de crachats' (28)). *Syllepsis* hints at de-*metaphorization* of the lover in the phrase 'ton rôle de Marie' (37), the addressee being both the Virgin Mary of the *metaphor* and potentially the Marie Daubrun of the poet's affections. Further *hypallage*, or paradoxical *antithesis*, conjures up the poet's mixed, and turbulent emotions, in his *apostrophe*, 'Volupté noire!' (39). Yet another *syllepsis* prepares for the catastrophic climax, when the poet in a *simile* compares himself to 'un jongleur insensible' (41). 'Jongleur' is a medieval term for a wandering poet as well as a modern term for a juggler. The poet will assassinate his lover with words, as the juggler will assassinate her with the seven swords. The obsessive and destructive climax is marked by a distinctively insistent rhythm in the three final hemistiches: *anaphoric reduplicatio* with the triple repetition of 'dans ton Cœur' and *homoioteleuton* with the triple repetition of the same adjectival ending '-ant' in stressed positions, supported by *alliteration* in /t/ and /l/.

A rhetorical reading of Baudelaire's poems helps to bring out the ambivalence that characterizes his verse. His *demonstrative* rhetoric in these two love poems is neither obviously praise nor obviously blame. It is a subtle exploration of those feelings of attraction and repulsion, desire and hatred, that define the emotional life of Baudelaire's lover-poet. The complexity of tone is supported by the dense and intriguing use of rhetorical *figures*. It may be an awareness of the rhetorical complexity of his poems that prompted Baudelaire, in the poem 'Epigraphe pour un livre condamné', to urge the rhetorically inexperienced reader to throw them away (*Nouvelles Fleurs du Mal*, 1866):[10]

> Si tu n'as fait ta rhétorique
> Chez Satan, le rusé doyen,
> Jette! tu n'y comprendrais rien,
> Ou tu me croirais hystérique.

3. RHETORIC AND NEGRITUDE: CÉSAIRE'S *CAHIER D'UN RETOUR AU PAYS NATAL*

Language and communication are at the symbolic heart of the intellectual issues raised by Césaire's long surrealist poem *Cahier d'un*

---

[10] Baudelaire, *Fleurs du Mal*, ed. Adam, 177.

retour au pays natal, a mixture of free verse and poetic prose.[11] Born
in Martinique in 1913 and educated at the *lycée* in the capital, Fort-
de-France, Césaire continued his education at the centre of the
French establishment in Paris, attending the *lycée* Louis-le-Grand
from 1931 to 1935 and then the École Normale Supérieure. He left
Paris to return to Martinique in 1939, the year in which the first edition of the *Cahier* was published (it is now usual to refer to the so-
called definitive edition, published in 1956). The poem explores the
problematic perception of black people by white people and of black
people by black people. It traces a range of attitudes before concluding with a triumphal celebration of hope in negritude, a concept originating with Césaire himself and his contemporary from
Senegal, Léopold Senghor. Whatever complex associations the term
'negritude' came to acquire, its origins lie in an attempt to assert a
positive black identity.

   Césaire's educational experiences situate him at a cultural and
linguistic crossroads. He knew the Creole language spoken by most
Martinicans. Yet at school in Fort-de-France, and even more so in
Paris, he learnt metropolitan French with its centuries of white cultural heritage. The author's unusual linguistic position makes its
mark on the *elocution* of the *Cahier*. It bristles with vocabulary that
means little or nothing to anyone not familiar with black culture in
the Antilles, without recourse to dictionaries or learned footnotes: 'le
morne' (p. 74), 'un balafon' (p. 78), 'une sapotille' (p. 80), 'cécropies'
(p. 86), 'jiculi' (p. 86), 'une couronne de daturas' (p. 96), 'le
Kaïlcédrat royal' (p. 114). Yet the language employed also requires
a knowledge of educated French. Césaire uses many technical terms
with erudite Greek or Latin etymologies: 'son hypoglosse' (p. 76), 'le
bulbe tératique' (p. 78), 'quelque milliers de mortiférés' (p. 88), 'mon
calcanéum' (p. 90), 'la membrane vitelline' (p. 100). Similarly, whilst
the syntax sometimes suggests the orality of black culture with colloquial turns of phrase ('Qu'y puis-je?/Il faut bien commencer./
Commencer quoi?' (p. 98)) and celebratory litanies ('Eia pour la

[11] A. Césaire, *A Notebook of a Return to my Native Land / Cahier d'un retour au pays natal*,
trans. M. Rosello with A. Pritchard (Newcastle-upon-Tyne: Bloodaxe Books, 1995). For
a critical introduction to Césaire's work, see G. Davis, *Aimé Césaire* (Cambridge:
Cambridge University Press, 1997). On matters of style see the excellent article by R.
Mercier, 'Processus d'intériorisation et procédés stylistiques dans le *Cahier d'un retour au
pays natal*', in J. Leiner (ed.), *Soleil éclaté: Mélanges offerts à Aimé Césaire à l'occasion de son soixante-dixième anniversaire par une équipe internationale d'artistes et de chercheurs* (Tübingen: Gunter
Narr Verlag, 1984), 273–84.

joie/Eia pour l'amour/Eia pour la douleur aux pis de larmes réin-carnées' (p. 116)), it also exploits sentence structures of *polysyndetic* complexity (p. 104):

> Et ce pays cria pendant des siècles que nous sommes des bêtes brutes; que les pulsations de l'humanité s'arrêtent aux portes de la nègrerie; que nous sommes un fumier ambulant hideusement prometteur de cannes tendres et de coton soyeux et l'on nous marquait en fer rouge et nous dormions dans nos excréments et l'on nous vendait sur les places et l'aune de drap anglais et la viande salée d'Irlande coûtaient moins cher que nous, et ce pays était calme, tranquille, disant que l'esprit de Dieu était dans ses actes.

There is a poignant irony here between the learned and controlled syntax (the two *anaphoric* sequences 'que [. . .] que [. . .] que [. . .]' and 'et [. . .] et [. . .] et [. . .] et [. . .]') and the black vision of exploitation, suffering, and oppression that it expresses. The poem's extreme linguistic range has serious implications for our view of the readership. It seems to be a poem for everybody and yet for nobody. This is important, because it means that anybody reading the poem, black or white, will find that they need to adjust their linguistic and cultural framework. The style is therefore central to the poem's effect on the reader.

This linguistic problem is foregrounded explicitly as part of the poem's subject-matter. One passage both describes and, in part, enacts the linguistic divide between schoolmaster and priest on the one hand and black child on the other (p. 76):

> Et ni l'instituteur dans sa classe, ni le prêtre au catéchisme ne pourront tirer un mot de ce négrillon somnolent, malgré leur manière si énergique à tous deux de tambouriner son crâne tondu, car c'est dans les marais de la faim que s'est enlisée sa voix d'inanition (un-mot-un-seul-mot et je-vous-en-tiens-quitte-de-la-reine-Blanche-de-Castille, un-mot-un-seul-mot, voyez-vous-ce-petit-sauvage-qui-ne-sait-pas-un-seul-des-dix-commandements-de-Dieu).

The verbal fluency of teacher and priest is suggested in the *paren-thesis* and contrasts with the linguistic impoverishment of the child, expressed *metaphorically* in terms of starvation. The poet's experiences relate to both sides of this linguistic divide, and the point in the poem is reached when he expresses *metaphorically* the linguistic tor-ture that white French culture has wrought on him (p. 96):

> Mais qui tourne ma voix? qui écorche ma voix? Me fourrant dans la gorge mille crocs de bambou. Mille pieux d'oursin. C'est toi sale bout de monde.

Sale bout de petit matin. C'est toi sale haine. C'est toi poids de l'insulte et
cent ans de coups de fouet. C'est toi cent ans de ma patience, cent ans de
mes soins juste à ne pas mourir.

This passage recognizing the linguistic taint left on him by white culture is one of the moments that lead up to the poet's whole-hearted
embrace of black culture. There is no neat *disposition* in the poem's
structure. Critics give different accounts of it. It rather resembles the
surging complexity of an oceanic movement which culminates in
what can reasonably be called a *peroration*, a celebration of the poet's
espousal of negritude. Along the way it is informed by a variety of
rhetorical perspectives.

Cynicism and Criticism

There are passages, predominantly in the first half of the poem, in
which the poet engages in *demonstrative* rhetoric assessing critically or
cynically aspects of Martinican life and culture. The rue Paille bears
testimony to the island's urban squalor (p. 84):

> [1] Et une honte, cette rue Paille,
> un appendice dégoûtant comme les parties honteuses du bourg qui étend
> à droite et à gauche, tout au long de la route coloniale, la houle grise de
> ses toits d'essentes. [2] Ici il n'y a que des toits de paille que l'embrun a
> brunis et que le vent a épilés.
>
> [3] Tout le monde la méprise la rue Paille. [4] C'est là que la jeunesse
> du bourg se débauche. [5] C'est là surtout que la mer déverse ses
> immondices, ses chats morts et ses chiens crevés. [6] Car la rue débouche
> sur la plage, et la plage ne suffit pas à la rage écumante de la mer.

The poet may be looking at this scene through European eyes,
but what he sees is also the local perception (3). The words
appeal to the reader's sense of horror and shame (*pathos*), an
appeal supported by numerous *figures*. The unusual word order of
the opening phrase (*hyperbaton*), along with the isolating typogra-
phy, stresses the emotional response to the scene even before the
description has started. The poet qualifies the street with a
metaphor and a *simile*, both charged with emotion before engaging
in any physical evocation. Both terms are anatomical, referring
respectively to the appendix and the genitalia, but the poet is less
concerned with parts of the anatomy in their own right than with
their associations. 'Appendice', qualified as 'dégoûtant', is chosen

as that part of the anatomy that is an irrelevance, best removed
(1). Genitalia are referred to not by anatomical vocabulary but by
periphrasis: 'les parties honteuses' (1). The rue Paille is a street that
polite members of society would rather not acknowledge. The
antithesis between shameful and polite areas is sketched in by the
geographical evocation of the lie of the street, perpendicular to
the 'route coloniale'. Two roofscapes strike the viewer, neither
appealing. One is monotonously grey and suggestive of uncom-
fortably packed housing: this is the significance of the *metaphor* 'la
houle grise' (1). The other is characterized by its poverty and
inadequate protection against the elements: the straw roofs 'que
l'embrun a brunis et que le vent a épilés' (2), the *isocolon* reinforcing the degree of exposure.

The next paragraph dwells on the response of the environment
to the street. After expressing the general scorn that the street evokes
(3), the poet concentrates on the reaction of the youth (4) and, unexpectedly, the reaction of the sea (5–6). This paragraph explores with
studied uncertainty the relationship of *cause* and *effect*: is it because
the street is so grim that the youth behave debauchedly there and the
sea uses it as a tipping ground, as the passage suggests? or is it the
behaviour of the youth and the action of the sea that makes the
street grim? The *anaphoric* opening of sentences 4 and 5 ('C'est là que
[. . .] C'est là surtout que [. . .]') has the effect of concentrating the
reader's perception of the street on the devastations wrought by
youth and sea. But most weight is attached to the sea, *personified* as
careless and uncontrollable. The revolting detritus it leaves on the
street is emphasized by a combination of *anaphora* and *epitrochasmus*:
'ses immondices, ses chats morts et ses chiens crevés' (5). And the
exploration of the *circumstances* that allow the sea to reach the street
(the inadequacy of the intervening strip of beach) are elaborated by
recourse to *geminatio* and *paronomasia* ('plage', 'plage', 'rage' (6)),
which, with its insistent phonetic repetitions, foregrounds the image,
at the end of the sentence, of the wildly beating waves. At this point
in the poem the emotions associated with scenes like this are rejection, shame, and despair; later in the poem, the years of suffering
and oppression that lie behind such scenes will prompt an urgent
revision of the black self-image.

Sometimes the poet's *demonstrative* rhetoric is conducted very
much through the eyes of an outsider, as in his description of a gan-
gling black man trying to squeeze on to a tram seat (p. 106):

[1] Un soir, dans un tramway en face de moi, un nègre.

[2] C'était un nègre grand comme un pongo qui essayait de se faire tout petit sur un banc de tramway. [3] Il essayait d'abandonner sur ce banc crasseux de tramway ses jambes gigantesques et ses mains tremblantes de boxeur affamé. [4] Et tout l'avait laissé, le laissait. [5] Son nez qui semblait une péninsule en dérade et sa négritude même qui se décolorait sous l'action d'une inlassable mégie. [6] Et le mégissier était la Misère. [7] Un gros oreillard subit dont les coups de griffes sur ce visage s'étaient cicatrisés en îlots scabieux. [8] Ou plutôt, c'était un ouvrier infatigable, la Misère, travaillant à quelque cartouche hideux. [9] On voyait très bien comment le pouce industrieux et malveillant avait modelé le front en bosse, percé le nez de deux tunnels parallèles et inquiétants, allongé la démesure de la lippe, et par un chef-d'œuvre caricatural, raboté, poli, verni la plus minuscule mignonne petite oreille de la création.

[10] C'était un nègre dégingandé sans rythme ni mesure.

[11] Un nègre dont les yeux roulaient une lassitude sanguinolente.

[12] Un nègre sans pudeur et ses orteils ricanaient de façon assez puante au fond de la tanière entrebâillée de ses souliers.

This portrait combines caricature and *pathos*. There is caricature in the explicit and implicit *similes* by means of which the man's enormous height and nose are conjured up: 'Son nez qui semblait une péninsule en dérade' (5), suggesting a protuberant nose with this *hyperbolic* image; 'ses mains tremblantes de boxeur affamé' (3); and 'grand comme un pongo' (2), the animal image participating in the conventional white racist derogatory discourse on black people. *Pathos* is invoked as further features of the man's physical appearance are described in an extended *metaphor*, which presents the action of poverty in terms of a tawer beating a hide in order to turn it into white leather. Two *parisonic* sequences of *metaphorical* verbs convey the beatings that have formed the man's head: three longer elements describe the shaping of the forehead, nose, and lip ('modelé [. . .] percé [. . .] allongé' (9)) and three verbs in rapid succession foreground the shaping of the ear ('raboté, poli, verni' (9)) in terms whose comic caricature is both explicit ('par un chef-d'œuvre caricatural' (9)) and implicit through the use of *alliteration* in /m/, *hyperbole*, and a redundant diminutive ('la plus minuscule mignonne petite oreille' (9)). Supporting the pathetic appeal is a different *metaphor*, presenting poverty as a violent and aggressive bat (7), with the black man as the victim of its attack. Yet it is the satirical voice that predominates in the sequence of three *anaphoric* sentences, emphasized typographically ('C'était un nègre [. . .]/Un nègre

[. . .]/Un nègre [. . .]' (10–12)), which present him at a comic distance as ungainly, idle, and untidy, paving the way for the portrait's conclusion a few sentences later: 'Il était COMIQUE ET LAID,/COMIQUE ET LAID pour sûr' (p. 108).

Yet, read in context, this *demonstrative* rhetoric is more complex than it seems when read in isolation. For, in its context, this passage acts as *external proof* in a *judicial* discourse, in which the poet is accusing himself of having looked at his fellow black people through the wrong eyes. The passage quoted above is immediately preceded by these words (p. 106):

> Et moi, et moi,
> moi qui chantais le poing dur
> Il faut savoir jusqu'où je poussai la lâcheté.

The description of the black man is thus introduced as evidence of the poet's cowardly use of an inappropriate European discourse. And the self-accusatory tone continues after the portrait. The poet does not spare himself for his complicity with the white European: 'J'arborai un grand sourire complice . . ./Ma lâcheté retrouvée!' (p. 108).

Celebration

It is shortly after this that the poet celebrates, in a *demonstrative* rhetoric of praise, his realization that he must embrace black culture; and it is here that the concept of negritude is first sung (pp. 112–14):

> ô lumière amicale
> ô fraîche source de la lumière
> ceux qui n'ont inventé ni la poudre ni la boussole
> ceux qui n'ont jamais su dompter la vapeur ni l'électricité
> ceux qui n'ont exploré ni les mers ni le ciel   5
> mais ceux sans qui la terre ne serait pas la terre
> gibbosité d'autant plus bienfaisante que la terre déserte
> davantage la terre
> silo où se préserve et mûrit ce que la terre a de plus terre
> ma négritude n'est pas une pierre, sa surdité ruée contre
>   la clameur du jour   10
> ma négritude n'est pas une taie d'eau morte sur l'œil
>   mort de la terre
> ma négritude n'est ni une tour ni une cathédrale

elle plonge dans la chair rouge du sol
elle plonge dans la chair ardente du ciel
elle troue l'accablement opaque de sa droite patience   15

The passages already quoted make use of various kinds of repetition, particularly *anaphora*. But it is only in the second half of the poem, and especially towards the end, that *anaphora* becomes the most compelling microstructural device, signalling the new-found confident and celebratory tone. This assertion of negritude is built around three *anaphoric* sequences, each supported by a variety of patterning devices. The celebration is introduced by the near-synonymous repetition of the happy *apostrophe* to light (1–2). The light is *metaphorical* and ambiguous. Is it the light that the poet has seen, the light that has revised and then reinforced his convictions? Or does the light represent the black race, in which case the following phrases introduced by 'ceux qui' would be read as standing in apposition to the *apostrophe*? The first *anaphoric* sequence evokes black people, and does so by drawing on the *place* of *opposites*: they are described in opposition to white Europeans. They did not first acquire those technical skills that have allowed Europeans to dominate other races. Each of these three lines (3–5) is *parisonic*, and each ends with a resounding couplet of nouns, emphasized by the particle 'ni' repeated five times. After three lines evoking black people in opposition to white people, a fourth line evokes them positively: 'ceux sans qui la terre ne serait pas la terre' (6). The black roots in the earth are asserted by means of the *syllepsis*, their earth being distinguished from earth tainted by European feet. This *syllepsis* is then repeated and embroidered in the following two *metaphorical* phrases (7–9), which present the black race first as a beneficial tumescence, then as a silo, stressing the natural fruitfulness of their life-style and the lands in which they live.

   This joyful assertion of the richness of black culture is followed by further *anaphoric* sequences, the first dismissing the negative view of negritude (10–12), the second promoting negritude in positive terms (13–15). The first sequence contrasts negritude with monumental passivity. What the negative *metaphors* of stone, stagnant water, tower, and cathedral have in common is a sense of completion and immutability. By contrast, negritude is defined positively by means of verbs suggesting movement and action: the repeated verb 'plonge' (*geminatio*) and 'troue'. Negritude is alive, organic, and far-reaching. Its associations are with living flesh, with both the earth

and the sky. These mutually reinforcing words of praise are given
added weight by both the verbal and the phonetic repetitions that
characterize them: 'dans la chair rouge du sol', 'dans la chair
ardente du ciel'. The repeated /R/ links the adjectives, and the
repeated /s/ and /l/ the terminal nouns. The last item in the
sequence is the most important: with all its qualities of action, negritude is a weapon with which to fight oppression.

The *anaphoric* lines become increasingly shorter and more frequent in the closing pages of the poem, and hence more effective as
an indication of the strong rhythms of the black peoples, as the poet
commits himself whole-heartedly and single-mindedly to them and
to their future (p. 134):

> et t'enroulant embrasse-moi d'un plus vaste frisson
> embrasse-moi jusqu'au nous furieux
> embrasse, embrasse NOUS
> mais nous ayant également mordus
> jusqu'au sang de notre sang mordus!   5
> embrasse, ma pureté ne se lie qu'à ta pureté
> mais alors embrasse
> comme un champ de justes filaos
> le soir
> nos multicolores puretés   10
> et lie, lie-moi sans remords
> lie-moi de tes vastes bras à l'argile lumineuse
> lie ma noire vibration au nombril même du monde
> lie, lie-moi, fraternité âpre
> puis, m'étranglant de ton lasso d'étoiles   15
> monte, Colombe
> monte
> monte
> monte
> Je te suis, imprimée en mon ancestrale cornée blanche.   20
> monte lécheur de ciel
> et le grand trou noir où je voulais me noyer l'autre lune
> c'est là que je veux pêcher maintenant la langue
>   maléfique de la nuit en son immobile verrition!

These are the poem's final lines, the climax of his *peroration*. What
comes across most vigorously is the multiple *geminatio*, *reduplicatio*,
and *anaphora* of first 'embrasse-moi', second 'lie-moi' (both imperatives addressed to the wind), and third, and most compellingly of all,
'monte', addressed to a dove. The sense implied by the first two of

these *metaphors* is one of complete commitment to, and unity with, the cause of black culture: the 'moi' of line 2 becomes the capitalized 'NOUS' of line 3. Supporting *metaphors* promote this sense of profound belonging: 'jusqu'au sang de notre sang mordus!' (5), 'lie ma noire vibration au nombril même du monde' (13). The degree of commitment to the cause is conveyed by these images of the sharing of bodily activity. At the same time, the poet celebrates unity in diversity with the *geminatio* ('pureté') in line 6 and the paradoxical *antithesis* ('multicolores puretés') in line 10. The upward ascent as the poem reaches its climax suggests hope for the future and determination, and this is explicitly contrasted with the hopeless position adopted by the poet in the past and evoked earlier in the poem (hence the imperfect tense and the *metaphors* of suicide and darkness in line 22). The poem's final word is a puzzle, an invention of the poet. It is significant, however, that the final phrase returns to the question of language with the suggestion of a final rejection of the 'langue maléfique de la nuit', the language that had always painted black people as a race to be oppressed and exploited. A poem which has highlighted the linguistic divide by deploying on the one hand a vocabulary comprehensible only to black people in the Antilles and on the other a range of technical and learned terms that only the most educated of native French people could understand ends with a word comprehensible to no one. But in its sheer novelty, in its suggestion of action (with its '-ion' ending), and in its fleeting evocation of glass and light (from 'verre'), it epitomizes the hope for a new future, towards which the whole poem has been tending.

Césaire's poem exemplifies the aesthetics of negritude as defined by Senghor.[12] Rhythm is crucial, in particular the rhythm created by the repetition of certain *figures* (p. 213):

Il faut noter certaines figures de vocabulaire—*allitérations, paronomases, anaphores*—qui, basées sur une répétition de *phonèmes* ou sons, forment des rythmes secondaires et renforcent l'effet d'ensemble.

Repetition of all kinds is a central part of what Senghor identifies as a poem's dramatic interest: 'L'intérêt dramatique y naît de la répétition: répétition d'un fait, d'un geste, d'un chant, de paroles qui font leitmotiv' (ibid.). He sees this stress on rhythm and repetition as a

---

[12] L. S. Senghor, 'L'Esthétique négro-africaine', in *Libertés I: Négritude et humanisme* (Seuil, 1964), 202–17.

feature distinguishing black from white European aesthetics. It is interesting, however, that he still draws on the terminology of traditional rhetoric to isolate stylistic features of his aesthetics of negritude.

As mayor of Fort-de-France for several decades and as author of the resounding *Discours sur le colonialisme* (1950), Césaire, like Senghor, is fully familiar with the techniques of the orator. Of course, the *Cahier* was written before his political career started. In it, consciously or not, the resources of rhetoric are deployed to express for the reader a new vision of black culture. Baudelaire's link with d'Aubigné was explicitly acknowledged in the epigraph to the first edition of *Les Fleurs du Mal* as consisting in the exploration of vice. Césaire's link with him consists in his ability to deploy rhetoric in such a way as to give intensely memorable expression to a vision of hope for the persecuted and oppressed.

6

THE SELF

Originally intended for the oratorical genres discussed in Chapter 2 (*judicial, deliberative, demonstrative*), where persuading an audience of an opinion is of prime importance, rhetoric adapts itself readily to the more flexible communicative situations of the fictional genres discussed in Chapters 3–5 (drama, prose fiction, poetry). But some types of discourse deal with neither opinion nor fiction. Christian preaching, philosophy, and autobiography are kinds of discourse that claim to offer truths, or even the Truth. There is a long history of tension between rhetoric and those who claim to tell the truth. On the one hand, there is a sense that the truth should be so obviously attractive that it needs no special means of expression. On the other is the suspicion that the truth will strike audiences or readers with greater impact if artfully expressed, especially as the truth might not always be immediately palatable.

Rhetoric and Truth

The tension between rhetoric and truth goes back to the early beginnings of the art. Aristotle's *Rhetoric* is as much a defence of the subject as an account of it. The earliest attacks are most vigorously expressed by Plato in his dialogues *Phaedrus* and *Gorgias*. He establishes an image of Socrates as the exponent of truth, unwilling to have recourse to rhetorical devices (*Gorgias*, 521d):[1]

I think I am one of the few Athenians, not to say the only one, in Athens who attempts the true art of statesmanship, and the only man of the present time who manages affairs of state: hence, as speeches that I make from time to time are not aimed at gratification, but at what is best instead of what is pleasant, and as I do not care to deal in these 'pretty toys' that you recommend, I shall have not a word to say at the bar.

[1] Plato, *Euthyphro, Apology, Crito, Phaedo, Phaedrus*, trans. H. N. Fowler, Loeb Classical Library (Cambridge, Mass.: Harvard University Press, 1914); *idem, Lysis, Symposium, Gorgias*, trans. W. R. M. Lamb, Loeb Classical Library (Cambridge, Mass.: Harvard University Press, 1925).

This quotation implies that rhetoric is something fancy ('pretty toys') that inevitably detracts from the truth; yet it is replete with rhetorical strategies, visible even in translation (particularly Socrates' exploitation of *ethos*).

This is a view with which Christian preachers have long had to contend. The most canonically established of seventeenth-century French preachers, Bossuet, wrestled with this very problem.[2] In his *Panégyrique de l'apôtre saint Paul* he praises Saint Paul for his alleged avoidance of rhetoric and its artifices (pp. 356–7):

N'attendez donc pas de l'Apôtre, ni qu'il vienne flatter les oreilles par des cadences harmonieuses, ni qu'il veuille charmer les esprits par de vaines curiosités. Écoutez ce qu'il dit lui-même: *Nous prêchons une sagesse cachée; nous prêchons un Dieu crucifié.* [. . .] C'est pour ces solides raisons que saint Paul rejette tous les artifices de la rhétorique. Son discours, bien loin de couler avec cette douceur agréable, avec cette égalité tempérée que nous admirons dans les orateurs, paraît égal et sans suite à ceux qui ne l'ont pas assez pénétré; [. . .] Le discours de saint Paul est simple, mais ses pensées sont toutes divines.

The feeling that rhetoric is not entirely respectable affects Bossuet's own practice as a preacher. He sometimes tells his audience explicitly that he is not speaking rhetorically, as in his funeral oration for the Oratorian Père François Bourgoing in 1662 (p. 24):

Pour orner une telle vie, je n'ai pas besoin d'emprunter les fausses couleurs de la rhétorique, et encore moins les détours de la flatterie. Ce n'est pas ici de ces discours où l'on ne parle qu'en tremblant, où il faut plutôt passer avec adresse que s'arrêter avec assurance, où la prudence et la discrétion tiennent toujours en contrainte l'amour de la vérité.

Of course, neither Saint Paul nor Bossuet does in fact avoid rhetoric, though they may prefer some devices to others. The quotation from Saint Paul, in French translation, offered by Bossuet as an example of the apostle's avoidance of rhetoric, creates its stark impact by means of *isocolon* (both phrases are constructed in the same way and are of the same length), *anaphora* ('Nous prêchons' is repeated twice in initial position), and *homoioteleuton* with the homo- phonic endings of 'cachée' and 'crucifié'. Bossuet's claim that he

[2] J. B. Bossuet, *Œuvres*, ed. abbé Velat and Y. Champailler (Gallimard, 1961). For discussions of Bossuet's attitude to rhetoric see P. France, *Rhetoric and Truth in France: Descartes to Diderot* (Oxford: Clarendon Press, 1972), ch. 4; P. Bayley, 'Accommodating Rhetoric', *Seventeenth-Century French Studies*, 19 (1997), 37–47.

does not need to use rhetoric to illustrate the life of the deceased Oratorian is a rhetorical device for implying that his life was so great that its glories will speak for themselves. In rhetorical terms, criticism of rhetoric, like Plato's and Bossuet's, is itself a rhetorical *topos* with a long history. One of its effects is to contribute to the *ethos* of the speaker, perhaps making him or her seem more honest and truthful than those who do not use this *topos*.

Rhetoric and the Self

Ethos and the anti-rhetoric *topos* are particularly important to writers who claim to write about themselves and wish to persuade readers of their sincerity. This applies most obviously to practitioners of the genre of autobiography. This is how Jean-Jacques Rousseau presents his writing in the prefatory paragraph of his *Confessions*:[3]

> Voici le seul portrait d'homme, peint exactement d'après nature et dans toute sa vérité, qui existe et qui probablement existera jamais. Qui que vous soyez, que ma destinée ou ma confiance ont fait l'arbitre du sort de ce cahier, je vous conjure par mes malheurs, par vos entrailles, et au nom de toute l'espèce humaine, de ne pas anéantir un ouvrage unique et utile, lequel peut servir de première pièce de comparaison pour l'étude des hommes, qui certainement est encore à commencer, et de ne pas ôter à l'honneur de ma mémoire le seul monument sûr de mon caractère qui n'ait pas été défiguré par mes ennemis.

The reader turns over the page to find the first words of the first book repeating some of the same themes (p. 33):

> Je forme une entreprise qui n'eut jamais d'exemple et dont l'exécution n'aura point d'imitateur. Je veux montrer à mes semblables un homme dans toute la vérité de la nature; et cet homme sera moi.
>
> Moi, seul. Je sens mon cœur et je connais les hommes. Je ne suis fait comme aucun de ceux que j'ai vus; j'ose croire n'être fait comme aucun de ceux qui existent.

A number of themes emerge forcefully from these passages that together constitute Rousseau's pact with his readers. Most loudly of all, it is the desire to represent himself truthfully that can be heard.

---

[3] J.-J. Rousseau, *Les Confessions*, ed. B. Gagnebin, M. Raymond, and C. Koenig (Gallimard, 1973), 31. Rousseau's attitude to rhetoric is discussed by France in *Rhetoric and Truth*, ch. 7; see also his *Rousseau, 'Confessions'* (Cambridge: Cambridge University Press, 1987). For an (at times) rhetorical approach to this autobiography see G. Py, 'Livres I à IV des *Confessions*', *L'Information littéraire*, 50(1) (1998), 8–20.

This is supported by the anti-rhetoric *topos* in the form of his claim that the confessions will not be carefully written, or literary, or bookish. A further claim to truth is his insistence on the uniqueness of the image that readers will find. Yet there is also the suggestion, not uncommon in autobiographies, that the writer is engaging in a kind of *judicial* discourse, defending himself against personal attacks, which, in Rousseau's case, were noisy and virulent.

Such claims are characteristic of much subsequent writing purporting to be explicitly autobiographical, but are common to all attempts by writers to speak the truth about themselves.[4] Representations of the self can be found not only in autobiographies, but in memoirs, correspondence, and diaries, as well as in that unique and unclassifiable work of self-representation, Montaigne's *Essais* (1580–95). In the light of the difficult history of relations between rhetoric and truth, and rhetoric and self, this chapter explores the ways in which three writers who represent themselves in different genres negotiate their position with respect to rhetoric in their writing practice: Montaigne, Madame de Sévigné in her correspondence (composed between 1648 and 1696), and Gide in his autobiography *Si le grain ne meurt* (1921). If there is any truth in Buffon's famous (and usually misquoted) dictum that 'Le style est l'homme même', then rhetorical analysis might reasonably be expected to illuminate writing about the self.[5]

I. A RHETORIC OF MUTABILITY: MONTAIGNE'S *ESSAIS*

Montaigne had an excellent knowledge of rhetoric, having attended one of the best humanist schools in France, the Collège de Guyenne in Bordeaux.[6] But he did not much like rhetoric, or so he keeps

---

[4] Most work on the genre of autobiography pays some attention to the tension between the truth and the way autobiographers represent it. See e.g. P. Lejeune, *L'Autobiographie en France* (Armand Colin, 1971); idem, *Le Pacte autobiographique* (Seuil, 1975, 1996); M. Sheringham, *French Autobiography: Devices and Desires: Rousseau to Perec* (Oxford: Clarendon Press, 1993); and J. Lecarme and E. Lecarme-Tabone, *L'Autobiographie* (Armand Colin, 1997).

[5] G. L., comte de Buffon, *Discours sur le style: A Facsimile Edition of the 1753 12mo Edition*, ed. C. E. Pickford (Hull: Department of French, 1978), p. xvii.

[6] M. de Montaigne, *Les Essais de Michel de Montaigne*, ed. P. Villey and V. L. Saulnier (Presses Universitaires de France, 1965). My references are to book, chapter, and page number. M. M. McGowan discusses the ways in which Montaigne seeks to influence his readers in *Montaigne's Deceits: The Art of Persuasion in the 'Essais'* (University of London Press,

telling us. He mocks orators for their preference for speech over action, calling them 'des Orateurs qui estudient à dire justice, non à la faire' (I, 25, 138). Rome's great rhetorician and orator, Cicero, bores him when he writes about philosophy, and it is Cicero's rhetorical approach to the subject that is clearly at fault, in Montaigne's eyes: 'ses prefaces, definitions, partitions, etymologies, consument la plus part de son ouvrage; ce qu'il y a de vif et de mouelle, est estouffé par ses longueries d'apprets' (II, 10, 413). One chapter, 'De la vanité des paroles' (I, 51), is a sustained attack on rhetoric's inflated grandeur and art of deception, as Montaigne perceives it. One way he depicts rhetoric unfavourably is by the suggestion that eloquence flourishes only in states that are ailing: 'L'eloquence a fleury le plus à Rome, lors que les affaires ont esté en plus mauvais estat, et que l'orage des guerres civiles les agitoit' (I, 51, 306). Here rhetoric suffers by association with the sickly city. Another way is by implicit comparison between the orator and Montaigne's caricatural portrait of an Italian butler he had met, pompous and painstaking in his distinctions and enumerations (I, 51, 306):

Je luy faisoy compter de sa charge. Il m'a fait un discours de cette science de gueule avec une gravité et contenance magistrale, comme s'il m'eust parlé de quelque grand poinct de Theologie. Il m'a dechifré une difference d'appetits: celuy qu'on a à jeun, qu'on a après le second et tiers service; les moyens, tantost de luy plaire simplement, tantost de l'eveiller et picquer; la police de ses sauces, premierement en general, et puis particularisant les qualitez des ingrediens et leurs effects; les differences des salades selon leur

1974). Two collections of essays focus on rhetoric in the *Essais*: F. Lestringant (ed.), *Rhétorique de Montaigne*, a special number of the *Bulletin de la Société des Amis de Montaigne*, 7(1–2) (1985) (in this collection see esp. G. Defaux, 'Rhétorique et représentation dans les *Essais*: De la peinture de l'autre à la peinture du moi', 21–48), and J. O'Brien, M. Quainton, and J. J. Supple (eds.), *Montaigne et la rhétorique: Actes du colloque de St Andrews (28–31 mars 1992)* (Champion, 1995) (in this collection see esp. A. Moss, ' "Des Coches": Une Rhétorique transportable', 77–87, showing how 'Montaigne déploie toutes les ressources de la rhétorique pour construire un monument, aussi beau qu'émouvant, à la mémoire de ce monde condamné au silence' (87)). J. Brody has published two collections of articles in which he offers readings of the *Essais* that are not strictly rhetorical but that attend closely to their verbal texture: *Lectures de Montaigne* (Lexington, Ky.: French Forum, 1982) and *Nouvelles Lectures de Montaigne* (Champion, 1994) (this latter collection includes a reading of III, 2, 'Du Repentir' (37–72)). Many critics have addressed the representational nature of the book: see e.g. R. A. Sayce, *The 'Essays' of Montaigne: A Critical Exploration* (Weidenfeld and Nicolson, 1972), ch. 4; R. Regosin, *The Matter of my Book: Montaigne's 'Essais' as the Book of the Self* (Berkeley: University of California Press, 1977); and C. Taylor, *Sources of the Self: The Making of the Modern Identity* (Cambridge: Cambridge University Press, 1989), 178–84.

saison, celle qui doit estre reschaufée, celle qui veut estre servie froide, la façon de les orner et embellir pour les rendre encores plaisantes à la veüe.

The butler talks about food with recourse to what Montaigne clearly sees as a similar range of tedious rhetorical devices, in particular the *places* (e.g. *divisions* and *effects*), to which Cicero has recourse when writing on philosophy. We shall see that Montaigne is more interesting when writing about his own differences from himself than the butler is when speaking about differences in salads.

For all his scepticism about rhetoric, Montaigne knows it too well to dismiss it completely. His attacks on it are variations of the anti-rhetoric *topos*. In one version of this *topos* Montaigne, while seeking to belittle rhetoric, in fact acknowledges its ubiquitousness and inevitability (I, 51, 307):

Oyez dire metonomie, metaphore, allegorie, et autres tels noms de la grammaire, semble-t-il pas qu'on signifie quelque forme de langage rare et pellegrin? Ce sont titres qui touchent le babil de vostre chambriere.

Montaigne here recognizes that there is nothing intrinsically abstruse or learned about the linguistic phenomena to which rhetoricians or grammarians have given complex names. Chambermaids use rhetorical *figures* in the same way that Molière's Monsieur Jourdain speaks prose—without realizing it.

Moreover, like any good user of rhetoric, Montaigne is highly conscious of his readers and of the way his writing will strike them. His preface 'Au lecteur' is at once another version of the anti-rhetoric *topos*, exploiting images of unaffected portraiture such as Rousseau reuses nearly 200 years later and a rhetorically crafted appeal to the reader's good will in the suggestion that the writer is an honest, modest, and unassuming man, even quite a witty one (*ethos*). There is wit, for example, in the insistent and unexpected claims that the *Essais* will be of no interest to the reader; they were written only for the benefit of Montaigne's family and friends: 'Je n'y ay eu nulle consideration de ton service, ny de ma gloire. [. . .] Je l'ay voué à la commodité particuliere de mes parens et amis' (I, 'Au lecteur', 3); 'ce n'est pas raison que tu employes ton loisir en un subject si frivole et si vain'. The imagery of portrayal is explicit about the claims to truth and the avoidance of artifice: 'Je veus qu'on m'y voie en ma façon simple, naturelle et ordinaire, sans contention et artifice: car c'est moy que je peins.' He is not writing his portrait with the rhetorical purpose of impressing people, he says:

'Si c'eust esté pour rechercher la faveur du monde, je me fusse mieux paré et me presanterois en une marche estudiée.' The 'Au lecteur' functions like a textbook example of an *exordium*, establishing a relationship of trust between writer and reader. He protests his honesty and sincerity, and demonstrates his ability to write in an arresting way; the reader is addressed directly, twice as 'lecteur' and five times as 'tu', 'te', or 'ton' within the space of a few sentences. The close relationship between writer and reader is fostered even more by Montaigne's conception of his reader as singular rather than plural.

The most arresting aspect of the 'Au lecteur', at least for the sixteenth-century reader less familiar than later readers with the concept of writers writing about themselves, is the claim to self-portrayal. Having used the imagery of portraiture several times, Montaigne sums up his book with *alliterative* memorability and *metaphorical* starkness: 'je suis moy-mesmes la matiere de mon livre'. This *metaphor*, suggesting an equivalence between the substance of the book and the man, is no idle one. It recurs later, and is in some sense a key to appreciating the unusual nature of Montaigne's project. The inseparability of man and book is forcefully reasserted in the claim that 'Je n'ay pas plus faict mon livre que mon livre m'a faict, livre consubstantiel à son autheur' (II, 18, 665). Here the *metaphor* of consubstantiality is introduced and reinforced by the *chiasmus* and *geminatio* of 'Je [. . .] faict mon livre [. . .] mon livre m'a faict'. A *metaphor* of companionship evokes the same consubstantiality elsewhere: 'Icy, nous allons conformément et tout d'un trein, mon livre et moy' (III, 2, 806). Whilst it is true that Montaigne tells readers about his nutritional likes and dislikes, about his tooth falling out, and even about the intimate details of his kidney stone, his portrait is no straightforwardly descriptive one in the manner of *demonstrative* rhetoric. Unlike d'Aubigné's portraits of political figures in *Les Tragiques*, Montaigne's is not an exercise in *ethopoeia*. Indeed, a reader glancing through the titles he gives to his chapters could be excused for thinking that the work does not deal in self-portraiture at all: 'Par divers moyens on arrive à pareille fin' (I, 1), 'De la tristesse' (I, 2), 'Nos affections s'emportent au dela de nous' (I, 3), 'Comme l'ame descharge ses passions sur des objects faux, quand les vrais luy defaillent' (I, 4), 'Si le chef d'une place assiégée doit sortir pour parlementer' (I, 5), 'L'heure des parlemens dangereuse' (I, 6). Even when these titles gesture towards matters of personal behaviour, they are framed in terms that are abstract and general rather than specific to one individual. Montaigne's portrait is so unusual because it is to be found not in a sequential narrative of his life's experiences, but in the manner of his writing, the very form of which conjures up for the reader Montaigne's mind at work on a wide range of topics. So Montaigne's portrait is a portrait of a mind, making links between what he feels, what he sees, and what he reads; and the words chosen, and their arrangement, are the expression of that mind.

Montaigne is acutely aware of the difficulties that this kind of writing represents for the reader. And it is a measure of his sensitivity to the rhetorical situation of writer and reader that his mind, and his words, so often dwell on these difficulties. In an *interrogation*, using striking *metaphors* of monstrosity, *alliteratively* linked, he invites the readers to agree with him that his book is badly organized, making clear his rejection of the orderliness of traditional *disposition*: 'Que sont-ce icy aussi, à la verité, que crotesques et corps monstrueux, rappiecez de divers membres, sans certaine figure, n'ayants ordre, suite ny proportion que fortuite?' (I, 28, 183). In the chapter 'De la vanité' (III, 9) he is more specific about his writing style as a representation of his mind at work: 'Mon stile et mon esprit vont vagabondant de mesmes' (994). And he is unapologetic about the careful attention that this diffusely wandering, apparently unfocused style requires of the reader. If readers lose their way, it is their own fault, not Montaigne's: 'C'est l'indiligent lecteur qui pert mon subject, non pas moy; il s'en trouvera tousjours en un coing quelque mot qui ne laisse pas d'estre bastant, quoy qu'il soit serré' (994). One of the reasons why Montaigne adopts this unusual style of self-portraiture without apology is his confidence in it as a rhetorical strategy. It is literally arresting. It makes readers stop and think: 'Puisque je ne puis arrester l'attention du lecteur par le pois, "*manco male*" [it's not so bad] s'il advient que je l'arreste par mon embrouilleure' (995). He writes in this way to be noticed. He cannot bear the thought of a lazy reader, and offers himself as a challenging writer: 'Qui est celuy qui n'ayme mieux n'estre pas leu que de l'estre en dormant ou en fuyant?' (995).

Capturing Movement in Words

Montaigne combines an evocation of his mental processes with reflections on his project in the opening of the chapter 'Du repentir', a passage that also attempts to persuade the reader of the value of his work (III, 2, 804–5):

[1] Les autres forment l'homme; je le recite et en represente un particulier bien mal formé, et lequel, si j'avoy à façonner de nouveau, je ferois vrayement bien autre qu'il n'est. [2] Meshuy c'est fait. [3] Or les traits de ma peinture ne forvoyent point, quoy qu'ils se changent et diversifient. [4] Le monde n'est qu'une branloire perenne. [5] Toutes choses y branlent sans cesse: la terre, les rochers du Caucase, les pyramides d'Aegypte, et du branle public et du leur. [6] La constance mesme n'est autre chose qu'un branle plus languissant. [7] Je ne puis asseurer mon object. [8] Il va trouble et chancelant, d'une yvresse naturelle. [9] Je le prends en ce point, comme il est, en l'instant que je m'amuse à luy. [10] Je ne peints pas l'estre. [11] Je peints le passage: non un passage d'aage en autre, ou, comme dict le peuple, de sept en sept ans, mais de jour en jour, de minute en minute. [12] Il faut accommoder mon histoire à l'heure. [13] Je pourray tantost changer, non de fortune seulement, mais aussi d'intention. [14] C'est un contrerolle de divers et muables accidens et d'imaginations irresoluës et, quand il y eschet, contraires; soit que je sois autre moy-mesme, soit que je saisisse les subjects par autres circonstances et considerations. [15] Tant y a que je me contredits bien à l'adventure, mais la verité, comme disoit Demades, je ne la contredy point. [16] Si mon ame pouvoit prendre pied, je ne m'essaierois pas, je me resoudrois: elle est toujours en apprentissage et en espreuve.

[17] Je propose une vie basse et sans lustre, c'est tout un. [18] On attache aussi bien toute la philosophie morale à une vie populaire et privée que à une vie de plus riche estoffe; chaque homme porte la forme entiere de l'humaine condition.

At first glance, there is order in this passage. It begins by claiming that Montaigne's self-portrait is original in conception, but modest (1–2). It then introduces the major theme of diversity (3), both in the world (4–6) and in Montaigne's life, and hence in his portrait (7–16). Finally it reasserts the modesty of the subject, whilst claiming that the portrait has universal significance (17–18).

But the apparent order, which a summary of the passage suggests, is deceptive, for several reasons. First of all, Montaigne makes a series of statements with few, if any, explicit links between them ('Or' (3) might count as an explicit indication that a new subject is being introduced). This means that it is the task of the reader to extract an argumentational framework from the sequence of statements, at which point, however, different emphases become possible. One might explain the argument as follows: Montaigne distinguishes his portrait as being that of an ordinary man at both the beginning and the end of the passage, and in between writes defensively about the inconsistencies and incoherences the reader will find in his portrait by drawing an analogy between the individual man and the world in which he lives, both subject to change; the stress on *ethos* with the modesty *topos* would reinforce this defensive approach, inviting readers to sympathize with the author. Alternatively, the argument might be much bolder: whilst making conventional gestures towards the modesty *topos*, Montaigne draws explicit attention to the novelty of his portrait; he insistently celebrates its incoherence as a feature of its truthfulness; and by making a link between his own incoherence and the incoherence of the world, he builds up to his extraordinary, even immodest, claim that his own allegedly ordinary life can, in a philosophical sense, embrace the life of every human being. Montaigne's sparing use of specifically argumentational phraseology allows the reader to interpret the argument in quite varied ways: careful self-defence in the *judicial* mode, bold self-assertion in the *demonstrative* mode.

Moreover, the attempt to extract an argument from Montaigne's sequence of statements might be seen to constitute a falsification of the text's message and its mode of operation. For any attempt to distil an argument tends to telescope his statements so that their individual significance and interest are diminished. For example, he expresses the view that he and his portrait are subject to flux in ten sentences (7–16). These sentences cannot really be said to constitute an argumentational progression. Each makes the same point, but in a different way, with different images and different words. To read for the argument is to ignore the verbal texture. Yet it could be argued that it is precisely the verbal texture that conveys Montaigne's mind at work. The passage is a densely woven pattern of rhetorical *figures*, teasingly inviting the reader to make links between them and press them into the service of an argument, but at the same time flaunting their linguistic independence by means of the repeated restatements: the *figures* keep changing, but the sense, by and large, does not. The linguistic independence of Montaigne's *elocution*, like that of Beckett discussed in Chapter 3, points to meaning beyond the explicitly referential: in Montaigne's case, to his love of words and his paradoxical vision of himself as similar and changing (the *invention* remains similar, the *elocution* changes); in Beckett's case, to his vision of a world empty of meaning, where words struggle vainly to refer to things.

The opening section relies above all on a ludic interplay of *metaphors*, with similar, yet slightly different values, relating to the evocation of man in words: 'forment', 'recite', 'represente', 'façonner', 'ferois' (1). 'Forment' describes the work of moral philosophers, those who envisage mankind in their writings only to tell people how they should be, how they should behave. The word reappears wittily in a different sense, and by means of *polyptoton*, when Montaigne describes himself as 'bien mal formé'. The image here refers most obviously to the work of nature, but Montaigne is also suggesting that, as an individual, he would not satisfy the requirements of moral philosophers. 'Recite' and 'represente' constitute an *antithesis* to 'forment', and evoke, in a combination of oral and pictural imagery, Montaigne's unique attempt to describe in words an individual as he is, rather than mankind as it should be. The other images, 'façonner' and 'ferois', evoking sculptural activity, participate in the modesty *topos*, though with a certain witty ambiguity. Montaigne is suggesting modestly that he would have liked nature to make him differently from the way he is; the wit and ambiguity lie in the way he makes himself the subject of the verbs of creation, assuming divine powers for the sake of verbal play. The momentary flight of fancy, that he could wish himself different from the way he is, is punctuated, and punctured, by the sharply concise sentence, 'Meshuy c'est fait' (2).

Retaining the imagery of artistic creation, but making it explicitly an image of painting, the next sentence (3) explains a key aspect of Montaigne's writing about himself in the form of a paradox. The features depicted are not erratic; they constitute an accurate portrait, even though they may appear not to cohere. The element of changeability is reinforced by the *hendiadys* ('se changent et diversifient'). The abrupt move in the next three sentences (4–6) to statements of a general nature about the world might disorientate the reader. But all these statements are motivated by the image of changeability, and are *metaphorical* variations on that theme. In retrospect, the generalized statements of changeability can be read as a context for the following images of Montaigne's own changeability: in rhetorical terms, the world is the *genus* of which Montaigne is a *species*. The first *metaphor* expressing changeability is that of the world as a kind of see-saw ('une branloire perenne' (4)). The word 'branloire' then nourishes further *metaphors* by means of *dérivation*: 'branlent' (5), 'branle' (5 and 6). This sort of gently graduated repetition helps to create the overwhelming sense of mutability as a prime feature of the natural world. This is further supported by the division of the world into a series of parts in an *epitrochasmus* ('la terre, les rochers du Caucase, les pyramides d'Aegypte' (5)) and also by Montaigne's distinction between the movement that affects everything, from the outside as it were, and the movement that individual features of the world produce of their own accord ('et du branle public et du leur' (5)). Montaigne strengthens his argument by taking the *opposite* of changeability, 'constance', and asserting *metaphorically* that this too is a kind of movement, albeit less noticeable (6). Moreover, the word 'constance' can be applied not only to features of the natural world, but to the ethical life of mankind. So although this sentence does not constitute an explicit link to the next, when Montaigne returns abruptly to the subject of himself, it does provide an implicit link.

In the next ten sentences (7–16) a plethora of *figures* suggest over and over again Montaigne's sense of his own mutability and his awareness of the demands it imposes on his writing as he attempts to convey it in words. First of all, his self's resistance to certainty and fixedness is conveyed by the difficulty the portraitist has in keeping it in his sights: 'Je ne puis asseurer mon object' (7). It is as if he has divided himself into two, the artist and the sitter. The sitter appears to have a life of his own and, in an implicit *simile*, is likened to a drunken man unable to stand straight: this is conveyed first *metaphorically* and emphasized by *hendiadys* ('trouble et chancelant' (8)), then more explicitly ('d'une yvresse naturelle' (8)). The consequences of his self's frequent changes are that, although he may try to convey it accurately at one moment, at the next it has to be conveyed differently. His portrait is inevitably unstable. Montaigne uses playful *polyptoton* to invite his reader to think about the difference between the 'être' that he paints and the 'être' that he does not paint: he portrays his self 'comme il est' (9), but 'Je ne peins pas l'estre' (10). It is the momentary being that is caught fleetingly before it changes; but there is no essence to be conveyed. The *polyptoton* in sentences 9 and 10 gives way, almost imperceptibly, to the *geminatio* in sentences 10 and 11, making the same point about the difference between essence and change: 'Je ne peins pas l'estre. Je peins le passage.' The point comes over clearly not only with the *geminatio*, but also with the *antithesis* between negative and affirmative and with the *alliterative* /p/. Montaigne then intensifies his understanding of the self's changeability in a series of *isocolonic* phrases (each incorporating a *geminatio*) that together form a *gradatio*, as he focuses on the frequency with which the self changes. In keeping with his fondness for restatement, particularly *geminatio*, the first element in the sequence, change over a period of years, which he rejects, is expressed twice, first more literally ('un passage d'aage en autre' (11)), then proverbially ('de sept en sept ans'). He promotes instead the idea of the self's much more frequent variations: from years to days ('de jour en jour'), from days to minutes ('de minute en minute'). This temporal vocabulary is resumed in the immediately following sentence (12), where Montaigne repeats the point about the relationship between his portrait's accuracy and the passage of time, but more pithily: 'Il faut accommoder mon histoire à l'heure.' Throughout this passage the thoughts are similar, but the *elocution* changes. In this way the writing enacts the mutability of Montaigne's self (one, but changing).

Still exploring the same theme of his mutability, he now shifts the focus from the frequency of change to the nature of change, and does so in such a way as to stress that change is not only accidental, but also intentional. Yet again, Montaigne makes the claim forcefully by means of restatement: on the one hand, the accidental ('non de fortune seulement' (13), 'divers et muables accidens' (14)), on the other, the intentional ('intention' (13), 'imaginations irresoluës et [. . .] contraires' (14)). The second part of this double *antithesis* is characterized by a *chiasmus* (two adjectives plus noun, followed by noun plus two adjectives). Then Montaigne delves further into the nature of his changing mind and its changing perceptions, offering two possibilities. The first is the more radical, involving profound internal change, and is expressed as a paradox ('soit que je sois autre moy-mesme' (14)). The second suggests that his changing mind is responding to the different light in which he perceives things: the key words in this possibility ('circonstances et considerations' (14)) reinforce each other by *hendiadys* and a degree of phonetic overlap (/k/ /i/ /ɔ̃/ /s/ /ʀ/). At this point Montaigne returns to a restatement of his main theme: that the truth lies in change and diversity. This is expressed in yet another paradoxical *antithesis*, reinforced by the repetition of the same verb (*geminatio*): 'je me contredits', 'la verité [. . .] je ne la contredy point' (15). The claim is further supported by an appeal to *external proof*, the authority of Demades, who, according to Plutarch, said that he never contradicted the public

interest, even though he sometimes contradicted himself. The inter-
textual reference bolsters Montaigne's own authority in the reader's
eyes, and covertly suggests that he too has his mind on the public
interest, as opposed to a strictly private one. This would certainly
contradict his claims in the 'Au lecteur' about the private interest of
his book, but it prepares us for the claim, in the next paragraph,
that his portrait has a universal application. Finally, he develops a
further sequence of *metaphors* to convey the instability of his self-
portraiture. There is a resumption of the earlier personalized
metaphor as his self unsteady on his feet ('Si mon ame pouvoit prendre pied' (16)). His writing is then described positively in three
metaphors, all suggesting its highly tentative nature: 'essaierois',
'apprentissage', 'espreuve' (16). The last two of these are highlighted
by *hendiadys* and their *isocolonic* form: 'en apprentissage et en
espreuve'.

In the final two sentences (17–18), Montaigne returns to the
explicit, yet increasingly ambiguous, deployment of *ethos* with which
the passage began. He insists on the modesty of his life ('une vie
basse et sans lustre' (17)). But this very sentence contains an intimation of the bold claim that follows: 'c'est tout un'. Montaigne claims
that his own allegedly humble life is as apt for illustrating issues of
moral philosophy as a richly distinguished life. After the repeatedly
restated claims of instability and tentativeness in the previous paragraph, this new claim stands out sharply. First of all, there is the
equation between the humble life and the rich life, which rings out
in *parisonic* form with the major element, the humble life, standing
out *alliteratively*: 'à une vie populaire et privée que à une vie de plus
riche estoffe' (18). More significantly, there is the suggestion, in the
phrase 'toute la philosophie morale', that this unstable portrait of
one modest individual has a universal dimension. This suggestion is
made explicit in the closing phrase, one of the most famous in the
whole of Montaigne's work: 'chaque homme porte la forme entiere
de l'humaine condition' (18). It is a phrase that resounds with its
hyperbole ('entiere') and its combination of *antithesis* and *dérivation*: one
man ('homme'), mankind ('humaine'). Its use of the word 'forme'
takes the reader back to the opening of the passage, defiantly inti-
mating that there is a form inherent in human beings that is quite
distinct from the form that moral philosophers would like to impose
on them. It is this natural, rather than *their* artificial, form in which
Montaigne claims to have an interest and which he wishes to

convey through the medium of his own self-portrait. In this short passage, the portrait itself has been alluded to through a wide range of *metaphors*, including 'recite', 'represente', 'peinture', 'histoire', 'contrerolle', 'essaierois', 'propose'. The varying *metaphors*, as well as all the other modulated *figures*, enact both the roaming mind and the shifting personality of the writer, and contribute to the uniqueness of his portrait.

Anti-colonialist Rhetoric

Yet to put the emphasis solely on Montaigne's unusual style and its consubstantiality with his mind at work is to succumb too readily to his rhetoric. As well as the teasing progress of Montaigne's mind that, to be sure, predominates in the *Essais* and that he himself is so happy to foreground in self-conscious comments on his writing, there are chapters and passages that are more solidly constructed and that seem to express a vision or a point of view with calculated vigour and in a more ostensibly persuasive style. A chapter like the 'Apologie de Raimond Sebond' (II, 12), by far the longest chapter and placed at the very centre of the *Essais*, is a logically and systematically constructed (though not entirely unambiguous) defence of Sebond's work, the *Theologia Naturalis*; similarly, 'De l'institution des enfans' (I, 26) defends a new and humane educational method. Sometimes, too, within a varied and digressive chapter, Montaigne writes passages that deploy an orderly and passionate rhetoric, designed to move and persuade the reader, as in his account of the Indians conquered by the Spaniards in 'Des coches', which rouses our sympathy and admiration for them and destabilizes our Eurocentric vision of the world (III, 6, 910):

[1] Quand je regarde cete ardeur indomptable dequoy tant de milliers d'hommes, femmes et enfans, se presentent et rejettent à tant de fois aux dangers inevitables, pour la deffence de leurs dieux et de leur liberté; céte genereuse obstination de souffrir toutes extremitez et difficultez, et la mort, plus volontiers que de se soubmettre à la domination de ceux de qui ils ont esté si honteusement abusez, et aucuns choisissans plustost de se laisser defaillir par faim et par jeusne, estans pris, que d'accepter le vivre des mains de leurs ennemis, si vilement victorieuses, je prevois que, à qui les eust attaquez pair à pair, et d'armes, et d'expérience, et de nombre, il y eust faict aussi dangereux, et plus, qu'en autre guerre que nous voyons.

[2] Que n'est tombée soubs Alexandre ou soubs ces anciens Grecs et

Romains une si noble conqueste, et une si grande mutation et alteration de tant d'empires et de peuples soubs des mains qui eussent doucement poly et defriché ce qu'il y avoit de sauvage, et eussent conforté et promeu les bonnes semences que nature y avoit produit, meslant non seulement à la culture des terres et ornement des villes les arts de deçà, en tant qu'elles y eussent esté necessaires, mais aussi meslant les vertus Grecques et Romaines aux originelles du pays! [3] Quelle reparation eust-ce esté, et quel amendement à toute cette machine, que les premiers exemples et deportemens nostres qui se sont presentez par delà eussent dressé entre eux et nous une fraternele societé et intelligence! [4] Combien il eust esté aisé de faire son profit d'ames si neuves, si affamées d'apprentissage, ayant pour la plus part de si beaux comencemens naturels! [5] Au rebours, nous nous sommes servis de leur ignorance et inexperience à les plier plus facilement vers la trahison, luxure, avarice et vers toute sorte d'inhumanité et de cruauté, à l'exemple et patron de nos meurs. [6] Qui mit jamais à tel pris le service de la mercadence et de la trafique? [7] Tant de villes rasées, tant de nations exterminées, tant de millions de peuples passez au fil de l'espée, et la plus riche et belle partie du monde bouleversée pour la negotiation des perles et du poivre: mechaniques victoires. [8] Jamais l'ambition, jamais les inimitiez publiques ne pousserent les hommes les uns contre les autres à si horribles hostilitez et calamitez si miserables.

It does not require detailed rhetorical analysis to sense major differences between this passage and that from the beginning of 'Du repentir'. Whereas the latter was characterized by short sentences and *parataxis*, making the reader work to form an argumentational framework, this passage from 'Des coches' contains mostly long sentences remarkable for their *hypotaxis*, making the argument generally clear. In three sharply delineated stages, Montaigne deplores the way in which the Spaniards conquered the Indians. First, he comments on the unequal forces: if the Indians had had at their disposal the experience and weapons of the Spaniards, they would have been a force to be reckoned with, such is their innate courage (1). Secondly, he points out the deficiencies of the Spaniards in implicit terms by contrasting them with the Greeks and Romans as conquerors (2–4). Finally, he spells out explicitly the shameful features of the Spanish conquests (5–8).

Montaigne makes transparent use of rhetorical devices to support this *judicial* discourse in which the Spaniards are condemned. *Ethos* paints the Indians as courageous victims and the Spaniards as disgraceful assailants (1). *Pathos* appeals to a sense of envy for the long-lost glories of the civilizations of the ancient world (2–4) and a sense of outrage and pity for the physical and moral ravages perpetrated by Spain. Indignation in the narrative voice is suggested by the insistent use of *exclamations* and *communicatio*, forcing the reader to engage with the issues and think about them: 'Que n'est tombée soubs Alexandre [. . .]' (2), 'Quelle reparation eust-ce esté [. . .]' (3), 'Combien il eust esté aisé [. . .]' (4), 'Qui mit jamais [. . .]' (6), 'Tant de ville rasées [. . .]' (7). Within these solid structures of arresting discourse, a prominence of *hyperbole, epitrochasmus*, and obtrusively balanced phrasing supports the effect of urgent indignation: for example, 'tant de milliers d'hommes, femmes et enfans' (1), 'toutes extremitez et difficultez' (1), 'et d'armes, et d'expérience, et de nombre' (1), 'une si noble conqueste, et une si grande mutation et alteration de tant d'empires et de peuples' (2), 'Quelle reparation [. . .] et quel amendement' (3), 'si neuves, si affamées' (4), 'vers la trahison, luxure, avarice et vers toute sorte d'inhumanité et de cruauté' (5), 'de la mercadence et de la trafique' (6), 'Tant de villes rasées, tant de nations exterminées, tant de millions de peuples passez au fil de l'espée' (7). Other devices figure too, like the *alliterative* /p/ in 'pour la negociation des perles et du poivre' (7), which foregrounds the scorn Montaigne feels for the greedy, exploitative conquerors. But it is above all the relentlessly and obviously patterned *hyperbolic* language that aims to rouse readers to revise their view of the conquest of the New World. These devices reach a dense climax in the last sentence (8), marked by its emphatically unusual word order (*hyperbaton*), its compelling *anaphora* ('Jamais l'ambition, jamais les inimitiez'), and its resounding combination of *chiasmus* and double *homoioteleuton* ('si horribles hostilitez et calamitez si miserables').

Yet one might start to feel that the greater the *hyperbole*, the more there is concealment of truth. There is no word here about human sacrifice or the bloody wars between the Aztecs and the Mayans. *Hyperbole* can be persuasive; it can also serve as a smokescreen. This is a very different kind of rhetoric, more obviously weighed, calculated, and shaped, from the one that Montaigne most often advertises as his preferred mode. But, in its very difference, it confirms the mutability and variety that Montaigne says is the distinctive mark of his own portrait, as of mankind's.

2. RHETORIC FOR FAMILY AND FRIENDS:
MME DE SÉVIGNÉ'S *CORRESPONDANCE*

Mme de Sévigné was happy to succumb to the unique illusion created by Montaigne's rhetoric of a real man communicating directly with his reader.[7] On one occasion when she travelled from Paris to Livry, she says how happy she was to discover that she had brought a volume of the *Essais* with her (6 October 1679):

> En voici un [un amusement] que j'ai trouvé: c'est un tome de Montaigne, que je ne croyais pas avoir apporté. Ah, l'aimable homme! qu'il est de bonne compagnie! C'est mon ancien ami, mais à force d'être ancien, il m'est nouveau.

The circumstances in which Sévigné wrote are very different from those of Montaigne, but her writing has much in common with Montaigne's project. Both have a strong sense of their relationship with their reader; and both wish to conjure up their presence for their reader in words. Unlike Montaigne, however, Sévigné did not explicitly say that she put pen to paper in order to write about herself. Indeed, she never thought that she was writing for publication or for consumption beyond her immediate circle of family and friends. This aristocratic woman whose voluminous correspondence covers the second half of the seventeenth century went into publication posthumously and piecemeal in the eighteenth century. It is only in the twentieth century that a complete text of her extant letters has been available to the reading public.

These circumstances ensure that it is no straightforward task to determine who is communicating with whom when we read the letters. It might be tempting to see the communication that they enact as narrow and closed: a real woman addressing a real letter to a real person at a real time, her rhetoric working within these closely defined limits. And it might also be thought that such letters,

---

[7] Mme de Sévigné, *Correspondance*, ed. R. Duchêne, Bibliothèque de la Pléiade (3 vols., Gallimard, 1972–8). Letters are referred to in my text simply by their date. There have been two contrasting approaches to Sévigné's writing. R. Duchêne sees it as informal correspondence that can be thought to have literary merit only incidentally (see his *Réalité vécue et art épistolaire: Mme de Sévigné et la lettre d'amour* (Bordas, 1970); B. Bray detects more of a systematic approach in her writing (see 'Quelques Aspects du système épistolaire de Mme de Sévigné', *Revue d'histoire littéraire de la France*, 69 (1969), 491–505). The enthusiastic little book by J. Cordelier, *Mme de Sévigné par elle-même* (Seuil, 1967), gives a good account of the evolution of her writing style.

without her necessarily intending them to do so, would reveal much about the personality of the writer. Yet, in the seventeenth century, the conventions of writing letters to friends and family and of receiving them allowed for a wider publication than the narrowly conceived model of communication suggests, and, hence, possibly favoured the cultivation of a style that would impress more than it would reveal. There are numerous indications within Sévigné's letters of a wider communicative circle. She writes to her daughter on 30 July 1677 promising to forward the letters she herself had received from Mme de Villars: 'elles vous divertiront'. Elsewhere, she comments on the superior style of her daughter's letters, which, although addressed to her mother alone, have been the subject of repeated readings and critical assessment not only by Sévigné herself, but by her friend, Corbinelli, and her son (11 August 1677):

Laissez-nous aimer et admirer vos lettres; votre style est un fleuve qui coule doucement et qui fait détester tous les autres. Ce n'est pas à vous d'en juger. Vous n'avez pas le plaisir; vous ne les lisez pas. Nous les lisons et les relisons; et nous ne sommes pas de trop mauvais juges. Quand je dis nous, c'est Corbinelli, le Baron et moi.

Clearly, private letters often had a wider, if small, audience among the recipient's family and friends. Moreover, collections of semi-private letters were published at the time, and there are moments when Sévigné teasingly refers to the possibility of such publication, at least of her daughter's letters, if not of her own. She writes to her daughter on 8 April 1671: 'que vos lettres sont aimables! Il y a des endroits dignes de l'impression'; and again on 19 May 1676: 'ce que vous m'en dites l'autre jour est à imprimer'. She can even conceive of her daughter's letters as a kind of book, referring to them as 'ce livre que vous m'envoyez' (6 November 1675).

There are probably many more numerous references in the letters, however, to their intimacy, privacy, spontaneity, and lack of calculated artistry. This approach might result in letters more likely to reveal the true personality of the writer. Sévigné sometimes compares her writing to the unpreparedness of conversation (3 November 1688):

Voilà bien de la conversation, car c'est ainsi qu'on peut appeler nos lettres. Si celle-ci vous ennuie, j'en suis fâchée, car je l'ai écrite de bon cœur, et *currente calamo* [with a flowing pen].

One of the ways in which she suggests her own lack of control over her writing is to *personify* her pen (30 July 1677):

Quand je commence, je ne sais point du tout où cela ira, si ma lettre sera longue ou si elle sera courte; j'écris tant qu'il plaît à ma plume, c'est elle qui gouverne tout.

She sometimes insists explicitly on her lack of interest in the traditional procedures of rhetoric: 'Voilà tout ce que mon imagination me fait jeter sur ce papier, sans art, sans arrangement, à course de plume' (23 January 1682).

But protestations about lack of artistry, especially when made so frequently and so elegantly, are cause for suspicion. Whilst it is true that Sévigné's letters reveal a great deal about the life-style, opinions, and emotions of their writer, they show us a woman becoming a writer; and she learns, as she writes to a variety of recipients, but above all to her daughter, how to modulate her tone, how to impress, how to amuse, how to appear confidential, distraught, and excited, how to express love and affection. Instinctively Sévigné senses the rhetorical nature of the letter: she must win and hold her reader's attention, just as in conversation she has to hold the attention of her interlocutor. In the case of her daughter, she wants more than attention; she wants to be assured of her love. By an extraordinary accident of survival, her letters are available for modern readers to participate in the communicative situation, whether by observing at a distance Sévigné's rhetoric at work on her original readers, or by treating the correspondence as a kind of letter-novel, becoming immersed in it and savouring, as it were directly, the impact of the writer's words.

The enormous bulk of the extant correspondence is to her daughter, Mme de Grignan. Widowed at 25 and never remarried, Sévigné cultivated a special relationship with her daughter. But the daughter's marriage to the comte de Grignan led to her departure to the south from the north of France, where she had lived with her mother in Paris and Brittany. Whenever they were apart, from 1671 until Sévigné's death in 1696, mother and daughter maintained a regular correspondence, twice a week, and eventually, when the postal service allowed it, three times. Mme de Grignan's replies, which have not survived, can only be imagined from Sévigné's letters themselves. What the modern reader of the correspondence sees is the rapid development of a letter-writing style which, for all the protestations of spontaneity, deploys a range of strategies to secure the interest and affection of the daughter. In depicting herself as a lively, loving, and lovable mother, Sévigné adopts a rhetoric which she uses either instinctively as an extension of her conversational skills or as a result of her broad reading. She read copiously and widely: Aristotle, Cicero, and the declamations then attributed to Quintilian were amongst her reading matter, although there is no evidence that it was specifically their rhetorical theory that she read.

Epistolary Informality

The following letter, written about a year after her daughter's first departure, at a time when Sévigné is looking forward to making her first visit south, clearly reveals the constant variety of subject and tone that characterizes her attempts to engage her daughter and to appear lively and spontaneous herself. It is necessary to quote the whole of the letter to appreciate Sévigné's particular sense of *disposition*:

A Paris, mercredi 16 mars [1672]

[1] Vous me parlez de mon départ. Ah! ma chère fille! je languis dans cet espoir charmant. Rien ne m'arrête que ma tante, qui se meurt de douleur et d'hydropisie. Elle me brise le cœur par l'état où elle est, et par tout ce qu'elle dit de tendresse et de bon sens. Son courage, sa patience, sa résignation, tout cela est admirable. M. d'Hacqueville et moi, nous suivons son mal jour à jour. Il voit mon cœur et la douleur que j'ai de n'être pas libre tout présentement. Je me conduis par ses avis; nous verrons entre ci et Pâques. Si son mal augmente, comme il a fait depuis que je suis ici, elle mourra entre nos bras; si elle reçoit quelque soulagement et qu'elle prenne le train de languir, je partirai dès que M. de Coulanges sera revenu. Notre pauvre abbé est au désespoir aussi bien que moi. Nous verrons comme cet excès de mal se tournera dans le mois d'avril. Je n'ai que cela dans la tête. Vous ne sauriez avoir tant d'envie de me voir que j'en ai de vous embrasser; bornez votre ambition, et ne croyez pas me pouvoir jamais égaler là-dessus.

[2] Mon fils me mande qu'ils sont misérables en Allemagne et ne savent ce qu'ils font. Il a été très affligé de la mort du chevalier de Grignan.

[3] Vous me demandez, ma chère enfant, si j'aime toujours bien la vie. Je vous avoue que j'y trouve des chagrins cuisants. Mais je suis encore plus dégoûtée de la mort; je me trouve si malheureuse d'avoir à finir tout ceci par elle, que si je pouvais retourner en arrière, je ne demanderais pas mieux. Je me trouve dans un engagement qui m'embarrasse; je suis embar-

quée dans la vie sans mon consentement. Il faut que j'en sorte; cela m'assomme. Et comment en sortirai-je? Par où? Par quelle porte? Quand sera-ce? En quelle disposition? Souffrirai-je mille et mille douleurs, qui me feront mourir désespérée? Aurai-je un transport au cerveau? Mourrai-je d'un accident? Comment serai-je avec Dieu? Qu'aurai-je à lui présenter? La crainte, la nécessité, feront-elles mon retour vers lui? N'aurai-je aucun autre sentiment que celui de la peur? Que puis-je espérer? Suis-je digne du paradis? Suis-je digne de l'enfer? Quelle alternative! Quel embarras! Rien n'est si fou que de mettre son salut dans l'incertitude, mais rien n'est si naturel, et la sotte vie que je mène est la chose du monde la plus aisée à comprendre. Je m'abîme dans ces pensées, et je trouve la mort si terrible que je hais plus la vie parce qu'elle m'y mène que par les épines qui s'y rencontrent. Vous me direz que je veux vivre éternellement. Point du tout, mais si on m'avait demandé mon avis, j'aurais bien aimé à mourir entre les bras de ma nourrice; cela m'aurait ôté bien des ennuis et m'aurait donné le ciel bien sûrement et bien aisément. Mais parlons d'autre chose.

[4] Je suis au désespoir que vous ayez eu *Bajazet* par d'autres que par moi. C'est ce chien de Barbin qui me hait, parce que je ne fais pas des *Princesses de Clèves et de Montpensier*. Vous en avez jugé très juste et très bien, et vous aurez vu que je suis de votre avis. Je voulais vous envoyer la Champmeslé pour vous réchauffer la pièce. Le personnage de Bajazet est glacé. Les mœurs des Turcs y sont mal observées; ils ne font point tant de façons pour se marier. Le dénouement n'est point bien préparé; on n'entre point dans les raisons de cette grande tuerie. Il y a pourtant des choses agréables; et rien de parfaitement beau, rien qui enlève, point de ces tirades de Corneille qui font frissonner. Ma fille, gardons-nous bien de lui comparer Racine; sentons-en la différence. Il y a des endroits froids et faibles, et jamais il n'ira plus loin qu'*Alexandre* et qu'*Andromaque*. *Bajazet* est au-dessous, au sentiment de bien des gens, et au mien si j'ose me citer. Racine fait des comédies pour la Champmeslé; ce n'est pas pour les siècles à venir. Si jamais il n'est plus jeune et qu'il cesse d'être amoureux, ce ne sera plus la même chose. Vive donc notre vieil ami Corneille! Pardonnons-lui de méchants vers, en faveur des divines et sublimes beautés qui nous transportent; ce sont des traits de maître qui sont inimitables. Despréaux en dit encore plus que moi, et en un mot, c'est le bon goût; tenez-vous-y.

[5] Voici un bon mot de Mme Cornuel, qui a fort réjoui le parterre. M. Tambonneau le fils a quitté la robe, et a mis une sangle au-dessous de son ventre et de son derrière. Avec ce bel air, il veut aller sur la mer; je ne sais ce que lui a fait la terre. On disait donc à Mme Cornuel qu'il s'en allait à la mer: 'Hélas! dit-elle, est-ce qu'il a été mordu d'un chien enragé?' Cela fut dit sans malice; c'est ce qui a fait rire extrêmement.

[6] Mme de Courcelles est fort embarrassée; on lui refuse toutes ses requêtes. Mais elle dit qu'elle espère qu'on aura pitié d'elle, puisque ce sont des hommes qui sont ses juges. Notre Coadjuteur ne lui ferait point de

grâce présentement; vous me le représentez dans les occupations de saint Ambroise.

[7] Il me semble que vous deviez vous contenter que votre fille fût faite à son image et semblance. Votre fils lui veut aussi ressembler, mais, sans offenser la beauté du Coadjuteur, où est donc la belle bouche de ce petit garçon? où sont ses agréments? Il ressemble donc à sa sœur; vous m'embarrassez fort par cette ressemblance. Je vous aime bien, ma chère fille, de n'être point grosse. Consolez-vous d'être belle *inutilement*, par le plaisir de n'être pas toujours mourante.

[8] Je ne saurais vous plaindre de n'avoir point de beurre en Provence, puisque vous avez de l'huile admirable et d'excellent poisson. Ah! ma fille, que je comprends bien ce que peuvent faire et penser des gens comme vous, au milieu de votre Provence! Je la trouverai comme vous, et je vous plaindrai toute ma vie d'y passer de si belles années de la vôtre. Je suis si peu désireuse de briller dans votre cour de Provence, et j'en juge si bien par celle de Bretagne, que par la même raison qu'au bout de trois jours à Vitré, je ne respirais que les Rochers, je vous jure devant Dieu que l'objet de mes désirs, c'est de passer l'été à Grignan avec vous; voilà où je vise, et rien au delà. Mon vin de Saint-Laurent est chez Adhémar; je l'aurai demain matin. Il y a longtemps que je vous en ai remerciée *in petto*; cela est bien obligeant.

[9] Monsieur de Laon aime bien cette manière d'être cardinal. On assure que l'autre jour M. de Montausier, parlant à Monsieur le Dauphin de la dignité des cardinaux, lui dit que cela dépendait du pape, et que s'il voulait faire cardinal un palefrenier, il le pourrait. Là-dessus le cardinal de Bonzi arrive. Monsieur le Dauphin lui dit: 'Monsieur, est-il vrai que si le pape le voulait, il ferait cardinal un palefrenier?' M. de Bonzi fut surpris, et devinant l'affaire, il lui répondit: 'Il est vrai, monsieur, que le pape choisit qui il lui plaît, mais nous n'avons pas vu, jusqu'ici, qu'il ait pris des cardinaux dans son écurie'. C'est le cardinal de Bouillon qui m'a conté ce détail.

[10] J'ai fort entretenu Monsieur d'Uzès. Il vous mandera la conférence qu'il a eue; elle est admirable. Il a un esprit posé et des paroles mesurées, qui sont d'un grand poids dans ces occasions. Il fait et dit toujours très bien partout.

[11] On disait de Jarzé ce qu'on vous a dit, mais cela est incertain. On prétend que la joie de la dame n'est pas médiocre pour le retour du chevalier de Lorraine. On dit aussi que le comte de Guiche et Mme de Brissac sont tellement sophistiqués qu'ils auraient besoin d'un truchement pour s'entendre eux-mêmes. Ecrivez un peu à notre Cardinal; il vous aime. Le faubourg vous aime. Mme Scarron vous aime; elle passe ici le carême, et céans presque tous les soirs, Barrillon y est encore, et plût à Dieu, ma belle, que vous y fussiez aussi! Adieu, mon enfant; je ne finis point. Je vous défie de pouvoir comprendre combien je vous aime.

At first glance the *disposition* seems quite removed from the traditional shape of a single discourse recommended by rhetoricians.
This may seem an obvious point; it is, after all, an informal letter.
Its structure is perhaps best characterized as *paratactic*. A series of
subjects seem to succeed each other with few explicit links. They
might be summed up as follows:

(1) Reasons standing in the way of Sévigné's visit to her daughter
(2) News of Sévigné's son on campaign in Germany
(3) Sévigné's reflections on death
(4) Sévigné's critical assessment of Racine's latest play *Bajazet*
(5) Anecdote about Mme Cornuel's wit
(6) Anecdote about Mme de Courcelles
(7) Sévigné's reflections on the resemblance between her grandchildren and their uncle
(8) Sévigné's reflections on provincial society
(9) Anecdote about a witty conversation involving the dauphin and
the cardinal de Bonzi
(10) Allusion to an address by the bishop of Uzès
(11) Sequence of summary anecdotes and farewells

The list of subjects might not suggest writing about the self; but, like
Montaigne, Sévigné writes about subjects other than herself in such
a way as to conjure up her own personality for the reader.

The transitions from one subject to another are extremely abrupt.
In most cases, there is none at all. So section 1 ends with the suggestion that Sévigné's desire to see her daughter surpasses her
daughter's desire to see her: 'et ne croyez pas me pouvoir jamais
égaler là-dessus'. With no transition, the next section begins with
news of her son: 'Mon fils me mande qu'ils sont misérables en
Allemagne.' When transitions exist, they are abrupt or elusive. She
moves from the discussion of death to the assessment of *Bajazet* with
the artless link 'Mais parlons d'autre chose' (3). She moves from an
expression of gratitude for wine to a comment on the bishop of
Laon with a hidden link that establishes a complicitous bond
between letter-writer and original recipient, but which is mystifying
for subsequent readers without the help of learned footnotes. She
writes about the wine: 'Il y a longtemps que je vous en ai remerciée
in petto [in my heart]' (8). The next sentence refers to the bishop of
Laon becoming a cardinal: 'Monsieur de Laon aime bien cette
manière d'être cardinal' (9). The link is between the way Sévigné

says thank you and the way the bishop accepts his elevation to the status of cardinal. Neither has spoken explicitly. Sévigné had not expressed her thanks verbally (until now); the bishop has not publicly declared the news that the Pope has made him a cardinal. The *parataxis* between the succeeding sections contributes to the appearance of spontaneity and conversational style in Sévigné's writing. So does the order in which the subjects are treated. There is no necessary reason that is made explicit as to why she relates the Mme Cornuel anecdote (5) before the one about Mme de Courcelles (6), why she treats death (3) before *Bajazet* (4), why she mentions her grandchildren (7) before provincial life (8). Sévigné's characteristic *disposition* is closely related to that part of *invention* that determines the character of the speaker (*ethos*) and the way in which speaker and addressee interrelate. The informality suggests honesty, frankness, and lack of affectation. The *disposition* is therefore one of the strategies that helps to create an image of Sévigné for her absent daughter, and an appealing image, she no doubt hopes.

One further remark needs to be made about Sévigné's *disposition*. For all its apparent informality, there are two respects in which it acknowledges the principles of formal *disposition*. The first is that it bears the traces of an *exordium* and a *peroration*. Rhetoricians claim that the beginning of a speech should arrest the attention of the audience and put the speaker in a favourable light (*ethos*). This principle clearly determines the way Sévigné begins her letter. She addresses Mme de Grignan directly on a topic that her daughter had herself discussed in her own most recent letter: 'Vous me parlez de mon départ' (1). This then allows Sévigné to express her affection for her daughter at some length by explaining her regret at not being able to make the journey to see her right away. Similarly, rhetoricians believe that the *peroration* is the place to appeal to *pathos* most explicitly. Sévigné does this in a short, but none the less resounding climax of expressions of love (11):

[Le Cardinal] vous aime. Le faubourg vous aime. Mme Scarron vous aime [. . .]. Barrillon y est encore, et plût à Dieu, ma belle, que vous y fussiez aussi! Adieu, mon enfant; je ne finis point. Je vous défie de pouvoir comprendre combien je vous aime.

The triple *isocolon* supports the insistent repetition of 'vous aime' (*reduplicatio*). The indications of the other people who love Mme de Grignan prepare an expectation for an even more overwhelming expression of love by Sévigné herself. She sets about this in two ways. First she establishes an *antithesis* between Barrillon's presence and her daughter's absence, expressing an urgent longing for her daughter to be present. Secondly, and most effectively, she ends her letter with a *litotes*: she does not try to say how much she loves her daughter, but suggests that the extent of her love is almost unimaginable. But it is not only these traces of an *exordium* and a *peroration* that suggest rhetorical principles at work in Sévigné's text. There is perhaps, after all, some principle governing the order in which the subjects are treated. Sévigné tends to treat the more substantial topics that have a marked bearing on the mother–daughter relationship in the first half of the letter, and, after this, yields to the lighter topics that deal more with other people. Whether conscious or not, significant artistry determines the *disposition* of Sévigné's letters.

Invention also plays its part in Sévigné's attempt to secure her daughter's attention and affection. The main principle is that any topic must relate directly to Mme de Grignan or must have the capacity to amuse her. The result of this is that most topics, and certainly those treated at greatest length, are a response to a stimulus in the daughter's most recent letter. Just as the discussion of Sévigné's inability to travel is introduced by an explicit reference to Mme de Grignan's letter ('Vous me parlez de mon départ' (1)), so too are her reflections on death ('Vous me demandez, ma chère enfant, si j'aime toujours bien la vie' (3)); and likewise the discussion of *Bajazet* ('Je suis au désespoir que vous ayez eu *Bajazet* par d'autres que par moi' (4)). Mention of the grandchildren seems also to respond to points made by Mme de Grignan (7). The general reflections on provincial life-style are a response to the daughter's complaint about the lack of butter in Provence (8). Even the anecdote about Mme de Courcelles is twisted to relate to a point made by Mme de Grignan about her uncle, the 'Coadjuteur': 'Notre Coadjuteur ne lui ferait point de grâce présentement; vous me le représentez dans les occupations de saint Ambroise' (6). When Sévigné mentions a topic not brought up by her daughter, she tries to incorporate her: her praise of the bishop of Uzès is accompanied by an indication that he will be writing to Mme de Grignan himself. Failing any explicit mention of Grignan, she tells entertaining stories about people known to both of them: hence the report of Mme Cornuel's witticism, based on the proverbial wisdom that the

sea is a cure for rabies, and responding to the news that
Tambonneau had given up the law to go to sea: 'est-ce qu'il a été
mordu d'un chien enragé?' (5); hence also the report of M. de
Bonzi's witticism when asked by the dauphin if the Pope had it in
his power to make even a stable-boy a cardinal: 'nous n'avons pas
vu, jusqu'ici, qu'il ait pris des cardinaux dans son écurie' (9).

As Sévigné's *invention* is governed by the need to secure her daughter's interest, so is her *elocution*. Both *invention* and *elocution* reveal considerable variety. With regard to *invention*, in addition to the witty
anecdotes and the satire on provincials, there is the intellectual discussion of *Bajazet*, in which she steers a path between agreeing with
her daughter's doubts about the play and asserting her own strong
preference for Corneille; there is the self-portrait of Sévigné as a
faithful niece, looking after her dying aunt, even to the extent of
depriving herself of an early visit to her daughter; and there is
Sévigné in meditative mood, verbally enacting her thoughts as she
contemplates death.

Devices of *elocution* change with the subject, but all are geared
towards painting an attractive and compelling image of the mother
and towards carrying her daughter with her in her thoughts
and concerns. For instance, conventional *metaphor* ('brise le cœur')
and *epitrochasmus* convey the picture of Sévigné as an admiring and
devoted niece: 'Elle me brise le cœur par l'état où elle est, et par
tout ce qu'elle dit de tendresse et de bon sens. Son courage, sa
patience, sa résignation, tout cela est admirable' (1). A torrent of
ratiocinatio reveals Sévigné's doubts as she anxiously contemplates
the manner of her death: 'Et comment en sortirai-je? Par où? Par
quelle porte? Quand sera-ce? En quelle disposition? Souffrirai-je
mille et mille douleurs, qui me feront mourir désespérée?' (3). The
insistent questions are reinforced by *metaphor* with which she alludes
to death (leaving by a door), and by the *hyperbole* evoking dreadful
degrees of pain ('mille et mille douleurs'). These questions arrest
the reader, but are not addressed to the reader. They create the
impression of an insight into Sévigné's mind, and therefore invite
Mme de Grignan's profound complicity with her mother. Fears of
the afterlife are conveyed by *reduplicatio* and *antithesis*: 'Suis-je digne
du paradis? Suis-je digne de l'enfer?' (3). For all the *figures* in this
passage, Sévigné maintains the impression of conversational informality, imagining her daughter's response ('Vous me direz que je
veux vivre éternellement') and replying with a moving and memo-

rable image ('j'aurais bien aimé à mourir entre les bras de ma nourrice').

The style changes again for the more intellectual discussion of Racine's play. Sévigné's attitude to it is interesting for the light it throws on her need constantly to retain her daughter's sympathy. She had seen the play earlier in the year and had enjoyed it, though with some reservations (letter of 15 January 1672). Now that it is in print, her daughter has read it and commented on it sooner than she had anticipated. And she clearly finds herself wanting to agree with her daughter's rather more devastating criticisms. She expresses her agreement with an amusing and winning *metaphor* ('Je voulais vous envoyer la Champmeslé pour vous réchauffer la pièce' (4), la Champmeslé being Racine's leading actress) and with a sequence of short *paratactic* sentences, which, as they pile up, suggest that much is wrong with the play: 'Le personnage de Bajazet est glacé. Les mœurs des Turcs y sont mal observées; ils ne font point tant de façons pour se marier. Le dénouement n'est point bien préparé; on n'entre point dans les raisons de cette grande tuerie' (4). Criticism of Racine turns into praise of Corneille, as Sévigné tries to encourage her daughter to share her enthusiasm for the older dramatist: 'Vive donc notre vieil ami Corneille!' (4).

There is no explicit rhetorical aim in this letter, or indeed in most of Sévigné's letters. This fact contributes to the appearance of spontaneity and informality. But both Mme de Grignan and the modern reader may see, in the relentless succession of such letters, an implicit *deliberative* aim. Sévigné writes in order to persuade her daughter to love her and to attend to her. Her success might be measured in two ways. The regular replies that Mme de Grignan sent her are testimony to Sévigné's persuasive powers. The time that mother and daughter actually spent in each other's presence, however, suggests that she was less good at persuading her daughter in person than on paper: when they were in the same place, relations were often strained. In writing, on the other hand, she used an informal *disposition* and a constantly varied *invention* and *elocution*, grounded in the personality and interests of her addressee, successfully to compel her daughter's attention. It is a most intimate kind of rhetorically executed communication that modern readers can feel privileged to witness.

Elocutionary Fireworks

Not that Sévigné always writes in this intimate and informal way to make herself attractive to Mme de Grignan. The mother–daughter correspondence is impressive for its bulk and its unique account of a real-life relationship. But Sévigné's anthologists have sometimes preferred those letters, often addressed to people other than her daughter, and often reproduced only in excerpts, where she is consciously writing what is commonly called 'purple prose', an obviously studied use of rhetorical *figures*. One such famous passage is the letter written to her uncle, Coulanges, announcing the suprising news of the intended marriage of the Grande Mademoiselle. This is the opening sentence (15 December 1670):

> Je m'en vais vous mander la chose la plus étonnante, la plus surprenante, la plus merveilleuse, la plus miraculeuse, la plus triomphante, la plus étourdissante, la plus inouïe, la plus singulière, la plus extraordinaire, la plus incroyable, la plus imprévue, la plus grande, la plus petite, la plus rare, la plus commune, la plus éclatante, la plus secrète jusqu'aujourd'hui, la plus brillante, la plus digne d'envie; enfin une chose dont on ne trouve qu'un exemple dans les siècles passés, encore cet exemple n'est-il pas juste; une chose que nous ne saurions croire à Paris (comment la pourrait-on croire à Lyon?); une chose qui fait crier miséricorde à tout le monde; une chose qui comble de joie Mme de Rohan et Mme de Hauterive; une chose enfin qui se fera dimanche, où ceux qui la verront croiront avoir la berlue; une chose qui se fera dimanche, et qui ne sera peut-être pas faite lundi.

The letter continues with comparable *elocutionary* fireworks and sustained *hyperbole*. The news is extraordinary because the Grande Mademoiselle was the immensely rich cousin of Louis XIV, whilst her intended husband was a relatively insignificant man, Lauzun, who had wormed his way into court circles. In the event, the marriage did not take place: the king forbade it. Sévigné's style in this letter is engineered with evident artistry to convey the excitement provoked by the unexpected and improbable news. She compels the reader's interest by announcing that she has news and then delaying it by means of an accumulation of *figures*, each treated in patently excessive detail. In the passage quoted, the first *figure* is the *conglobatio* of superlative adjectives (nineteen in all), and the next is the *parisonic* and *anaphoric* sequence of phrases beginning 'une chose', and each developed in a relative clause (six in all). Her treatment of the *figures* is as extraordinary as the news she has to relate.

This is a letter with a tone quite different from the apparent spontaneity that Sévigné so often says is characteristic of her style. Although addressed to Coulanges, it is written with such conscious artistry that her expectation must have been that it would be read by, or recited to, many others. It shows Sévigné supremely aware of the relationship between herself, her words, and her reader. Our response to a passage like this should not be to see it as an exception to the rule of her self-professed informality. Rather, it should alert us to Sévigné's finely tuned sense of the rhetorical nature of the exercise of writing letters to family and friends. Whatever she conveys about herself is expressed in the way most appropriate to the letter's immediate recipient. Her protestations of spontaneity need to be set alongside her explicit references to rhetoric, which are not infrequent. She tells her daughter about Pomponne's comment on her conversations with Mlle Ladvocat: 'Il y a des entr'actes à nos conversations, que M. de Pomponne appelle des traits de rhétorique pour capter la bienveillance des auditeurs' (11 December 1673). On another occasion she tells her about her attempt to speak consolingly to the comte de Vaux: 'Je ne sais si ma rhétorique lui parut bonne' (1 July 1676). Mme de Grignan has written to calm her mother's anxieties about her son's expensive life-style; showing her ability to read with an eye alert to the writer's rhetorical practice, Sévigné replies: 'Quelque bonne opinion que j'aie de votre rhétorique, je vous avoue, ma bonne, que j'en douterais en cette occasion' (6 March 1680). Elsewhere she praises her daughter's rhetoric and describes its effect on her: 'Votre récit a toute la force de la rhétorique; il suspend l'attention, il augmente la curiosité, et conduit à un événement si triste et si surprenant que j'en fus tout émue et fis un cri qui fit peur à mon fils' (1 January 1690). Most interestingly, she comments to her daughter about one of the sons of the Rochebonne family, and praises 'toutes ses petites pensées, tous ses petits raisonnements, ses finesses, sa petite rhétorique naturelle' (20 July 1689). Some might see the juxtaposition of 'rhétorique' and 'naturelle' as paradoxical; but Sévigné has in mind all those ways in which one wins over one's audience, however uncalculated they may be. She too is a supreme practitioner of natural rhetoric.

3. RHETORIC AND SEXUAL REVELATION:
GIDE'S *SI LE GRAIN NE MEURT*

In contrast to Mme de Sévigné, Gide refers to rhetoric mostly with distaste.[8] He was educated in the 1870s and 1880s, when rhetoric was still nominally on the school syllabus in France, but when the subject had suffered the onslaught of the romantics and was, as a curriculum subject, very much in its death throes. For Gide, rhetoric is a distinctly negative term, much used by him in the literary criticism to be found in his *Journal*. He quite enjoys the last act of Corneille's tragedy *Rodogune*, but dismisses the rest, rather vaguely, as rhetoric: 'Par delà des amoncellements de rhétorique presque insupportable, un presque admirable cinquième acte' (21 March 1930). The same word is used to refer to those works of Beethoven he does not like: 'Beethoven m'a paru lourd de rhétorique et de redondance' (12 July 1934). His measured assessment of Shakespeare's *Venus and Adonis* uses the word 'rhetoric' to refer to what he does not like about the poem: 'Quelques passages de très fâcheuse rhétorique, et concession au goût du temps, ne déparent qu'à peine l'admirable foisonnement du poème' (5 July 1937). As an exception to these negative associations, he praises Hugo's rhetoric in *Les Orientales*: 'Quelle prodigieuse invention rhétorique! Tout y est: la force, la grâce, le sourire et les plus pathétiques sanglots' (18 November 1929). All these comments suggest that Gide is in tune with his times in thinking of rhetoric in a narrow sense as *elocution* drawing attention to itself by its very obviousness, mostly, if not always, with unfortunate results.

Gide seems not to think of rhetoric in its much broader sense of the art of persuasion. His writing practice, however, certainly embraces this art. His first-person fictional works depict characters who may use rhetoric deliberately to delude others and, in the process, often delude themselves (see Chapter 4). But he makes par-

---

[8] Gide's journal is published in two volumes: *Journal, 1889–1939*, Bibliothèque de la Pléiade (Gallimard, 1951), and *Journal, 1939–49*, Bibliothèque de la Pléiade (Gallimard, 1954). His autobiography is *Si le grain ne meurt* (Gallimard, 1972); and his work that most explicitly discusses homosexuality is *Corydon* (Gallimard, 1947). For subtle writing about his autobiography see Lejeune, *Le Pacte autobiographique*, 165–97, and *idem*, *Exercices d'ambiguïté: Lectures de 'Si le grain ne meurt'* (Lettres modernes, 1974), with its penetrating discussions of Gide's self-referential comments in the work, and also Sheringham, *French Autobiography*, 183–93.

ticular use of rhetoric when he deals with the topic of homosexuality. *Corydon*, published after years of delay and much soul-searching in 1922, is a series of four dialogues in which a homosexual defends homosexuality to an interested acquaintance. Gide claimed it was his most important work (*Journal*, 19 October 1942), though posterity has not agreed with him. It did, at least, pave the way for the work in which he wrote explicitly about himself as a homosexual. His autobiography, *Si le grain ne meurt*, was published in 1926. When he writes about this book during its composition, he does so in terms that irresistibly evoke the rhetorical nature of the situation existing between writer and readers: 'Je n'écris pas ces Mémoires pour me défendre. Je n'ai point à me défendre, puisque je ne suis pas accusé. Je les écris avant d'être accusé. Je les écris pour qu'on m'accuse' (*Journal*, 19 January 1917). Implicitly, this comment indicates the centrality, in Gide's autobiographical enterprise, of the revelation of his sexuality. It is not a work about his early life in which mention of his homosexuality is incidental; the revelation of his sexuality is a core feature of the writing process and one which he expects to be controversial. In other respects, this comment is ambiguous. *Judicial* rhetoric is evoked, but whereas we might expect such an autobiography to be a self-defence, Gide seems to want his readers to accuse him. Readers judging his homosexuality negatively should then expect to have their eyes opened to the prejudices underlying their judgement.

Si le grain is now a famously ambiguous autobiography. If homosexuality is central, why is the book divided into one long part in which the topic is hardly mentioned, and one short part in which it is? Why does Gide terminate the story with his engagement to Emmanuèle (his wife's real name was Madeleine)? Why does he paint such a negative picture of Oscar Wilde and Lord Alfred Douglas? Why, as the narrator of his earlier life, does he decline to pass any judgement on it, explaining himself as follows: 'D'autant que ce jugement a plus d'une fois varié et que je regarde ma vie tour à tour d'un œil indulgent ou sévère suivant qu'il fait plus ou moins clair au-dedans de moi' (p. 283)? The answers to some of these questions lie in Gide's lifelong insistence on the complexity of personality. No account of a life can hope to conjure up a personality in any clear or sharply delineated way, and, in the varied images he presents of himself, then and now, the narrator of *Si le grain* studiously prevents the reader from making fixed interpretations of his character. The work contains images of its subject, but not *an* image.

Gide's fondness for ambiguity by no means implies that his work is non-rhetorical. Several comments within the work itself indicate the narrator's awareness of his relationship with his readers. Indeed, at the very end of part 1 he refers to the reactions of a real reader of the book in its draft form: 'Roger Martin du Gard, à qui je donne à lire ces Mémoires, leur reproche de ne jamais dire assez, et de laisser le lecteur sur sa soif' (p. 280). The narrator responds to this criticism with characteristic ambiguity. On the one hand, he has wanted to say everything: 'Mon intention pourtant a toujours été de tout dire.' On the other, the task of self-revelation requires simplification and selection: 'un besoin de mon esprit m'amène, pour tracer plus purement chaque trait, à simplifier tout à l'excès; on ne dessine pas sans choisir'. The reason he gives for the need for selection is interesting: the more explicitly confidential a writer is, the more artifice is required, whereas Gide says of himself: 'je cherche surtout le naturel'. Yet this very process of rationalizing his method suggests how carefully calculated his naturalness is. To complicate the question even further, there are comments in the *Journal* that suggest that he thought his writing in this work too artificial, that he did not always attain the naturalness after which he strove: 'à mon goût, tout cela est trop écrit, d'un style trop précieux, trop conscient' (23 December 1916). Further comments in the text itself suggest calculated strategies that the narrator is advertising to the reader: 'mon récit n'a raison d'être que véridique' (p. 10), 'Je ne veux point me peindre plus vertueux que je ne suis' (pp. 249–50), 'Ce n'est pas ma défense, c'est mon histoire que j'écris' (p. 309), 'Il y aurait là-dessus beaucoup à dire; mais je me suis défendu les digressions' (p. 301). Though Gide's metatextual comments may sometimes pull in opposite directions, they all conspire to suggest a work whose narrator is keen to maintain the good will, trust, and attention of the reader. Frank, if sometimes apparently conflicting, statements about the process of writing promote a favourable image of the narrator as an honest man: they fulfil an important rhetorical function, the *ethos* of *invention*.

Notwithstanding the ambiguities to which the work gives rise, Gide seems to write in such a way as to prevent any potentially hostile reader from becoming alienated. The revelation of his homosexuality is handled delicately and patiently. It would be possible to see the *disposition* of the whole work as part of this strategy. Part 1, with its ten chapters, each made up of a variety of short and often amusing anecdotes about his childhood and portraits of his family and friends, no more than hints at Gide's sexuality, with the references, for instance, to the games played under the table with the concierge's son (p. 9) and to the momentary passion he felt for a Russian boy at school (p. 83). Gide seeks in this part to entertain the reader with the sheer variety of the child's experiences. *Ethos* is crucial: the character of the child amuses, and wins sympathy, with his sickliness, his curiosity, his varied interests, and his feelings of difference from others. In the last chapter of part 1, the tone changes: the subject is now in his early twenties, his offer of marriage to Emmanuèle is declined, and he spends his time in the claustrophobic atmosphere of Symbolist circles in Paris. This atmosphere prepares for the marked contrast with the liberating experiences of the visits to Algeria narrated in part 2. The narrative in this part is much more sustained, and is preceded by several pages of general reflections on the subject's sexuality and questions of morality. It is as if part 1 is a long *captatio benevolentiae* for the narrative of sexual experience that constitutes part 2. One passage from each part will reveal the very different rhetorical skills that Gide deploys at different stages of his interaction with his reader.

Captatio benevolentiae

Entertainment predominates in part 1. One of the strands of the young Gide's life was his interest in music, his piano lessons, and in particular the attempt to find a decent piano teacher. A series of teachers is presented to the reader: nearly all of them, with comic predictability, turn out to be flawed. M. Merriman's fault was to lack any musical sensibility, which Gide conveys with all the skill of the satirical portraitist (pp. 156–7):

[1] Les leçons de Mlle Gœklin ayant été jugées insuffisantes, je fus confié à un professeur mâle, qui ne valait, hélas! pas beaucoup mieux. [2] M. Merriman était essayeur chez Pleyel; il avait fait du métier de pianiste sa profession, sans vocation aucune; à force de travail il était parvenu à décrocher au Conservatoire un premier prix, si je ne m'abuse; son jeu correct, luisant, glacé, ressortissait plutôt à l'arithmétique qu'à l'art; quand il se mettait au piano, on croyait voir un comptable devant sa caisse; sous ses doigts, blanches, noires et croches s'additionnaient; il faisait la vérification

du morceau. [3] Assurément il aurait pu m'entraîner pour le mécanisme; mais il ne prenait aucun plaisir à enseigner. [4] Avec lui, la musique devenait un pensum aride; ses maîtres étaient Cramer, Steibelt, Dussek, du moins ceux dont il préconisait pour moi la férule. [5] Beethoven lui paraissait libidineux. [6] Deux fois par semaine, il venait, ponctuel; la leçon consistait dans la répétition monotone de quelques exercices, et encore point des plus profitables pour les doigts, mais des plus niaisement routiniers; quelques gammes, quelques arpèges, puis je commençais de rabâcher 'les huit dernières mesures' du morceau en cours, c'est-à-dire les dernières étudiées; après quoi, huit pas plus loin, il faisait une sorte de grand V au crayon, marquant la besogne à abattre, comme on désigne dans une coupe de bois les arbres à exécuter; puis disait, en se levant, tandis que sonnait la pendule:

—Pour la prochaine fois, vous étudierez les huit mesures suivantes.

[7] Jamais la moindre explication. [8] Jamais le moindre appel, je ne dis pas à mon goût musical ou à ma sensibilité (comment en eût-il été question?) mais non plus seulement à ma mémoire ou à mon jugement. [9] A cet âge de développement, de souplesse et d'assimilation, quels progrès n'eussé-je point faits, si ma mère m'avait aussitôt confié au maître incomparable que fut pour moi, un peu plus tard (trop tard, hélas!) M. de la Nux. [10] Hélas, après deux ans d'ânonnements mortels, je ne fus délivré de Merriman que pour tomber en Schifmacker.

In rhetorical terms, this is an *ethopoeia*, a portrait rendered comic and pointed by the concentrated presentation of Merriman uniquely in terms of his weakness. For him, music is technique without art. Various devices of *elocution* help the narrator to focus his satire. Above all, there is his use of *metaphor* and *simile*, which present the man and his playing in the driest possible terms. The sound he makes is compared to arithmetic (2); his manner of playing is likened to an accountant's work at his desk; a surrealistic *metaphorical personification* transforms the different kinds of notes into numbers to be added up; and the piece of music is like a calculation to be checked. This *extended metaphor* of music as accountancy gives way to a variety of other indications, some literal, some *metaphorical*, about Merriman's approach. The *concession* that he might have been good at teaching the technical side of performance counts against him when the narrator admits that Merriman did not enjoy teaching (3). The dryness of the subject, in his hands, is made explicit: 'la musique devenait un pensum aride' (4). And a comically devastating *antithesis* contrasts Merriman's preferred composers (Cramer, Steibelt, and Dussek) with one whom he regards as suspiciously pleasurable (Beethoven). The favoured ones are known for their mechanical exercises, not for their musical quality. The narrator associates them *metaphorically* with 'la férule' (4), with its connotations of painful discipline. Beethoven is dismissed with comic and baffling *hyperbole* as 'libidineux' (5). Any reader with even the slightest smattering of culture will be amused by Merriman's perversely quirky musical taste.

His behaviour and conduct of the lessons tally with his playing. The adjective 'ponctuel' is emphasized by its preceding comma in the phrase: 'il venait, ponctuel' (6). A liberal use of explicitly negative adjectives expresses a dim view of the exercises the boy was made to play: 'monotone', 'encore point des plus profitables', 'des plus niaisement routiniers', the superlatives helping to drive the critical point home. *Hyperbaton* and *anaphora* conspire to suggest the uninteresting thinness of Merriman's lessons: 'quelques gammes, quelques arpèges, puis je commençais de rabâcher' (6). One detail in particular is singled out as an illustration of his mechanical approach in action, his insistence that each week the next eight bars of the composition be practised: the implication is that the piece is divided up into groups of eight bars without any regard to its musical sense. A further *simile*, rich in associations, conveys the mechanical nature of this method. Merriman is like the woodcutter marking with a nick those trees to be felled. The use of the words 'abattre' for the bars of music and 'exécuter' for the trees, suggests the destruction that Merriman's method wreaks on any musical composition. The last stage in the lesson is his departure. The narrator neatly juxtaposes two events: Merriman stands up, the clock chimes, which shows the man's punctuality in practice (6). The monotony of the whole experience is summed up by the treatment of the lesson in one long sentence which begins and ends with an indication of the teacher's clockwork mentality.

The entertaining portrait is followed by the narrator's mature reflections on Merriman (7–10). The rhetorical task here is not only to insist on the bad light in which Merriman should be seen; it is also to portray the narrator himself favourably as a critically intelligent and modest man (*ethos*). *Anaphora* and *isocolon* stress Merriman's lack of interest in musicality. He never said anything interesting about a piece: 'Jamais la moindre explication. Jamais le moindre appel' (7–8). The narrator's modesty about his musical abilities is conveyed by his use of *correctio* ('je ne dis pas à mon goût musical ou à ma sensibilité' (8)) and it is further emphasized by the *parenthetical* indication that the narrator thinks that he had, at least as a boy, no musical sensibility: '(comment en eût-il été question?)' (8). The *parenthesis* is of course ambiguous. As well as suggesting the narrator's modesty about his musical talent as a boy, it is a further criticism of the musical incompetence of the teachers he had had. As if to allay the reader's objection that the boy was hard to satisfy, the narrator mentions proleptically a later piano teacher who was a great success, M. de la Nux (9). In doing so, he manages to convey, without any damage to his modesty, the musical potential that he had as a child: 'A cet âge de développement, de souplesse et d'assimilation, quels progrès n'eussé-je point faits' (9). Here the *epitrochasmus* and the implicit *exclamation* combine to suggest a wealth of ability that needed only to be channelled. A further *correctio*, expressed in a *parenthesis*, insists on the narrator's modest musical competence even after the lessons with M. de la Nux, 'plus tard (trop tard, hélas!)' (9). The story's punchline includes another verbally felicitous attack on Merriman ('deux ans d'ânonnements mortels' (10)) and climactically suggests that to move from Merriman to the next teacher was to jump from the frying pan into the fire.

Revelation

In anecdotes and portraits like that of Merriman, Gide wins over the reader with his protestations of modesty and above all his skill in gently comic narrative. It is only when he might hope that the reader has been won over that he broaches the topic of his homosexuality more overtly. Even in the early stages of part 2, however, his style is characterized more by *litotes* than by direct statement: the narrator suggests more than he says. The reader is prepared for the liberating experiences awaiting the young Gide in the warm climate of North Africa, released from his family and circle of Parisian friends, except for his companion Paul Laurens, with whom he travelled. This is how he narrates his first homosexual experience, when he went out walking with his Algerian guide Ali (pp. 298–9):

[1] L'hôtel était situé hors la ville, dont les abords, de ce côté, sont sablonneux. [2] C'était pitié de voir les oliviers, si beaux dans la campagne environnante, à demi submergés par la dune mouvante. [3] Un peu plus loin, on était tout surpris de rencontrer une rivière, un maigre cours d'eau, surgi du sable juste à temps pour refléter un peu de ciel avant de rallier la

mer. [4] Une assemblée de négresses lavandières, accroupies près de ce peu d'eau douce, tel était le motif devant lequel venait s'installer Paul. [5] J'avais promis de le rejoindre; mais, si fatiguante que fût la marche dans le sable, je me laissai entraîner dans la dune par Ali—c'était le nom de mon jeune porteur; nous atteignîmes bientôt une sorte d'entonnoir ou de cratère, dont les bords dominaient un peu la contrée, et d'où l'on pouvait voir venir. [6] Sitôt arrivé là, sur le sable en pente, Ali jette châle et manteau; il s'y jette lui-même, et, tout étendu sur le dos, les bras en croix, commence à me regarder en riant. [7] Je n'étais pas niais au point de ne comprendre pas son invite; toutefois je n'y répondis pas aussitôt. [8] Je m'assis, non loin de lui, mais pas trop près pourtant, et, le regardant fixement à mon tour, j'attendis, fort curieux de ce qu'il allait faire.

[9] J'attendis! J'admire aujourd'hui ma constance . . . [10] Mais était-ce bien la curiosité qui me retenait? [11] Je ne sais plus. [12] Le motif secret de nos actes, et j'entends: des plus décisifs, nous échappe; et non seulement dans le souvenir que nous en gardons, mais bien au moment même. [13] Sur le seuil de ce que l'on appelle: péché, hésitais-je encore? [14] Non, j'eusse été trop déçu si l'aventure eût dû se terminer par le triomphe de ma vertu—que déjà j'avais prise en dédain, en horreur. [15] Non; c'est bien la curiosité qui me faisait attendre . . . [16] Et je vis son rire lentement se faner, ses lèvres se refermer sur ses dents blanches; une expression de déconvenue, de tristesse assombrit son visage charmant. [17] Enfin il se leva:

—Alors, adieu, dit-il.

[18] Mais, saisissant la main qu'il me tendait, je le fis rouler à terre. [19] Son rire aussitôt reparut. [20] Il ne s'impatienta pas longtemps aux nœuds compliqués des lacets qui lui tenaient lieu de ceinture; sortant de sa poche un petit poignard, il en trancha d'un coup l'embrouillement. [21] Le vêtement tomba; il rejeta au loin sa veste, et se dressa nu comme un dieu. [22] Un instant il tendit vers le ciel ses bras grêles, puis, en riant, se laissa tomber contre moi. [23] Son corps était peut-être brûlant, mais reparut à mes mains aussi rafraîchissant que l'ombre. [24] Que le sable était beau! [25] Dans la splendeur adorable du soir, de quels rayons se vêtait ma joie! . . .

This is a narrative about a sexual encounter. But with great concern to manipulate his own and his younger self's image (*ethos*) so as to retain the reader's good will, the narrator avoids any explicit account of physical relations between Ali and the youthful Gide. His technique is one of *insinuation*. One of the narrator's main devices is to imply that things happened without his active participation, creating the impression that he simply followed passively the natural flow of events. This is noticeable even in the first few sentences (1–5), where narration masquerades as description. What seems to be a depersonalized evocation of the hotel just outside the town, of olive trees, and of sand dunes is in fact a subtle indication of the walk Gide and Ali took away from civilization towards nature. Gide's failure to meet up with his travelling companion, Paul, receives no explanation: he apparently followed Ali passively and unthinkingly: 'je me laissai entraîner dans la dune par Ali' (5). When they reached a crater in the dunes, it was Ali who took control. The narrator's style concentrates the reader's attention on Ali's actions. That is the effect of the *geminatio*: 'Ali jette châle et manteau; il s'y jette lui-même' (6); and it is the effect of the use of suspenseful clauses before a main verb: 'et, tout étendu sur le dos, les bras en croix, commence à me regarder en riant' (6). When the narrator makes himself the subject of his verbs, he uses verbs that insist on his passivity, his lack of response. Rather than throw himself down as Ali had done, he sat down ('Je m'assis' (8)); 'je n'y répondis pas' (7). A further *geminatio*, coupled with *exclamation* conveys his passivity forcefully: 'j'attendis' (8), 'J'attendis!' (9). When the suspense is broken, it is not by Gide but by Ali: 'Enfin il se leva' (17). It is Ali who spoke, held out a hand, tossed off his clothes, and fell on to the seated Gide. A passive recipient, Gide recalls the touch of Ali's warm body.

Further devices aim to suggest Gide's passivity and, at this most sensual of narrative moments, inspire the reader's sympathy for him as a thoughtful and reflecting narrator. *Correctio* conveys his tentativeness: 'Je m'assis, non loin de lui, mais pas trop près pourtant' (8). A long and extraordinarily positioned *parenthesis* (9–15) breaks the narrative flow, and creates an image of the narrator thinking probingly and with apparent frankness about his motivation as a young man in waiting for Ali's next move. Self-probing is suggested by the recourse to *ratiocinatio*: 'Mais était-ce bien la curiosité qui me retenait?' (10), 'Sur le seuil de ce que l'on appelle: péché, hésitais-je encore?' (13). These questions, and their answers, help to foster a complicity between narrator and readers at the very moment at which the narrator is about to make his boldest and most intimate revelation. After an indication of real doubt about his personal motivation and a suggestion that the self is ultimately unknowable (11–12), the narrator openly celebrates his curiosity: he was taking pleasure in the expectation of what Ali might do next. This is an important point: it foregrounds the ambiguity that pervades this passage.

Despite the narrator's attempts to paint himself as a passive participant in the encounter by recourse to *insinuation* and other verbal

and narrative devices that seem to diminish his responsibility for
what happens, there are also indications, even if fewer, that the
young Gide was rather more of an active participant than it might
at first appear. When they reached the crater, the narrator describes
it as a place 'd'où l'on pouvait voir venir' (5). This is not an innocent description. It subtly suggests that there might have been in the
young Gide's mind an expectation that something secretive would
happen. The narrator's insistence on his passivity is not total. The
adverb in the phrase 'je n'y répondis pas aussitôt' (7) is crucial in
suggesting a willingness to participate actively. And his insistence on
his curiosity is so strong (8, 10, 14–15) that his waiting for Ali can be
interpreted as waiting of a pleasurably active rather than a passive
kind. Indeed, the *parenthesis* explicitly rejects constancy and a conventional sense of virtue as being the motivation for waiting in preference for a more active curiosity. Moreover, in the rapid sequence
of events that lead up to their embrace, one key verb gives Gide a
vital role. When Ali held out his hand, Gide responded in an unusually active way: 'je le fis rouler à terre' (18).

The ambiguities in this account of the young Gide's first homosexual experience are no more effectively conveyed than through
the use of *aposiopesis*, speechlessness or silence. Gide enjoys recourse
to silences of various kinds, all pregnant with suggestion, but of an
indeterminate nature. The narrator seems to resort to *aposiopesis* on
three occasions, conveyed by *points de suspension*. The pause after the
sentence 'J'admire aujourd'hui ma constance . . .' (9) could encourage the reader (misleadingly) to dwell on Gide's constancy before
temptation, or it could invite the reader to think questioningly about
the adequacy of this explanation for his behaviour. The pause at the
end of the sentence 'c'est bien la curiosité qui me faisait attendre
. . .' (15) might likewise help to stress curiosity, invite further questioning, or indicate the narrator's mental adjustment as he moves
from reflection to the resumption of his narrative. The third example, coming at the end of the narrative, works together with two
exclamations to gesture towards the sexual act without any explicit
mention of it: 'Que le sable était beau! Dans la splendeur adorable
du soir, de quels rayons se vêtait ma joie! . . .' (24–5). Here we have
the speechlessness of ecstasy, of modesty, and of reflection. As the
passage moves towards its sexual climax, Gide also deploys silence
of a different sort. It is an unusual kind of *irony*, whereby he speaks
of sexual pleasure not explicitly, but by evoking pleasures of a

different kind. Ali's nakedness is quickly clothed in a *simile*: 'nu comme un dieu' (21). His warm body is paradoxically compared to the shade: 'aussi rafraîchissant que l'ombre' (23). Gide's joy is explained with reference not to Ali, but to nature: the beautiful sand and the rays of the evening sun. These silences, ambiguities, and indirections combine to persuade readers (some potentially hostile) to listen with respect to a man with a wife and a substantial literary reputation as he reveals to a predominantly heterosexual bourgeois public his first sexual experience with an Algerian youth.

Why does Gide explicitly evoke, and then reject, the possibility of his having been deterred from engaging in this homosexual act by a concern for his virtue and an awareness of sin (13–14)? Perhaps he does so as part of his strategy to make his readers accuse him: he pushes them into making a conventionally negative assessment of his morality, but through his further reflections and his presentation of the narrative he leads readers to question the appropriateness of blaming him here. Gide's concern with the judgement of his reader links him to Montaigne and Sévigné. For all three writers, self-presentation involves a delicate balance of praise and blame, self-accusation and self-defence. Montaigne says he is 'un particulier bien mal formé'; Sévigné asks anxiously if she is worthy of a place in heaven; Gide invites readers to condemn his sinfulness. But at the same time Montaigne claims that he is in a sense the model of all humanity; Sévigné invites her daughter's affection and approval; and Gide makes readers question their conventional moral yard-sticks. Writing about the self is a uniquely complex blend of *judicial* and *demonstrative* rhetoric.

Such writing reserves a privileged role for the anti-rhetoric *topos*. Those who write about themselves, whether in a spirit of complete self-portraiture (like Montaigne), of social and familial cohesiveness (like Sévigné), or of public self-revelation (like Gide) might, on the surface, be thought to be the writers least likely to have recourse to rhetorical procedures. All claim explicitly, though in different ways, that their writing aims to be honest, direct, and unaffected. But such claims are rhetorical devices in themselves, fostering an image of openness and frankness. There is no escape from rhetoric. Those who claim to reject it cannot help but use it, whether consciously or not. The self is a rhetorical construct.

CONCLUSION

In this book I have advocated an approach to the close reading of French literary texts based on rhetoric in all its breadth, rather than on its individual parts. Students of rhetoric as the art of persuasion need always to distinguish who is speaking and to whom. Accordingly, the approach adopted here has emphasized the different communicative axes in play in any given text. I hope that readers have been persuaded of the fruitfulness of traditional rhetoric as a tool of critical analysis of a wide range of texts, whether or not those texts were written in a consciously rhetorical spirit, and whether or not they are the work of writers who received a rhetorical education.

Whilst this book is in no sense out of tune with the work of those critics who in the last forty years have attempted to renew interest in rhetoric and in rhetorical approaches to literature, it has sought to take their work further. A few quotations, arranged in chronological order, will suggest in what ways.

Gérard Genette is a critic profoundly interested in rhetoric, but he sees it as having only a historical importance: 'Pour nous, aujourd'hui, l'œuvre de la rhétorique n'a plus, dans son contenu, qu'un intérêt historique (d'ailleurs sous-estimé). L'idée de ressusciter son code pour l'appliquer à notre littérature serait un anachronisme stérile' (1966).[1] A. Kibédi Varga was among the first modern critics to argue that *invention* and *disposition* could be as useful for literary criticism as *elocution* is. Although he restricts himself to the early modern period, he envisages the application of rhetorical analysis to works of the modern period: 'pourquoi ne pas en poursuivre l'étude au-delà du XVIIIe siècle?' He thinks the results would be attractive for poetry, but not for the novel: 'L'entreprise serait sans doute plus difficile dans le domaine du roman, pour lequel la rhétorique ne contient guère de préceptes; c'est un genre dont la situation ne correspond à aucune situation du discours rhétorico-classique' (1970).[2] In his powerful defence of rhetoric, Brian Vickers bolsters his

---

[1] G. Genette, *Figures*, vol. i (Seuil, 1966), 221.

[2] A. Kibédi Varga, *Rhétorique et littérature: Étude de structures classiques* (Didier, 1970), 125, 126.

theoretical claims with practical examples, and includes a chapter on rhetoric in the modern novel, demonstrating the rhetorical density of James Joyce's *Ulysses*, George Orwell's *Nineteen Eighty-Four*, and Randall Jarrell's *Pictures from an Institution*. But the rhetoric he observes is the *figures* of *elocution*, and he does not distinguish the different communicative axes on which they operate: 'analysis of the rhetorical element in fiction must concern itself with the details of style' (1988).[3] In a sophisticated attempt to identify a rhetorical framework for the analysis of the modern novel, Albert Halsall stresses the writer–reader axis: 'l'analyse sémio-rhétorique ici proposée servira à étudier les effets potentiels sur des interprètes virtuels par le signe complexe que représente un récit pragmatique' (1988).[4] The effect is to diminish the significance of the rhetoric represented on the character axis, which is one of the narrator's main resources for influencing his readers' responses. I hope that in my own analyses I have convinced readers both that rhetoric is as applicable to modern as to early modern literature and that rhetorical critics must attend to the representation of rhetorical behaviour within texts as well as to the writer's communication with readers and audiences: the writer–reader axis cannot properly be understood without scrutiny of the character axis.

In suggesting that very different kinds of texts lend themselves to rhetorical analysis, I do not mean to imply that at some fundamental level all texts are the same. Even when the same rhetorical device is used by different writers, its connotations turn out to be polysemic, and different effects can be observed. For example, *anaphora* is often combined with either *isocolon* or *parison* for purposes of emphasis. But the specific ways in which these devices work in different texts is a function of their contexts. Compare the way they are used by Racine's Agrippine (*Britannicus*, 1288–94) and by Aimé Césaire (*Cahier d'un retour au pays natal*, p. 112):

> De mes accusateurs qu'on punisse l'audace;
> Que de Britannicus on calme le courroux;
> Que Junie à son choix puisse prendre un époux;
> Qu'ils soient libres tous deux, et que Pallas demeure; ·
> Que vous me permettiez de vous voir à toute heure;
> Que ce même Burrhus qui nous vient écouter,
> A votre porte enfin n'ose plus m'arrêter.

---

[3] B. Vickers, *In Defence of Rhetoric* (Oxford: Clarendon Press, 1988), 375.

[4] A. W. Halsall, *L'Art de convaincre: Le Récit pragmatique: rhétorique, idéologie, propagande* (Toronto: Paratexte, 1990), 30–1.

ceux qui n'ont inventé ni la poudre ni la boussole
ceux qui n'ont jamais su dompter la vapeur ni l'électricité
ceux qui n'ont exploré ni les mers ni le ciel
mais ceux sans qui la terre ne serait pas la terre

Agrippine uses these emphatic *figures* of repetition and sentence structure in order to show her son that she has once again taken control. Racine uses them to create for the theatre audience an image of a domineering mother and to create a retrospective irony, whereby her apparent triumph at this juncture will soon be shown to be very hollow. The *figures* play an important role in the power game between the emperor and his mother, and contribute substantially to the dramatic excitement. The same *figures* function quite differently in Césaire's verses, where they shape the celebratory tone of the poet's depiction of black people as a race innocent of those technological advances that led white Westerners into the ways of exploitative colonization. The *figures* may be the same, but the effects are quite different: a desire for domination on the one hand, celebration on the other.

The impact of rhetorical devices can be gauged only after scrutiny of their context. Hence the importance placed in this book on close reading. One of the main virtues of a rhetorical, as opposed to a thematic, approach to texts is (or should be) the emphasis accorded the evolution of textual detail within a text. Listening to a speech, watching a play, and reading a novel or a poem are temporal activities. We see the first scene of a play before the second, and read the first page of a novel before the second (usually). Since rhetoric stresses the way in which a text communicates with its audience, rhetorical readings need to attend closely to the gradual accumulation of interrelating signifiers in the order in which they are presented. That is why I have examined substantial passages from the texts I have discussed.

Readers should not think that I am trying to promote rhetorical approaches at the expense of other approaches. Rhetoric does, however, have the advantage over some approaches to literature of attending to matters of communication and verbal detail, which are peculiar to literary study. Even so, rhetoric has its limitations. Stylistics would claim to take the study of *elocution* further than the rhetoricians have done. Versification is a crucial topic in the analysis of verse, and is not part of traditional rhetoric. Narratology will take readers much further in understanding the complex interrelation of different axes of communication in works of prose fiction. But whilst rhetoric does not cater for all technical issues relevant to the literary critic, its range is none the less wide. Moreover, it does not distinguish between 'literary' and 'non-literary' communication, and it is therefore of much potential use to students of culture more generally.[5]

There is no reason to confine rhetorical analysis to literary texts. The work of today's advertisers, politicians, customer-care departments, and government information services is centrally concerned with the art of persuasion, and the features of traditional rhetoric can still explain much of what they do. Certain *figures* recur frequently in advertising campaigns to lodge a product or a message in the audience's memory. *Alliteration, polyptoton,* and *antithesis* are used over and over again: 'Stratégies et Solutions Internet' (*alliteration* in /s/), 'Pages jaunes: l'adresse de toutes les adresses' (*polyptoton*), 'Investir c'est bien, mais en s'investissant' (*polyptoton*), 'Monte Carlo: derrière chaque petit séjour se cache toujours un grand talent' (*antithesis*). Advertisers also have constant recourse to *ethos* and *pathos.* They try repeatedly to sell motor cars to men by appealing to their customers' perceived desire to be attractive to beautiful young women. A rather different use of *pathos* was found in British Government attempts in the 1980s to prevent the spread of AIDS by encouraging the use of condoms: images of sex were terrifyingly associated with death. Of course, today's communicators have at their disposal new resources that the ancient rhetoricians never dreamt of. Moving images, colour photography, the combination of music and words, and the immediate access to a mass public via the new technologies offer today's persuaders new tools of communication.[6] But when we think how these novelties work, they do not so much suggest the inadequacy of traditional rhetoric to cope with the modern world as demonstrate the durability of rhetoric's core procedures.

---

[5] For links between rhetoric and the visual arts, and rhetoric and music, see Vickers, *In Defence of Rhetoric*, ch. 7, 'Rhetoric and the Sister Arts'. Specifically on rhetoric and the visual arts in France, see J. Lichtenstein, *La Couleur éloquente: Rhétorique et peinture à l'âge classique* (Flammarion, 1989).

[6] On these modern methods of persuasion, see R. Barthes, 'Rhétorique de l'image', in *L'Obvie et l'obtus: Essais critiques III* (Seuil, 1982), 25–42; D. Victoroff, *La Publicité et l'image* (Denoël–Gonthier, 1978); J.-N. Kapferer, *Les Chemins de la persuasion* (Dunod, 1988).

Rhetoric has always had its detractors, from Socrates and Plato onwards. There are those who regret that it is not more centrally concerned with the pursuit, and expression, of truth. There are those who regret the technical terminology that it has engendered. But rhetoric is viscerally connected with human life: there was rhetorical behaviour before the discipline of rhetoric was invented to codify it.[7] How human beings communicate, and how they choose to represent human communication in their fictions, are proper subjects for the student of language and literature; they are subjects that cannot properly be studied without reference to rhetoric. Two and a half thousand years on, rhetoric starts the new millennium with a promising future ahead of it. The world is incredibly full of traditional rhetoric.

[7] See G. A. Kennedy, *Comparative Rhetoric: An Historical and Cross-Cultural Introduction* (New York: Oxford University Press, 1998). This book broadens the horizon of rhetorical study very significantly. Kennedy considers rhetorical forms in societies without writing (including Aboriginal and North American Indian culture) and in ancient literate societies (including the Near East, China, and India).

APPENDIX: OUTLINE OF CHAPTER 1

The following outline presents rhetorical terms in the order in which they are explained and illustrated in Chapter 1. The numbers in parentheses are page references.

Kinds of Oratory (11)
  Judicial Discourse (12)
  Deliberative Discourse (12)
  Demonstrative Discourse (13)
Invention (13)
  Ethos (14)
  Pathos (14)
  Logos (15)
    External proofs (15)
    Internal proofs (or places) (16): *Definition* (16); *Division* (16); *Genus and species* (16); *Cause and effect* (16); *Comparison* (16); *Opposites* (16); *Circumstances* (16)
    Topics (17)
    Forms of Argument (18)
      Deductive reasoning (18)
        Syllogism (major premiss, minor premiss, conclusion) (18)
        Enthymeme (18)
      Inductive reasoning (19)
        Example (19)
Disposition (20)
  Exordium (captatio benevolentiae, insinuation) (20)
  Proposition (20)
  Narration (20)
  Digression (20)
  Confirmation (21)
  Refutation (21)
  Peroration (recapitulation, amplification) (21)
Elocution (*Ornaments*) (22)
  Kinds of Style (23)
    Grand style (23)
    Medium style (23)
    Low style (23)
  Figures of Imagery (including tropes) (24)

SELECT BIBLIOGRAPHY

The bibliography on the authors discussed in this book and on rhetoric in general is vast. The following list is a selection of works that I have found particularly useful. It includes rhetorical treatises both ancient and modern, editions of all the texts discussed in Chapters 2–6 of this book, and some critical studies of those texts, especially if they exploit rhetoric. Many of the works listed here contain further bibliographical information. Works with English titles are published in London, and with French titles in Paris, unless it is stated otherwise.

ARISTOTLE, *The Art of Rhetoric*, trans. J. H. Freese, Loeb Classical Library (Cambridge, Mass.: Harvard University Press, 1926).

AUBIGNAC, F. HÉDELIN, ABBÉ D', *La Pratique du théâtre*, ed. P. Martino (Champion, 1927; Geneva: Slatkine Reprints, 1996).

AUBIGNÉ, A. D', *Les Tragiques*, ed. J.-R. Fanlo (2 vols., Champion, 1995).

AYRES-BENNETT, W., and O'DONOVAN, P. (eds.), *Syntax and the Literary System: New Approaches to the Interface between Literature and Linguistics* (Cambridge: Cambridge French Colloquia, 1995).

BACRY, P., *Les Figures de style et autres procédés stylistiques* (Belin, 1992).

BAILBÉ, J., *Agrippa d'Aubigné, poète des 'Tragiques'* (Caen: Publications de la Faculté des Lettres et Sciences Humaines, 1968).

BALES, R., *Persuasion in the French Personal Novel: Studies of Chateaubriand, Constant, Balzac, Nerval, and Fromentin* (Birmingham, Ala.: Summa Publications, 1997).

BARTHES, R., *S/Z* (Seuil, 1970).

—— 'L'Ancienne Rhétorique: Aide-mémoire', in *Recherches rhétoriques (q.v.)*, 254–333.

—— 'Rhétorique de l'image', in *L'Obvie et l'obtus: Essais critiques III* (Seuil, 1982), 25–42.

BARY, R., *La Rhétorique françoise* (1673).

BAUDELAIRE, C., *Les Fleurs du Mal*, ed. A. Adam (Garnier, 1961).

—— *Curiosités esthétiques, L'Art romantique, et autres œuvres critiques*, ed. H. Lemaitre (Garnier, 1962).

BAYLEY, P., *French Pulpit Oratory (1598–1650): A Study in Themes and Styles with a Descriptive Catalogue of Printed Texts* (Cambridge: Cambridge University Press, 1980).

—— 'Accommodating Rhetoric', *Seventeenth-Century French Studies*, 19 (1997), 37–47.

BECKETT, S., *En attendant Godot*, ed. C. Duckworth (Walton-on-Thames: Nelson, 1985).

BELLARD-THOMSON, C. A., *The Literary Stylistics of French* (Manchester: Manchester University Press, 1992).

BEUGNOT, B., *Les Muses classiques: Essai de bibliographie rhétorique et poétique* (Klincksieck, 1996).

BOILEAU-DESPRÉAUX, N., *Œuvres*, ed. J. Vercruysse (2 vols., Garnier–Flammarion, 1969).

BOOTH, W. C., *Rhetoric of Fiction* (Chicago: University of Chicago Press, 1961).

BOSSUET, J. B., *Œuvres*, ed. abbé Velat and Y. Champailler (Gallimard, 1961).

BRADFORD, R., *Stylistics* (Routledge, 1997).

BRAY, B., 'Quelques Aspects du système épistolaire de Mme de Sévigné', *Revue d'histoire littéraire de la France*, 69 (1969), 491–505.

BRODY, J., *Lectures de Montaigne* (Lexington, Ky.: French Forum, 1982).

—— *Nouvelles Lectures de Montaigne* (Champion, 1994).

BUFFON, G. L., COMTE DE, *Discours sur le style: A Facsimile Edition of the 1753 12ᵐᵒ Edition*, ed. C. E. Pickford (Hull: Department of French, 1978).

BUFFUM, I., *Agrippa d'Aubigné's 'Les Tragiques': A Study in the Baroque Style in Poetry* (New Haven: Yale University Press, 1951).

CAMUS, A., *La Chute* (Gallimard, 1956).

CARR, T. M., JR., *Descartes and the Resilience of Rhetoric: Varieties of Cartesian Rhetorical Theory* (Carbondale and Edwardsville: Southern Illinois University Press, 1990).

CARRUTHERS, M., *The Book of Memory: A Study of Memory in Medieval Culture* (Cambridge: Cambridge University Press, 1990).

CASTOR, G., *La Poétique de la Pléiade: Étude sur la pensée et la terminologie du XVIᵉ siècle*, trans. Y. Bellenger (Champion, 1998) (first pub. as *Pléiade Poetics* (Cambridge: Cambridge University Press, 1964)).

CAVE, T., *The Cornucopian Text: Problems of Writing in the French Renaissance* (Oxford: Clarendon Press, 1979).

CÉSAIRE, A., *Notebook of a Return to My Native Land/Cahier d'un retour au pays natal*, trans. M. Rosello with A. Pritchard (Newcastle-upon-Tyne: Bloodaxe Books, 1995).

CHÉNIER, A., *Poems*, ed. F. Scarfe (Oxford: Blackwell, 1961).

CHESTERS, G., *Baudelaire and the Poetics of Craft* (Cambridge: Cambridge University Press, 1988).

CICERO, *Brutus, Orator*, trans. G. L. Hendrickson and H. M. Hubbell, Loeb Classical Library (Cambridge, Mass.: Harvard University Press, 1962).

—— *De Inventione, De Optimo Genere Oratorum, Topica*, trans. H. M. Hubbell, Loeb Classical Library (Cambridge, Mass.: Harvard University Press, 1949).

—— *De Oratore*, trans. E. W. Sutton and H. Rackham (Loeb Classical Library (2 vols., Cambridge, Mass.: Harvard University Press, 1942).

CLÉMENT, B., *L'Œuvre sans qualités: Rhétorique de Samuel Beckett* (Seuil, 1994).

CONLEY, T. M., *Rhetoric in the European Tradition* (Chicago: University of Chicago Press, 1994).

CORBETT, E. P. J., *Classical Rhetoric for the Modern Student*, 3rd edn. (New York: Oxford University Press, 1990).

CORDELIER, J., *Mme de Sévigné par elle-même* (Seuil, 1967).

CORNEILLE, P., *Writings on the Theatre*, ed. H. T. Barnwell, (Oxford: Blackwell, 1965).

CRÉVIER, J.-B., *La Rhétorique française* (2 vols., 1765).

CULLER, J., *Structuralist Poetics* (Routledge and Kegan Paul, 1975).

CURTIUS, E. R., *European Literature and the Latin Middle Ages*, trans. W. R. Trask (Routledge and Kegan Paul, 1953).

DAVIDSON, H. M., *Audience, Words, and Art: Studies in Seventeenth-Century Rhetoric* ([Columbus], Oh.: Ohio State University Press, 1965).

DAVIS, G., *Aimé Césaire* (Cambridge: Cambridge University Press, 1997).

DECLERCQ, G., 'Crime et argument: La Persuasion dans *Britannicus* acte IV, scène 4', in *Lalies: Actes des sessions de linguistique et de littérature (Aussois, 1er–6 septembre 1981)* (1984), 165–75.

—— 'Stylistique et rhétorique au XVIIe siècle: L'Analyse du texte littéraire classique', *Dix-septième siècle*, 150 (1986), 43–60.

—— *L'Art d'argumenter: Structures rhétoriques et littéraires* (Éditions Universitaires, 1992).

DEFAUX, G., 'Un Cannibale en haut de chausses: Montaigne, la différence et la logique de l'identité', *Modern Language Notes*, 97 (1982), 919–57.

—— 'Rhétorique et représentation dans les *Essais*: De la peinture de l'autre à la peinture du moi', in Lestringant (ed.), *Rhétorique de Montaigne*, 21–48.

DIXON, P., *Rhetoric* (Methuen, 1971).

DUCHÊNE, R., *Réalité vécue et art épistolaire: Mme de Sévigné et la lettre d'amour* (Bordas, 1970).

DUCROT, O., *Dire et ne pas dire: Principes de sémantique linguistique*, 2nd edn. (Hermann, 1980).

DUMARSAIS, C. C., and FONTANIER, P., *Des Tropes*, ed. G. Genette (Geneva: Slatkine Reprints, 1984).

—— *Traité des tropes*, ed. F. Douay (Flammarion, 1988).

DUPRIEZ, B., *Gradus: Les Procédés littéraires* (10/18, Union Générale d'Editions, 1980).

ECO, U., *The Role of the Reader: Explorations in the Semiotics of Texts* (Hutchinson, 1981).

FISH, S. E., *Is There a Text in this Class? The Authority of Interpretative Communities* (Cambridge, Mass.: Harvard University Press, 1980).

FITCH, B., *The Narcissistic Text: A Reading of Camus's Fiction* (Toronto: University of Toronto Press, 1982).

FLAUBERT, G., *Correspondance*, ed. J. Bruneau (2 vols., Gallimard, 1973–80).

—— *Madame Bovary*, ed. B. Ajac (Garnier–Flammarion, 1986).

FLEMING, J. A., 'The Imagery of Tropism in the Novels of Nathalie Sarraute', in W. M. Frohock (ed.), *Image and Theme: Studies in Modern French Fiction* (Cambridge, Mass.: Harvard University Press, 1969), 74–98.

FONTANIER, P., *Les Figures du discours*, ed. G. Genette (Flammarion, 1968).

FORESTIER, G., *Introduction à l'analyse des textes classiques: Eléments de rhétorique et de poétique du XVIIᵉ siècle* (Nathan, 1993).

FOSSIER, F., *Au Pays des immortels: L'Institut de France hier et aujourd'hui* (Fayard–Mazarine, 1987).

FRANCE, P., *Racine's Rhetoric* (Oxford: Clarendon Press, 1965).

—— *Rhetoric and Truth in France: Descartes to Diderot* (Oxford: Clarendon Press, 1972).

—— 'Rhetoric and Modern Literary Analysis', *Essays in Poetics*, 5 (1980), 1–14.

—— 'The Uses of Rhetoric', *History of European Ideas*, 1 (1981), 133–41.

—— *Rousseau, 'Confessions'* (Cambridge: Cambridge University Press, 1987).

FROMILHAGUE, C., *Les Figures de style* (Nathan, 1995).

—— and SANCIER-CHATEAU, A., *Introduction à l'analyse stylistique*, 2nd edn. (Dunod, 1996).

FUMAROLI, M., *L'Âge de l'éloquence: Rhétorique et 'res litteraria' de la Renaissance au seuil de l'époque classique* (Geneva: Droz, 1980).

—— *Héros et orateurs: Rhétorique et dramaturgie cornéliennes* (Geneva: Droz, 1990).

GARDES-TAMINE, J., *La Rhétorique* (Armand Colin, 1996).

GAULLE, C. DE, *Discours et messages: Pendant la guerre, juin 1940–janvier 1946* (Plon, 1970).

GENETTE, G., *Figures* (3 vols., Seuil, 1966–72).

—— 'Rhétorique et enseignement', in *Figures*, ii. 23–42.

—— 'La Rhétorique restreinte', in *Recherches rhétoriques* (q.v.), 233–53.

GIBERT, B., *La Rhétorique ou les Règles de l'Eloquence* (1730).

GIDE, A., *L'Immoraliste* (Gallimard, 1972).

—— *Si le grain ne meurt* (Gallimard, 1972).

—— *Corydon* (Gallimard, 1947).

—— *Journal, 1889–1939*, Bibliothèque de la Pléiade (Gallimard, 1951).

—— *Journal, 1939–49*, Bibliothèque de la Pléiade (Gallimard, 1954).

GOODDEN, A., *'Actio' and Persuasion: Dramatic Performance in Eighteenth-Century France* (Oxford: Clarendon Press, 1986).

GORDON, A. L., *Ronsard et la rhétorique* (Geneva: Droz, 1970).

GREAR, A., 'Rhetoric and the Art of the French Tragic Actor (1620–1750): The Place of *Pronuntiatio* in the Stage Tradition' (Ph.D. thesis, University of St Andrews, 1982).

GRIFFITHS, R., *The Dramatic Technique of Antoine de Montchrestien: Rhetoric and Style in French Renaissance Tragedy* (Oxford: Clarendon Press, 1970).

GRIMAREST, J.-L., LE GALLOIS, SIEUR DE, *La Vie de M. de Molière*, ed. G. Mongrédien (Brient, 1955).

GROUPE MU, *Rhétorique générale* (Larousse, 1970; Seuil, 1982).

—— *Rhétorique de la poésie* (Complexe, 1977; Seuil, 1990).

HALSALL, A. W., *L'Art de convaincre: Le Récit pragmatique: rhétorique, idéologie, propagande* (Toronto: Paratexte, 1990).

—— *Victor Hugo et l'art de convaincre: Le Récit hugolien: Rhétorique, argumentation, persuasion* (Montreal: Les Éditions Balzac, 1995).

HAMMOND, N., 'Racine et la mémoire', in Volker Kapp (ed.), *Les Lieux de mémoire et la fabrique de l'œuvre, Actes du 1er colloque du Centre International de Rencontres sur le XVIIe siècle (Kiel, 29 juin–1er jullet 1993)*, Papers on French Seventeenth-Century Literature (Paris, Seattle, Tübingen: Biblio 17, 1993), 307–19.

HAMON, P., 'Un Discours contraint', in R. Barthes, L. Bersani, P. Hamon, M. Riffaterre, and I. Watt (eds.), *Littérature et réalité*, (Seuil, 1982), 119–80.

HARWOOD, S., *Rhetoric in the Tragedies of Corneille* (New Orleans: Tulane University, 1977).

HAWCROFT, M., *Word as Action: Racine, Rhetoric, and Theatrical Language* (Oxford: Clarendon Press, 1992).

HIGMAN, F. M., *The Style of John Calvin in his French Polemical Treatises* (Oxford: Clarendon Press, 1967).

HORN, P. L., *Marguerite Yourcenar* (Boston: Twayne Publishers, 1985).

HOUSTON, J. P., *The Traditions of French Prose Style: A Rhetorical Study* (Baton Rouge, La.: Louisiana State University Press, 1981) .

—— *The Rhetoric of Poetry in the Renaissance and Seventeenth Century* (Baton Rouge, La.: Louisiana State University Press, 1983).

HUGO, V., *Les Contemplations*, ed. P. Albouy (Gallimard, 1973).

ISER, W., *The Implied Reader: Patterns of Communication in Prose Fiction from Bunyan to Beckett* (Baltimore: Johns Hopkins University Press, 1974).

—— *The Act of Reading: A Theory of Aesthetic Response* (Baltimore: Johns Hopkins University Press, 1978).

JAKOBSON, R., 'Closing Statement: Linguistics and Poetics', in T. A. Sebeok (ed.), *Style and Language* (Cambridge, Mass.: MIT Press, 1960), 350–77.

—— *Essais de linguistique générale*, trans. N. Ruwet (Éditions de Minuit, 1963).

JEFFERSON, A., *The Nouveau Roman and the Poetics of Fiction* (Cambridge: Cambridge University Press, 1980).

JONDORF, G., *French Renaissance Tragedy: The Dramatic Word* (Cambridge: Cambridge University Press, 1990).

JONES, R., 'Modes of Discourse in *La Chute*', *Nottingham French Studies*, 15(2) (1976), 27–35.

KAPFERER, J.-N., *Les Chemins de la persuasion* (Dunod, 1988).

KENNEDY, G. A., *The Art of Persuasion in Greece* (Princeton: Princeton University Press, 1963).

—— *The Art of Rhetoric in the Roman World* (Princeton: Princeton University Press, 1972).

—— *Classical Rhetoric and its Christian and Secular Tradition from Ancient to Modern Times* (Croom Helms, 1980).

—— *Greek Rhetoric under Christian Emperors* (Princeton: Princeton University Press, 1983).

—— *Comparative Rhetoric: An Historical and Cross-Cultural Introduction* (New York: Oxford University Press, 1998).

KIBÉDI VARGA, A., *Rhétorique et littérature: Études de structures classiques* (Didier, 1970).

KÜNTZ, P., 'Esquisse d'un inventaire des ouvrages de langue française traitant de la rhétorique entre 1610 et 1715', *Dix-septième siècle*, 80–1 (1968), 133–42.

LACAPRA, D., *'Madame Bovary' on Trial* (Ithaca, NY: Cornell University Press, 1982).

LACLOS, C. DE, *Les Liaisons dangereuses*, ed. R. Pomeau (Flammarion, 1981).

LAMY, B., *La Rhétorique ou l'Art de parler*, 4th edn. (Amsterdam, 1699; Brighton: Sussex Reprints, 1969).

—— *La Rhétorique ou l'Art de parler*, ed. B. Timmermans (Presses Universitaires de France, 1998).

LANHAM, R. A., *A Handlist of Rhetorical Terms*, 2nd edn. (Berkeley: University of California Press, 1991).

LAUSBERG, H., *Handbuch der literarischen Rhetorik*, 2nd edn. (Munich: Max Hueber Verlag, 1973).

LECARME, J., and LECARME-TABONE, E., *L'Autobiographie* (Armand Colin, 1997).

LE GRAS, *La Réthorique* [*sic*] *française ou les préceptes de l'ancienne et vraye eloquence* (1676).

LEJEUNE, P., *L'Autobiographie en France* (Armand Colin, 1971).

—— *Exercices d'ambiguïté: Lectures de 'Si le grain ne meurt'* (Lettres modernes, 1974).

—— *Le Pacte autobiographique* (Seuil, 1975, 1996).

LESTRINGANT, F. (ed.), *Rhétorique de Montaigne* (a special no. of the *Bulletin de la Société des Amis de Montaigne*, 7(1–2) (1985)).

LÉVI-VALENSI, J., '*La Chute* ou la parole en procès', *Cahiers Albert Camus*, 3 (1970), 33–57.

LICHTENSTEIN, J., *La Couleur éloquente: Rhétorique et peinture à l'âge classique* (Flammarion, 1989).

MCGOWAN, M. M., *Montaigne's Deceits: The Art of Persuasion in the 'Essais'* (University of London Press, 1974).

MAINGUENEAU, D., *Eléments de linguistique pour le texte littéraire* (Bordas, 1986).

MASKELL, D., *Racine: A Theatrical Reading* (Oxford: Clarendon Press, 1991).

MERCIER, R., 'Processus d'intériorisation et procédés stylistiques dans le *Cahier d'un retour au pays natal*', in J. Leiner (ed.), *Soleil éclaté: Mélanges offerts à Aimé Césaire à l'occasion de son soixante-dixième anniversaire par une équipe internationale d'artistes et de chercheurs* (Tübingen: Gunter Narr Verlag, 1984), 273–84.

MICHEL, A., *La Parole et la beauté: Rhétorique et esthétique dans la tradition occidentale* (Les Belles Lettres, 1982).

MINOGUE, V., *Nathalie Sarraute and the War of Words* (Edinburgh: Edinburgh University Press, 1981).

MOLIÈRE, *Œuvres complètes*, ed. G. Couton, Bibliothèque de la Pléiade (2 vols., Gallimard, 1971).

—— *Le Tartuffe*, ed. R. Parish (Bristol Classical Press, 1994).

MOLINIÉ, G., *Dictionnaire de rhétorique* (Le Livre de Poche, 1992).

—— *La Stylistique* (Presses Universitaires de France, 1993).

MONTAIGNE, M. DE, *Les Essais de Michel de Montaigne*, ed. P. Villey and V. L. Saulnier (Presses Universitaires de France, 1965).

MOREL, J., 'Rhétorique et tragédie au XVIIe siècle', *Dix-septième siècle*, 80–1 (1968), 89–105.

MORIER, H., *Dictionnaire de poétique et de rhétorique* (Presses Universitaires de France, 1961).

MORNET, D., *Histoire de la clarté française* (Payot, 1929).

MOSS, A., ' "Des Coches": Une Rhétorique transportable', in O'Brien, Quainton, and Supple (eds.), *Montaigne et la rhétorique*, 77–87.

MUNTEANO, B., *Constantes dialectiques en littérature et en histoire* (Didier, 1967).

NASH, W., *Rhetoric: The Wit of Persuasion* (Oxford: Blackwell, 1989).

NURSE, P. H. (ed.), *The Art of Criticism: Essays in French Literary Analysis* (Edinburgh: Edinburgh University Press, 1969).

O'BRIEN, J., QUAINTON, M., and SUPPLE, J. J. (eds.), *Montaigne et la rhétorique: Actes du colloque de St Andrews (28–31 mars 1992)* (Champion, 1995).

PARISH, R., *Racine: The Limits of Tragedy*, Papers on French Seventeenth-Century Literature (Paris, Seattle, Tübingen: Biblio 17, 1993).

PERELMAN, C., *L'Empire rhétorique: Rhétorique et argumentation* (Vrin, 1977).

—— and OLBRECHTS-TYTECA, L., *Traité de l'argumentation: La Nouvelle Rhétorique*, 5th edn. (Brussels: University of Brussels, 1988).

PLATO, *Euthyphro, Apology, Crito, Phaedo, Phaedrus*, trans. H. N. Fowler, Loeb Classical Library (Cambridge, Mass.: Harvard University Press, 1914).

—— *Lysis, Symposium, Gorgias*, trans. W. R. M. Lamb, Loeb Classical Library (Cambridge, Mass.: Harvard University Press, 1925).

POTTS, D. C., ' "Une carrière épineuse": Neoplatonism and the Poet's Vocation in Boileau's *Art poétique*', *French Studies*, 47 (1993), 20–32.

PY, G., 'Livres I à IV des *Confessions*', *L'Information littéraire*, 50(1) (1998), 8–20.

QUAINTON, M., *D'Aubigné: 'Les Tragiques'* (Grant and Cutler, 1990).

QUINTILIAN, *Institutio Oratoria*, trans. H. E. Butler, Loeb Classical Library (4 vols. Cambridge, Mass.: Harvard University Press, 1920–2).

RACINE, J., *Théâtre complet*, ed. J. Morel and A. Viala (Garnier, 1980; Dunod, 1995).

REBOUL, O., *La Rhétorique*, Que sais-je? (Presses Universitaires de France, 1984).

—— *Introduction à la rhétorique* (Presses Universitaires de France, 1991).

Recherches rhétoriques (Seuil, 1970) (includes articles by G. Genette and R. Barthes (*q.v.*)).

REGOSIN, R., *The Matter of my Book: Montaigne's 'Essais' as the Book of the Self* (Berkeley: University of California Press, 1977).

Rhetorica ad Herennium, trans. H. Caplan, Loeb Classical Library (Cambridge, Mass.: Harvard University Press, 1954).

RICHARDS, I. A., *The Philosophy of Rhetoric* (New York: Oxford University Press, 1936).

RIMMON-KENAN, S., *Narrative Fiction: Contemporary Poetics* (Routledge, 1983).

ROBRIEUX, J.-J., *Eléments de rhétorique et d'argumentation* (Dunod, 1993).

RONSARD, P. DE, *Œuvres complètes*, ed. P. Laumonier, I. Silver, and R. Lebègue (20 vols., Hachette, then Droz, then Didier, 1914–75).

ROUSSEAU, J.-J., *Les Confessions*, ed. B. Gagnebin, M. Raymond, and C. Koenig (Gallimard: 1973).

RYNGAERT, J.-P., *Lire 'En attendant Godot'* (Dunod, 1993).

SAINT-GÉRAND, J.-P., ' "Une singulière noirceur d'expression": Baudelaire et la rhétorique', *L'Information grammaticale*, 39 (1988), 30–7.

SARRAUTE, N., *L'Ère du soupçon* (Gallimard, 1956).

—— *Le Planétarium* (Gallimard, 1959).

SAYCE, R. A., *Style in French Prose: A Method of Analysis* (Oxford: Clarendon Press, 1953).

—— *The 'Essays' of Montaigne: A Critical Exploration* (Weidenfeld and Nicolson, 1972).

SCHERER, J., *La Dramaturgie classique en France* (Nizet, 1950).

SCOTT, C., *The Poetics of French Verse: Studies in Reading* (Oxford: Clarendon Press, 1998).

SELLSTROM, A. D., 'Rhetoric and the Poetics of French Classicism', *French Review*, 34 (1961), 39–48.

SENGHOR, L. S., 'L'Esthétique négro-africaine', in *Libertés I: Négritude et humanisme* (Seuil, 1964), 202–17 (essay originally pub. in 1956).

SERMAIN, J.-P., 'Rhétorique et roman au XVIIIᵉ siècle: L'Exemple de Prévost et de Marivaux (1728–42)', *Studies on Voltaire and the Eighteenth Century*, 233 (1985).

SÉVIGNÉ, M., MARQUISE DE, *Correspondance*, ed. R. Duchêne, Bibliothèque de la Pléiade (3 vols. Gallimard, 1972–8).

SEYLAZ, J.-L., 'Les Liaisons dangereuses' et la création romanesque chez Laclos (Geneva: Droz, 1958).

SHERINGHAM, M., French Autobiography: Devices and Desires: Rousseau to Perec (Oxford: Clarendon Press, 1993).

SÖTÉR, I., La Doctrine stylistique des rhétoriques du XVIIᵉ siècle (Budapest: Eggenberger, 1937).

STARKIE, E., Flaubert: The Making of the Master (Weidenfeld and Nicolson, 1967).

STEINER, W., The Colors of Rhetoric: Problems in the Relation between Modern Literature and Painting (Chicago: University of Chicago Press, 1982).

TAYLOR, C., Sources of the Self: The Making of the Modern Identity (Cambridge: Cambridge University Press, 1989).

TOPLISS, P., The Rhetoric of Pascal (Leicester: Leicester University Press, 1966).

TRUCHET, J., La Prédication de Bossuet (2 vols., Éditions du Cerf, 1960).

VALÉRY, P., Œuvres, ed. J. Hytier, Bibliothèque de la Pléiade (2 vols., Gallimard, 1957–60).

VAN RUTTEN, P., Stylistique littéraire (San Francisco: International Scholars Publications, 1995).

VENESOEN, C., 'Le Néron de Racine: Un Cas curieux d'impuissance verbale', L'Information littéraire, 33 (1981), 130–6.

VERLAINE, P., Œuvres poétiques, ed. J. Robichez (Garnier, 1969).

VICKERS, B., In Defence of Rhetoric (Oxford: Clarendon Press, 1988).

VICTOROFF, D., La Publicité et l'image (Denoël–Gonthier, 1978).

WALES, K., A Dictionary of Stylistics (Longman, 1989).

WALKER, D., André Gide (Basingstoke: Macmillan, 1990).

WILLIAMS, C., The Last Great Frenchman: A Life of General de Gaulle, 2nd edn. (Abacus, 1995).

WING, N., 'The Stylistic Function of Rhetoric in Baudelaire's "Au lecteur"', Kentucky Romance Quarterly, 19 (1972), 447–60.

YATES, F., The Art of Memory (Harmondsworth: Penguin Books, 1969).

YOURCENAR, M., Discours de réception de Mme Marguerite Yourcenar à l'Académie Française et réponse de M. Jean d'Ormesson (Gallimard, 1981).

ZOLA, E., Germinal, ed. A. Dezalay (Le Livre de Poche, 1983).

INDEX OF RHETORICAL TERMS

INDEX OF NAMES AND WORKS

This is an index of primary authors and their works, and does not include the authors of
critical writings or other authors mentioned incidentally.